Penguin Handbooks
*Malaysian Cookery*

Rafi Fernandez was born in Secunderabad, India, in June 1944 and has lived in England since 1965. A science graduate, she diverted to a secretarial course in order to qualify for a UK work permit and join her boyfriend, whom she married in England in 1968. Until 1980 she worked as a secretary in a travel agency, then for Air-India. The latter position enabled her to travel to many parts of the world, and in doing so she became very interested in cooking for pleasure; even today her husband, who works for American Express, brings her back new ideas.

After resigning in 1980 to live in the country with her two young sons, Kevin and Lee, she was invited to do an interview for *Good Housekeeping* magazine, in conjunction with the Festival of India in the UK; she had helped to organize this when working for Air-India. She then attended the Culinary Techniques Workshop at the Carrier Seminar of Cooking and in 1983 started to organize her own catering events, 'West Meets East Through Food', at which she introduces Eastern custom and culture related to the menu being served.

Her husband, who is a Malaysian Indian, encouraged her to write this book, which is her first. He became her pen-friend when she was only twelve years old, and they met in India when she was sixteen, but owing to their different religions were not allowed to marry until she was twenty-three. Her husband is a Roman Catholic and she is a Muslim.

Rafi Fernandez's second main hobby is producing unusual plants from seeds, and bonsais from different parts of the world.

# Malaysian Cookery

### Rafi Fernandez

Penguin Books

PENGUIN BOOKS

Published by the Penguin Group
27 Wrights Lane, London W8 5TZ, England
Viking Penguin Inc., 40 West 23rd Street, New York, New York 10010, USA
Penguin Books Australia Ltd, Ringwood, Victoria, Australia
Penguin Books Canada Ltd, 2801 John Street, Markham, Ontario, Canada L3R 1B4
Penguin Books (NZ) Ltd, 182–190 Wairau Road, Auckland 10, New Zealand

Penguin Books Ltd, Registered Offices: Harmondsworth, Middlesex, England

First published 1985
10 9 8 7 6 5 4 3 2

Printed and bound in Great Britain by
Cox & Wyman Ltd, Reading
Typeset in Linotron Aldus by
Rowland Phototypesetting Ltd,
Bury St Edmunds, Suffolk

Illustrations by Ruan Martin

*With all my love to*
*Eddy, Kevin and Lee,*
*and a big thank you to*
*my dear mother, without*
*whose permission I could not*
*have married a Malaysian*
*and this book would not have*
*been written.*

# Contents

Preface 9

Acknowledgements 11

1. Introduction

Malaysia: the country, its people, and its cuisine 15

Utensils and other equipment 20

Weights and measures 23

Basic preparations and cooking methods 24

Herbs, spices and other essential ingredients 32

Glossary 45

2. Malay Cuisine

Introduction 53

Soups and starters 55

Poultry and egg dishes 60

Meat and offal dishes 67

Seafood dishes 74

Vegetable dishes 81

Rice, noodles and bread dishes 92

Condiments 104

Sweets and drinks 106

3. Chinese Cuisine

Introduction 115

Soups 117

Poultry dishes 123

Meat and offal dishes 134

Seafood dishes 144

Vegetable dishes 154

Rice, noodles and bread dishes 163

Condiments 175

Sweets and drinks 177

Chinese tea 181

Steamboat (Chinese fondue) 182

8    *Contents*

*4. Indian Cuisine*    Introduction                            189
                       Soups and snacks                        191
                       Poultry and egg dishes                  196
                       Meat and offal dishes                   207
                       Seafood dishes                          219
                       Vegetable and lentil
                         dishes                                229
                       Rice and bread dishes                   243
                       Condiments and
                         accompaniments                        250
                       Sweets and drinks                       255

*5. Menu Suggestions*  Malay menus                             265
                       Chinese menus                           267
                       Indian menus                            269
                       Multi-racial menus                      271

                       Index                                   273

*Preface*    I was born in India, and for the first twenty-one years of my life I was very sheltered and pampered by my parents and did not know much about the outside world. I first became aware of Malaysia when I became the pen-friend of a young Indian Roman Catholic Malaysian. Through his letters I grew to know Malaysia, not knowing then that I would one day marry him and how deeply involved I would become with the Malaysians and the country itself.

When I arrived in England in 1965 I was totally ignorant about cooking. With the aid of a recipe book I started to learn, but only out of necessity. When I got married in 1968 my interest in cooking increased, however, as my husband loves good food of all kinds, and once I had acquired a knowledge of authentic Indian cooking, I began to try Malay and Chinese recipes with his help and advice. Much of the credit for this book is due to him.

In my recipes I have used authentic oriental herbs, spices and other ingredients, most of which are now widely available. If you have difficulty in obtaining any of these, you will find suggestions for substitutes on pages 32–45. In fact, I often have to use substitute ingredients myself, as I live in a rural area of England where the authentic ones are not easily obtained.

It is very difficult to be precise in giving exact measurements, particularly of spices. Follow my suggestions for your first attempt, and once you have acquired confidence you can increase or decrease the spices and other ingredients to suit your own taste.

People often say that they would love to cook eastern food but feel the ingredients and preparation are very complicated. The solution is very simple. Don't decide to cook eastern dishes on the spur of the moment. Carefully read through the book, particularly the early chapters, then use my menu suggestions (page 263) as guide lines. Study each recipe carefully, and make a list of all the ingredients you will need to buy. Buy spices in small quantities and keep them in airtight containers, clearly labelled. You can build up a spice larder gradually. Always include as many 'do-it-ahead' dishes as possible in your menu, and never try out a new recipe if you are having guests – keep to recipes you know will be a success.

Thousands of cookery books have been written, from which we can learn to prepare food of every nationality, but it is not easy to produce authentic results outside the country of origin. Ingredients may have different textures and strengths in different countries, and even the water can change the flavour to a certain degree. Also, cooks are individualists and it is unlikely that two cooks following the same recipe exactly will produce identical results. However, Malaysian cooking is well worth trying, and once you have learned to appreciate the taste of spices such as blacan/terasi and ingredients such as ikan bilis and dried prawns, it will rank high on your list of national cuisine.

I hope you will enjoy reading my book, and that it will give you, your family and your friends many hours of happy eating. I must end by saying, 'If I can do it, so can you.'

*Rafi Fernandez*

11

*Acknowledgements*  The author wishes to thank the Malaysian Tourist Office, London, for permission to reproduce their slide of their Hotel Tanjung Jara in Terangganu, Malaysia, which received one of H.H. Prince Karim Aga Khan's awards for architecture in 1983.

My thanks are also due to the following: Anne Waller, Rosamond Richardson, Margaret Williamson, Lesley Bryant, Trish Thompson and Basil Ross; everyone at Penguin who was involved with the book; Felicity Bryan, who made this, my first book, possible; Eddy, my husband, for bearing with my tensions and for his helpful criticisms and guidance; my sons, Kevin and Lee, for just being there.

# 1.

# *Introduction*

# Malaysia: the country, its people and its cuisine

The Federation of Malaysia is divided into two regions – Peninsular Malaysia (West Malaysia) and Sabah and Sarawak (East Malaysia). The country is surrounded on three sides by the sea, and enjoys a mild humid climate, with an average temperature of 15–20°C throughout the year. It rains practically every day, which accounts for the luscious fauna and foliage and the variety of unusual and delicious fruits and vegetables. Rice is grown in abundance and forms the staple food. (Second in line is seafood of all kinds, which the surrounding seas will never stop producing.) It is thought that rice was introduced to Malaysia by Indian merchants only 1,000 years ago. Until recently only one crop was produced each year, but today there are two, providing 85 per cent of the rice consumed by the country. Two-thirds of the country is still dense jungle, and only the Orang Asli (the original man), the Ibans and the Dyaks still live within, as they did over forty generations ago.

Malaysia is a plural society with a rich cultural heritage based on the separate traditions which constitute Malaysian society. Because of its geographical position, Malaysia has maintained close relationships with India and China for centuries and today large numbers of people from India and China have become part of its permanent population. Although today the Chinese outnumber the Indians in Malaysia, it was India that influenced its early civilization.

The name 'Malay' is the ethnic term for the Muslims who make up more than half the population of Malaysia. The other seven million are made up of Chinese, Indians, Ceylonese, Eurasians, Portuguese, tribesmen and aborigines. The soft-spoken and harmonious Malay language is a blend of Arabic, Sanskritik and Portuguese. The original Malays were animists but were influenced by Hinduism, Buddhism and, later, Islam. Islam, the country's national religion, came to Malaysia in the fifteenth century from India when a Hindu prince converted and took up the title of 'Sultan Muzaffar Shah'. Today Malaysia has fourteen states, each ruled in pomp by a sultan. Every five years they elect one of their own number and crown him 'King of Malaysia'.

Though modern ideas are gaining ground in Malay society,

orthodox religious beliefs still have a considerable hold. Islam affects not only people's method of worship, but their whole way of life – it plays a prominent role in Malay culture, architecture and cuisine. Five times a day all over Malaysia the *imams* (Muslim priests) call out the *azaan* (a notification to Muslims that it is time for prayers) from the minarets of the thousands of *masjids* (mosques) throughout the country. Islam prohibits the Malays from eating pork because it has been described in the Koran (the holy book of the Muslims) as an unclean animal, and according to the laws laid down in the Koran they can only eat other meats and fish if they are *halal* – slaughtered according to Muslim law. The Malays aim for the day when they can go on a holy pilgrimage to Mecca, where Islam took birth under the auspicious teachings of Mohammed the Prophet. (Peace be on Him.)

The Chinese first came to Malaysia as traders in Malacca, and the first immigrants who settled were men who had to leave their families behind in China as hostages. Some never returned to their families but underwent assimilation; these men are called *babas*, the women they married are *nonyas*, and when spoken of as a couple they are known as *peranakan* or Straits Chinese. Today they are found mostly in Penang, Malacca and Singapore. The main influx of Chinese into Malaysia came in 1840 when new tin mines were found; they came from the southern provinces of China, bringing with them their customs, religion and language with different dialects. The main Chinese dialects are Cantonese, Hokkien and Mandarin, but when they converse with each other it is usually in Malay. The Chinese in Malaysia have always remained a separate community, self-sufficient and independent. They have built many schools in order to ensure that the Malaysian Chinese do not forget their cultural background. Some Chinese have adopted Christianity or Islam, but Buddhism is still the main religion. Chinese cooking in Malaysia is still authentic except for that of the Straits Chinese, which has a distinctive Malay influence.

Indian traders had been coming to Malaysia for centuries, but the main community of Indian immigrants was only established in the late nineteenth century. The Malaysian Indians who form 10 per cent of the population arrived after hearing rumours of the good fortunes of the country. Their dreams were soon shattered when they were able to work only as labourers on the rubber plantations, which were a new industry, and many returned to India. Hinduism is the main religion, as most of the Indians came from South India, but there is a strong Christian community and smaller communities of Indian Muslims, Sikhs, Sindhis and Bengalis. Hindus are mostly vegetarians, and those who are not do not eat beef because the cow is sacred and worshipped. Tamil and Malyalam are the most widely spoken languages. Although the Indians stay in a close-knit community with very strong family bonds, there have been some social contacts and intermarriages with Malays and Indian Muslims. There is a small Ceylonese community; they are mostly Hindus and have a great deal in common with the Indians. Their cuisine differs only slightly from the Indian cuisine.

Malaysia is one of the richest and most exciting countries in the world from a gastronomic point of view; every kind of cuisine can be found. There are three main ones, however – Malay, Chinese and Indian – and I have divided the book into these three sections.

My personal experience of eating any meal in Malaysia is that it is greatly enjoyable, prepared with great love, and the hospitality is incomparable. Even eating at stalls or getting the street hawker with his mobile kitchen in your drive is an occasion to be remembered. In fact, my most memorable meals have been at the stalls which are a big feature of Malaysian life. Seats are laid out around 10–15 stalls, each the size of a kiosk and each preparing its own speciality. You can order a variety of dishes from each of the stalls, and your meal may end up a fascinating combination of Malay, Chinese and Indian dishes. The drinks arrive first and you slowly sip while the food is being prepared. The meal usually ends with a selection of fresh fruits, colourfully served on a bed of crushed ice. When you have finished, each owner comes to clear his crockery and chopsticks or cutlery and to settle his bill. It is amazing how organized they are, and although a cluster of stalls works as if the members were all one big family, they each return to their own traditions and religions once they are within their own four walls.

Meals in Malaysia are not prepared as they are in the West. The number of persons is not taken into account, but several dishes are prepared each day and placed on the table under nets, for family members and friends to help themselves. Indians and Malays generally eat their food cold. Usually what is prepared for lunch is served again for dinner, with a fresh vegetable or egg dish in addition to the lunch menu.

For family meals the Chinese serve all the dishes together, but for special occasions one dish at a time is served and each person uses his chopsticks to help himself to a portion in his small bowl. Rice or noodles are brought in with the first course and left until the meal ends. Chinese meals usually end with a soup.

In Malaysia, verbal or formal invitations are sent out for special occasions but one usually visits friends and relatives on the spur of the moment. Malaysian hospitality is incomplete without a snack or a meal, and this is a ritual – the hostess offers her guests food, the guests politely refuse, she insists, they refuse and so on. She has already given instructions for the meal to be prepared, so she has to win, and invariably she does.

Printed menus are a recent introduction, but you will rarely find them at stalls or small restaurants. Each group tells the restaurateur what they would like and how they would like the dishes prepared. A selection of dishes are ordered, including rice and noodles, and the restaurateur adjusts the portions according to the number dining. Quantities served in Malaysia are large, but if you are not able to finish all the food you ordered you can have it packed up to take away. Scented paper towels are always provided before and after a meal, even at most stalls.

Meals are available twenty-four hours a day. Two years ago I visited Malaysia with my husband and two sons, to celebrate Christmas with his family. Although we arrived at 1 a.m. after a tedious journey, our first halt was the open-air stalls just outside Kelang where we had a feast of satay, giant prawns in a rich sauce, kankong (a local spinach) with a hot chilli sauce, squid with black beans and oyster sauce, and finally a platter of delicious fresh fruits. My husband told the boys about his young days, when he and his friends went out for a feast of satay with limited money between them. In those days you ordered satay and the vendor charged according to the number of empty sticks left on the table. The young lads broke and hid some of the sticks in order to avoid a hefty bill. Today, I am afraid the vendor has already counted the number of sticks before serving.

I will never forget that Christmas. My mother-in-law's home was turned into an open house for 25 December. She has four daughters and five sons, so imagine all the spouses and grand-children, plus all their friends and family friends and countless aunts, uncles and cousins – we estimated that 300 people would have to be fed. The preparations had started on 23 December, but the actual cooking did not begin till about 5 a.m. on the 25th. Everyone shared kitchen duties, and most of the dishes were cooked on open charcoal fires in the courtyard outside the kitchen. The menu for the day was:

    10 turkeys, roasted in woks.
    25 deep-fried chickens. A Chinese woman was hired for the day
       to prepare these as the guests arrived, and as her fee she kept
       all the giblets.
    10 roasted ducks. The Chinese woman kept all these giblets
       too.
    10 kg deep-fried fish.
    10 kg large prawns, made into a hot curry.
    10 chickens, made into a spicy curry.
    20 kg mutton, made into a hot dry curry (my mother-in-law's
       speciality).
    5 kg lentils, made into a curry.

All the above dishes were served cold with bread and Appam. There were several other snacks, and of course the Christmas cake. As we were visiting we provided the traditional British Christmas pudding, and I even took over some fresh holly which we kept in the refrigerator until the day. Whether one is Malay, Chinese or Indian, all occasions are celebrated with great pomp.

   Malaysians do not generally serve a dessert or pudding at the end of their meal. I have included a selection of recipes in each section, but in Malaysia these would be eaten as a snack. There is a wide range of delicious cold and hot non-alcoholic drinks – a skill perfected because the majority of the population are Muslims and their religion forbids the drinking of alcohol. Stalls are everywhere, and where in the West we would drink tea or coffee, Malaysians will drink one of these – Cendol, Champok, Ice Kacang, rose syrup, soya bean milk (natural or with a variety of flavourings), Chinese tea, chrysanthemum tea, herb tea, mango juice, lychee juice, lime juice, tamarind juice, sugar cane juice, etc., etc. Oh, I forgot the strong, sweet, sticky black coffee. I found that tea was not too popular at stalls, even though Malaysia grows excellent tea. When I did find an Indian man selling tea it was interesting to stand and watch him cool a cup of tea for his customers. I called it 'the yard of tea' – he poured it from one cup to another with a yard in between where the cooling took place. All drinks to take away (even hot ones) are packed in little pink plastic bags with a straw stuck in and the end sealed with a piece of pink plastic string. It is amazing how rarely it leaks. Even if you select a bottled drink it is emptied into a plastic bag. Cartons are coming in strong and fast, but I do hope the little pink plastic bags do not disappear.

Malaysians love the outdoor life, and evenings and weekends are always fully booked socially. Food, of course, plays a most important role. Annual holidays are not planned as they are in the West – sometimes a trip to the zoo, the seaside, gardens, even the museum is considered a holiday. One does not really have to bother about packing a picnic, because there is no area or street where snacks or full meals are not available.

I have often heard people in Malaysia say that 'good food and happiness go hand in hand', and from my own personal experiences I find this very true.

## Utensils and other equipment

Having learned to cook in the UK, I began with ordinary saucepans, knives and a pestle and mortar. I soon realized that I would need more suitable equipment, and I invested my money in three items – a traditional wok with a lid, a heavy cleaver, and an electric blender. A cook is good when he or she considers the actual cooking procedure enjoyable and not a chore, therefore I recommend highly that you consider acquiring these three items.

### Wok

Because of the wok's shape the heat is spread evenly, and you can stir-fry, shallow-fry, deep-fry, steam and, by using a lid, braise, simmer or boil.

Traditional woks are made from thin metal and work best on a gas cooker. Although you can get a grid to rest the wok on if your cooker is an electric one, I am afraid it will not be as efficient. If you have an electric cooker it is more advisable to purchase a flat-bottomed wok. These are usually non-stick, so you have only to follow the non-stick rules. Traditional woks need to be seasoned before they are used. Heat the wok, pour in some oil, and continue heating until the oil begins to smoke. Swirl the wok around to cover the inside with the oil. Add an egg and some salt and stir-fry quickly. The egg will burn and the inner base of the wok will begin to turn black. Do not worry – this is meant to happen. When the egg is fully dry, discard it, and wipe away the excess oil with a soft paper towel. To use the wok, just rinse it in hot water and wipe dry. Wash the wok in very hot water after each use, but do not use detergent and do dry it thoroughly. Keep it in a cool dry place. Gradually your wok will get blacker, and it will finally be fully seasoned.

When using a wok, always ensure that it is fully heated before adding the oil. If more oil or fluid has to be added during the cooking process, always pour it around the sides of the wok and not directly over the ingredients. The spoon usually used has a shovel-like shape, but you can use any flat spoon, and of course a wooden one if you have a non-stick wok. A perforated spoon is handy when you have to remove ingredients from oil or gravy.

One more word of advice. Before using your wok, study your recipe carefully. Have all the ingredients prepared, spices and seasonings weighed and measured, and put them close to hand. When you are using a wok, particularly a traditional one, cooking time is greatly speeded and you will not be able to go and hunt for the odd spice or ingredient in between. Once the cooking has started the heat should be maintained according to the instructions in each recipe, especially if you are making stir-fry dishes.

You may take a little while to get used to your wok, as I did, but soon it will be your best friend and you will use it every day.

*Cleaver*    The Chinese are masters of knives. If you can learn the art you will save yourself a great deal of time and energy. The most commonly used knife is the cleaver (also known as a chopper). It is large and heavy, and at first you will find it too much for your hands. You can buy authentic Chinese cleavers from Chinese grocers and shops, but you may be able to pick up a French version from a good department store. I prefer the complete steel cleaver, made from one piece of heavy steel with a steel handle.

When using a cleaver, make sure you have a firm heavy chopping board. With a cleaver you can cut very thin slices, and you can use the flat side to crush garlic or nuts. You can also use it for chopping finely and mincing: hold the handle with your right hand, and with the fingers of the left hand hold the square top of the cleaver. Keep your right hand stationary and move the blade backwards and forwards with the left hand. This way you can chop ingredients like herbs, garlic, ginger and spring onions very finely, or mince meat and fish. As the cleaver has a large flat blade, you can use it to transfer the chopped ingredients straight from the chopping board to the cooking utensil.

Always wash and dry the cleaver thoroughly after each use, and make sure you store it well out of the reach of children and of those who have not learned the art of handling it.

## Electric blender

This is a vital piece of equipment, as so many recipes call for ingredients and spices to be ground. A heavy pestle and mortar is fairly adequate, but harder work and more time-consuming. (See notes on how to grind spices and herbs on page 24.)

## Chopsticks

It took me quite a while to learn how to eat with chopsticks, but now I use them even during the actual cooking. I find them very handy for turning over fish or meat pieces, for stir-frying, and for holding on to pieces while deep-frying. If you use chopsticks for cooking make sure they are either metal or plain wooden ones. Painted or ivory chopsticks could dissolve in extreme heat.

The diagrams show how to hold the chopsticks. Practise using chopsticks on cold food to avoid accidents.

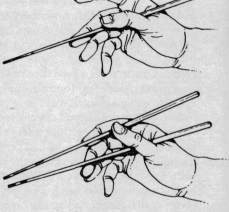

1. Place one chopstick between the inside of the thumb and the palm. Rest the pointed or thinner end on the third finger. This should be held firmly and it should remain stationary while in use.

2. Place the second chopstick between the upper part of the thumb and the index finger. This stick should be moved with leverage from the thumb and the index finger.

# Weights and measures

Throughout the book both imperial and metric weights and measures have been given. Use only one set of weights and measures, as they are not interchangeable.

For measuring rice and water I have used cup measures. Use the same cup to measure both the rice and the water.

Cup and spoon measurements are level. Most recipes serve 4–6 persons, unless otherwise stated. The following charts will give you an idea how I worked out the conversions.

## Weights

| Imperial | Metric | Imperial | Metric | Imperial | Metric |
|---|---|---|---|---|---|
| ½ oz | 15g | 8 oz/ ½ lb | 225 g | 15 oz | 425 g |
| 1 oz | 25 g | 9 oz | 250 g | 16 oz/ 1 lb | 450 g |
| 2 oz | 50 g | 10 oz | 275 g | 32 oz/ 2 lb | 900 g |
| 3 oz | 75g | 11 oz | 300 g | 3 lb | 1·3 kg |
| 4 oz | 100 g | 12 oz | 350 g | 4 lb | 1·8 kg |
| 5 oz | 150 g | 13 oz | 375 g | | |
| 6 oz | 175g | 14 oz | 400 g | | |
| 7 oz | 200 g | | | | |

## Fluid Measures

Up to 3 fl oz use spoon measures if possible. When using spoon measures they should be level.

| Imperial | Metric | Imperial | Metric |
|---|---|---|---|
| 4 fl oz | 110 ml | ½ pt | 300 ml |
| 5 fl oz/ ¼ pt | 150 ml | ¾ pt | 450 ml |
| | | 1 pt | 600 ml |
| 6 fl oz | 175 ml | 2 pts | 1·2 litres |

# Basic preparations and cooking methods

## How to grind or pound spices and herbs

This task is performed every day in the East, and once it is done the actual cooking is very basic. In many of the recipes which follow you will notice that I have listed separately the ingredients that have to be ground or pounded. These can be prepared by using a heavy pestle and mortar, as it is still done in Malaysia. Grind and pound the spices and herbs, using a little oil, until they form a smooth paste. This can also be done in an electric blender, which will save you a lot of time and hard work. Grind the ingredients, gradually adding oil, which will prolong the blender's life by acting as a lubricant (water and other liquids tend to rust the motor). Occasionally you will need to move the ingredients from the sides with a spatula. If you have used oil for grinding, the ground paste can be fried without oil. Whole spices are best dry-roasted individually before being ground (see page 29).

## How to make coconut milk

In some recipes I have specifically mentioned creamed or desiccated coconut, but in general the recipes call for either thick or thin coconut milk. There are three methods, and I leave you to choose the one which will suit you best.

### Thick and thin coconut milk from fresh coconuts

Break the shell, reserving the coconut water which is delicious when chilled. Remove the brown skin and cut the coconut flesh into small pieces. Place in a blender and liquidize the coconut flesh gradually on medium speed, adding a little ordinary milk or warm water. Empty the contents into a large sieve and vigorously squeeze out as much thick milk as you can. Return the flesh to the blender and add the amount of water required by the particular recipe you are using. Blend again on medium speed for 1–2 minutes. Empty the contents into the sieve, but squeeze out the thin milk into a separate bowl. I find that the coconuts available here do not yield more than ¾–1 cup of thick milk per coconut, so you may need more than one. If you have any milk left over, seal it in an airtight plastic tumbler and either freeze it if you do not anticipate using it for a while, or keep it in the refrigerator for up to 4 days.

Usually, the thin coconut milk is added first during cooking and the thick milk is added during the last few minutes of cooking time. Once the thick milk has been added, stir constantly as it curdles easily, and do not cover the pan.

## Thick and thin coconut milk from desiccated coconut

Soak 2 lb (900 g) of desiccated coconut in ½ pt (300 ml) of hot water for 1–2 hours, then transfer to a blender and liquidize on medium speed for 1–2 minutes. Empty the contents into a large sieve and squeeze out the thick coconut milk. This should produce about 6–8 fl oz (175–225 ml). Return the coconut to the blender and add the amount of water required by the recipe you are using. Liquidize again for 1–2 minutes. Empty the contents into the large sieve and squeeze out the thin coconut milk into a separate bowl.

## Thick and thin coconut milk from creamed coconut blocks

Soak 3 oz (75 g) of chopped creamed coconut and a pinch of salt in 6 fl oz (175 ml) of hot water. Stir well till dissolved and your thick milk is ready. For thin coconut milk, follow the same procedure but use only 1 oz (25 g) of coconut. An alternative method is to soak 4 oz (100 g) of chopped creamed coconut in 12 fl oz (350 ml) of hot water with ½ teaspoon of salt, stir till dissolved, and chill in the refrigerator. When it is fully chilled the cream will separate from the water and rise to the top. This can be spooned out and used as the thick milk, and the remaining liquid can be used as the thin milk.

Sometimes tinned coconut milk is available. Check the labels carefully, because often it has been sweetened. Tinned coconut milk does not have a very thick consistency, so if you are using it, add a little creamed coconut.

*Rice*    The Malays call it *beras* (*nasi* when cooked), the Chinese
call it *fan* (pronounced 'fun') and the Indians call it *arisi*
(Tamil) or *chawal* (Hindi). In Malaysia rice is the staple diet, and in
many homes it is cooked for all the three main meals. There are
many varieties of rice, and in Malaysia you can also get different
colours like purple, grey, black and blue as well as the common
white and brown. I generally use Patna rice, also described as
long-grain or American long-grain, for daily consumption. For
special occasions or special dishes I use *basmati*, which is now
available from some large supermarkets. *Basmati* rice has a rich
aroma, and when cooked the grains are longer, slender and very
delicate. In recipes where the rice is sautéd first, I recommend you
use *basmati*. In some recipes I have used glutinous rice. The grains
are short and fat and contain more starch. You can substitute pudding rice. Those who have health problems or are conscientious
about wholefood can use natural brown unpolished rice, but this
will require extra water and a longer cooking time.

## Preparing rice for cooking

I always wash rice before using it, to remove the starchy powder
from the grains. First I pick out any husks or stones, then I wash the
rice in several changes of water. Sometimes five or six changes are
necessary before the water remains clear. I use my hand as a sieve
when changing the water, but if you are worried about losing rice
grains, use a proper sieve. Soak the washed rice in water for about
20–30 minutes before cooking – this will produce a better yield
when cooked.

## How to measure rice and water

With millions of people cooking rice daily, there are bound to be
several methods. My mother, for example, measures four fistfuls of
rice per person, washes it, puts it in a pan, places her second finger at
a right angle, allowing the tip of the finger to touch the base of the
pan, and pours in water until it reaches the second line of her finger.
She uses this method when cooking for 2 or 20 people, and her
cooked rice is always perfect.

Every cookery writer has adopted his or her method from
experience, and no one can prove that any one method is more

accurate. Throughout the book I have used imperial and metric measures but when it came to the rice dishes in each section I have used cup measures. Be sure to use the same cup to measure both the rice and the water.

1 cup of uncooked rice + 1½ cups of water = 2 persons.

2 cups of uncooked rice + 3 cups of water = 4 persons.

3 cups of uncooked rice + 4½ cups of water = 6 persons.

I have never failed using this method, and I often cook for 40–50 persons in one go.

## How to cook rice

Here again there are many methods. Many people still boil the rice in plenty of water until the grains are cooked, then drain off the water (not wasting the water but using it to starch clothes), and rinse the cooked grains in a colander under running cold water. However, this method removes all the vitamin content. The most popular method is by evaporation.

Always use a heavy pan with a tight-fitting lid which will not allow any of the essential steam to escape. If your lid does not fit tightly, cover the pan with a sheet of foil as well as the lid. Measure and wash the rice, leave it to soak for 20–30 minutes, then drain it thoroughly. Place the rice in a pan with the measured water, a pinch of salt and a knob of margarine or a few drops of olive oil. Leave the pan uncovered and bring to the boil, then turn the heat as low as possible, cover the pan tightly, and leave to cook till the rice is fluffy. This usually takes 20–25 minutes. When cooking rice it is important to lower the heat as quickly as possible after the water has come to the boil. On a gas stove this is very easy, but if your cooker is electric, like mine, I suggest that while you bring the rice and water to the boil on a highly heated ring you have a second ring ready at the lowest possible setting. This way you can make a quick transfer, covering the pan to seal in all the essential steam. Be sure to remember to turn off the first ring, for your own safety and also if there are youngsters around. (I was once careless this way – it can so easily happen, especially with a ceramic hob.)

To check if your rice is cooked, lift the lid a little after about 15–20 minutes and peep to see if small steam holes (called 'fish eyes' by the Chinese) have formed on the surface. Close the lid again immediately, turn off the heat, and allow to rest for 5–8 minutes. Then loosen the grains gently with a fork and serve. Use a flat spoon to dish out cooked rice, pushing the spoon down to the base and lifting the rice out in sections. Loosen the grains gently once they are placed on the serving plate. Never spoon out in layers, as you may damage the cooked grains.

If you are planning a dish which requires cooked rice for stir-frying, prepare the rice either a day earlier or several hours ahead to enable you to loosen and cool the grains. Hot rice tends to stick together when fried.

Glutinous rice or pudding rice requires more water and takes longer to cook. Instructions are given in the recipes where it is used.

Most families in Malaysia own an electric rice cooker, and I take my hat off to the genius who invented it. They are available in various sizes from Chinese grocers and shops and some large departmental stores. I highly recommend that you invest in one of these – it can save time and fuel, and it can also be used as a steamboat (see pages 182–5), for a dish like Yong Tau Fu (see page 159), or even to steam fish, meats and vegetables. The rice cooker is sold with accurate instructions which you can follow, or you can use my measuring method. Put in the rice and water with a pinch of salt and a knob of margarine, switch on the cooker, and the rest is done automatically. Once the rice is done, the cooker will switch itself off and continue to look after the rice by keeping it warm till you are ready to serve it.

## Noodles

A variety of noodles are available, both fresh and dry. Egg or yellow noodles are called *mee* and rice noodles are called *beehoon*. See the Glossary (page 45) for other names. In the Malay and Chinese sections of the book I have specified the kind of noodles to be used for each recipe.

Fresh noodles are available ready to use from Chinese grocers. Just soak them in fairly hot water with a few drops of oil for a few minutes to loosen the threads, then drain. Some recipes call for crisply fried noodles, in which case drain them for longer. When I make a trip to my nearest Chinese grocer I often pick up extra quantities of fresh noodles, as any variety freezes well. To use, thaw completely then follow the same procedure as with fresh noodles.

Nowadays, dried noodles are available at most supermarkets. Use them according to the instructions on the packet. When using rice sticks (vermicelli), I recommend soaking them in *warm* water until the threads are soft and loose – boiling water will break the threads.

*Seafood*    Seafood is the second staple food of Malaysia. Pomfret is my favourite, and this and several other Malaysian fish can be bought frozen from Chinese grocers. For each recipe I have recommended the type of fish, prawns or other seafood you can use. Here are few more suggestions: sea bream, plaice, sea bass, grey or red mullet, cod, whiting, fresh tuna, carp, mackerel, halibut, sole, rainbow trout, garfish, coley, saury, haddock, sardine, rock salmon, red snapper, turbot, salmon, conger eel, herring and whitebait. All these are suitable for grilling, steaming and frying. They can all be used for curries too, but I recommend that you first coat the fish pieces with some salt, a pinch of turmeric and a little cornflour and fry them in shallow oil. This seals the fish and also reduces the cooking time so that the pieces are less likely to break.

Raw frozen prawns and scampi, shelled or unshelled, are available in various sizes from Chinese grocers. You can use cooked shelled or unshelled prawns or scampi, available from fishmongers and supermarkets, but remember to reduce the cooking time. The same applies when using dressed crabs, crayfish and lobsters.

Fish balls, raw or fried, squid balls and fish cakes are available from Chinese grocers and they freeze well. It is always handy to have some for making up quick soups or stir-fried dishes.

*'Dry-roasting' method*    When whole spices need to be ground I recommend that they are first dry-roasted. Heat a griddle or heavy frying pan and fry each spice individually without oil until fragrant. Turn the spices regularly to avoid burning. Roasting whole spices brings out the flavour and also makes grinding easier. If you are attempting a Ceylon curry, roast the spices a few shades darker.

## Final fry
## (tarka *or* baghar)

This is used mostly in vegetable and lentil dishes. Heat the oil until fairly hot and fry the whole spices until they begin to splatter. Standing well back, pour the oil and spices on to the vegetables or lentils and cover the pan immediately. Mustard seeds are generally fried first, and when these start to pop, drop in the remaining ingredients in the order given.

## Addition of spices while cooking

Always reduce the heat before adding any powdered spices, as they burn very easily and will give your dish a bitter taste. When I am using powdered spices, I mix them with a little water and fry them gently till the water has evaporated.

## Cooking meat, fish and vegetables in their own juices

I like to add the least possible amount of water when cooking meat, fish or vegetables into a curry, unless the recipe specifies a gravy of thin consistency. In order to prevent them from charring by the evaporation of water inside the utensil, you can cover the pan with a Pyrex plate and pour some water on the plate.

## Hot curries

If your curry has become too hot, temper it down with some lemon juice and a little sugar. Alternatively, serve natural yogurt as an accompaniment – I have nicknamed this 'fire extinguisher'. Cool your mouth with none other than pure water, and you can end the meal by eating a little plain rice or a piece of bread, which will absorb the chilli taste.

*Salt*   If one of your dishes has accidentally become too salty, correct this by adding a few drops of lemon juice. If the dish is a curry you can add a piece of bread, which will absorb some of the excess salt but should be discarded before serving. My husband says I use too little salt, so please use my suggestions as a guide but adjust the salt to suit your own taste.

## General preparation and planning a menu

Always plan your menu well ahead and study the recipes carefully. Make sure you have all the necessary ingredients or adequate substitutes. In Malaysian cooking it is the preparation that takes the time. Once you have found all the ingredients, prepare them according to the recipe and lay them out in the order they are to be used. Prepare as many dishes as you can well in advance, leaving only stir-fried dishes till last. Each of my recipes gives the number of persons it will serve, but this should be used as a guide only – it depends on the appetite of your family and friends.

*Stains*   Curries tend to leave marks on some crockery. To remove stains, soak the crockery in hot water to which used tea leaves have been added. To remove marks from cutlery and pans, rub them with some softened tamarind (see page 44) and leave aside for a few minutes before rinsing. Try to avoid using a plain white tablecloth when serving curries, as the dye from turmeric is very strong and the stains are very difficult to remove. If curry is spilt on any tablecloth or clothes and you cannot attend to it immediately, sprinkle on some talcum powder or dry flour to absorb some of the stain.

*Shopping*   When I first arrived in London there was one Chinese grocer and perhaps a few Indian ones. Today there are hundreds, especially in London and most large cities. Furthermore, supermarkets and large departmental stores with food halls now offer a good range of oriental ingredients.

# Herbs, spices and other essential ingredients

For translation into local languages see pages 45–50. All these items are readily available from Chinese or Indian grocers, and those usually also available in supermarkets have been indicated with an asterisk.

### Agar-agar

A seaweed gelatine. Tasteless, transparent and sold in strands. Sets without refrigeration. Ordinary gelatine can be substituted, but the texture will not be as firm as with agar-agar. Agar-agar takes longer to dissolve and should be soaked overnight in a little water. Keeps indefinitely in a dry place.

### Anchovy, dried

Fresh whitebait, salted and dried in the sun. To use, split each fish and discard the head and intestines. Best deep-fried until golden and crisp. Serve as a garnish or to hand round while your guests are having their drinks. Store in an airtight jar.

### Aniseed*

Has a liquorice taste and aids digestion. One of the spices that makes up the 'five-spice' mixture. Keeps indefinitely.

### Asafoetida

Mainly used by Indians. Obtained from a resin gum, and although it has a very unpleasant smell when raw, it leaves the cooked dish with a delicious flavour. Used in minute quantities. Stores indefinitely in a tightly sealed jar.

### Bah Kuk tea

A blend of ten Chinese herbs and spices with a high medicinal value. Ideal for soups. Packed in sachets like *bouquet garni*. Available only from Chinese grocers and Chinese medicine shops. Stores indefinitely.

### Bamboo shoots*

Sold in cans, packed with brine or braised. Unlike fresh shoots, canned varieties require very little cooking. Any leftovers can be transferred to a plastic container and frozen.

*Bay leaves**   See *Laurel leaves*

*Bean pastes**   Crushed soya beans, rice flour and salt, fermented until a thick paste forms. Many varieties available. I have used the yellow and red varieties in this book. Available in jars or tins, both in paste form and in cubes. Keeps for a considerable period in the refrigerator. You can also get bean paste with chillies blended in, so read the labels carefully. The yellow variety can be found in some supermarkets.

*Beansprouts**   Two basic varieties: green pea (mung bean) sprouts or yellow soya bean sprouts. Only the first variety available in supermarkets. Also available canned, but these are soft as they are packed in brine – if fresh sprouts are not available I substitute thin shreds of celery. I very rarely cook beansprouts as they are very high in protein. Where a recipe suggests that you tail them, this is done only to give the dish a perfect appearance and is therefore not essential.

*Blacan or terasi*   Prawns and salt, allowed to ferment and then mashed into a paste. It has a very strong smell but is essential in Malay cooking. Once cooked the smell disappears, leaving the dish with a gentle taste and aroma. Sold in blocks or cakes. Keeps indefinitely, but once opened wrap it in two or three layers of cling film or foil to protect other ingredients in your larder. There is no real substitute, but if you are desperate use Hei-ko (shrimp paste) or anchovy paste mixed in thick soya sauce. Hei-ko is available from Chinese grocers and anchovy paste is available in tubes from some supermarkets.

*Candlenuts*   Fruits of the candleberry tree, originally used by the Orang Asli and aborigines as candles as they are rich in oil and burn for a long time. They are heart-shaped, and the Malays use them as a thickening agent in curries. Use almonds, macadamia nuts, or Brazil nuts as substitutes.

*Cardamom**   Also called 'the seeds of paradise', and the second most expensive spice in the world. Available in pods and powder form. Can be used whole by bruising the skin, but either discard before serving or warn the diners. They are edible, but if chewed unawares the strong taste could give you a shock. Used in both savoury and sweet dishes, and also to spice tea and coffee. The seeds can be chewed on their own to refresh your mouth like mint does.

## *Chilli sauce**
A wide range readily available. You have to try a few to find the one that will suit your taste. If you wish to make your own, see pages 104–5.

## *Chillies, fresh and dried**
Fresh chillies are green or red and in various sizes. The larger variety are not so hot, but the tiny ones called 'bird's eye' are fiery. Fresh chillies are rich in Vitamin C and indispensable in Indian and Malay cooking. Chillies also help stimulate the appetite, which tends to wilt in a hot climate. Although in my recipes I have suggested the quantities, only you can judge the taste of your family and friends, so increase or decrease accordingly. When you have handled chillies, make sure you wash your hands two or three times and avoid touching your face and eyes. Another useful hint is to smear the hands with a little oil before handling the chillies. This will prevent any burning sensation.

If you find fresh chillies difficult to come by regularly, purchase extra quantities when they are available, wash and dry them thoroughly and open freeze them. You can also grind them with oil in an electric blender and freeze in ice trays. When the cubes are set, remove and seal in plastic bags. Jars of ground red chillies in oil are available from Chinese and Indian grocers and some supermarkets, and are useful to keep in the larder.

Frozen chillies cannot be used to make 'chilli flowers', which are very popular for garnishing, but if you run them under water and slice them thinly while still frozen you can use them as a garnish. For chilli flowers, use long firm chillies and slit them half-way through. Gently remove the seeds and slit each half three or four times more. Soak in cold water and the slits will curl and look like petals.

You can grow chillies by planting the seeds removed from fresh chillies. I grow my own each summer, enough to see me through the year.

Dried chillies are red and available in many sizes and strengths. The small ones are the hottest. The large Kashmiri ones will give a lovely colour to curries but are quite mild. Red chilli powders also vary in strength, so use the quantities I have recommended as a guide and adjust accordingly. Both fresh and dried chillies will have a milder flavour if you discard the seeds.

## Chinese cabbage*

There are two main varieties: long pale green leaves with wide white ribs, and long dark green leaves with wide white ribs. The pale variety is now widely sold in supermarkets and greengrocers. The dark variety has a slightly bitter taste. Use either. The pale variety can also be used raw in salads and as a garnish.

## Chinese dried mushrooms

Dried whole and fairly expensive. Available only from Chinese grocers. Will keep indefinitely in a dry place. I regret that there is no substitute, and if you cannot obtain them, omit them from the recipe. To use, soak in warm water until soft, then discard stems and thinly slice caps. The water can be strained and used if the recipe requires water to be added.

## Chinese sausage

Two varieties are available: the first a light-coloured variety made from lean pork and pork fat cubes, and the second a mixture of liver, pork and pork fat. Available only from Chinese grocers and some restaurants. Stores indefinitely in the refrigerator. To use, always slice the sausage diagonally.

## Chinese taste powder*

Also called Wei Fen. A blend of twelve Chinese herbs and spices. Can be used as a substitute for monosodium glutamate. Use sparingly. Stores indefinitely.

## Cinnamon*

Tender bark of a perennial tree, thinly peeled and rolled into quills. The true species is grown in Sri Lanka, although different varieties can be found in other South-East Asian countries. If a recipe calls for a 1-inch (2.5-cm) piece of cinnamon, this does not apply to the thickness but to the length of a rolled quill. Readily available in quills and in powder form.

*Cloves**   A highly aromatic and medicinal spice, used in the East since 200 B.C. Has a sweet, pungent flavour. The Malays and Indians use it to enhance the flavour of curries, rice dishes and sweets. Also used to spice tea and coffee. The Indians rub the juice of cloves on the temples when they have a fever, as it is said to draw the fever out. Available whole and in powder form.

*Coconut milk**   See pages 24–5.

*Coriander: seeds,**
*powder* and fresh*   An essential ingredient in Malay and Indian cooking, and also used by the Straits Chinese in some dishes. Seeds and powder readily available.

   The lacy leaves and tender stems of fresh coriander are used to flavour curries, and the leaves are almost always used as a garnish. Fresh coriander can be grown from seed, and can be bought in bunches from Indian, Chinese and Greek grocers. It will stay fairly fresh for up to a week in the refrigerator. It can be frozen by two methods. A simple method is to break the leaves and the very tender stems and freeze in an airtight box. To use, just crush a little with your fingers while still frozen and return the rest to the freezer. Alternatively, you can grind the leaves and tender stems with oil in an electric blender and freeze in ice trays. When the cubes are set, store in plastic bags.

   Frozen coriander leaves cannot be used for garnish, unfortunately, but if you have added some to flavour the dish you can garnish with nuts, mustard and cress, parsley, fresh mint, etc.

*Cumin**   Another essential ingredient for curries. Available as seeds or powder. Do not use caraway seeds as a substitute, as they are very different in flavour.

*Curry leaves*   Fresh and dried varieties available from Indian and Chinese grocers. Used in curries and 'final fry' (*tarka*), see page 30. In Malaysia a housewife can pick these in her garden or can just buy the quantity she needs each day. If you are planning to buy a packet, here are two hints for storage. Place the leaves open in a wicker basket in a dry place. Gradually they will turn a dull brown and become brittle. Do not cover or seal the dried leaves or they will become mouldy. In fact, I leave a selection of dried chillies, curry leaves, unpeeled garlic and bay leaves in a wicker basket and it makes a charming display as well as being handy. An alternative is to seal the fresh leaves in an airtight container and freeze. The leaves remain separate, so you can easily remove only the number required.

## Curry powder*

A taboo to Indians, who blend their own each day. The Malays blend their own too, and it is not dissimilar to the Indian varieties, but they call it *rempah*. If you wish to use a commercial curry powder of your choice, delete coriander, cumin, turmeric, fenugreek and chilli powders from the recipe. Use 2 tablespoons of curry powder for every pound of meat or fish but only 1 tablespoon for every pound of vegetables.

## Fennel*

Very similar in appearance to cumin seed, and nicknamed 'sweet cumin', but one cannot be substituted for the other. Fennel has a liquorice flavour.

## Fenugreek*

This has a slightly bitter flavour and should be used sparingly. It is often very noticeable in commercial curry powders. The leaves of the plant are used in salads or combined with other vegetables to make a curry, and are sometimes even cooked with mutton into a dry curry.

## Fish, dried

A wide range is available from Chinese grocers and some non-vegetarian Indian grocers. To use, soak in warm water until soft and then cut into small pieces or slices. If you wish to fry the pieces of fish you should dry them thoroughly, otherwise they will not get crisp and will also splatter a lot. If you find difficulty in obtaining dried fish use Bombay Duck. This can now be found in some supermarkets, but should be used without soaking.

## Fish sauce

When fish is soaked in salt, the fermented juice becomes fish sauce. Available from Chinese grocers only. Use light soya sauce as a substitute. Fish sauce keeps indefinitely.

## Five-spice powder*

Also called Wu Hsiang Fen. Widely used in Malaysia and essential in Chinese cooking. A blend of star anise, fennel, cinnamon, cloves and Szechuan pepper. Use sparingly. Try a pinch on stewed fruit, apple pie and even in casseroles. Stores indefinitely.

## Fruits

Fresh or tinned. Malaysia has a wide range of fresh fruits and sometimes one comes across a few in Chinatowns or Indian grocers. Most of them are available in tins. Most meals in Malaysia end with a platter of fresh fruits – here is a short list: custard apples, durians, guavas, jackfruit, longans, lychees, mangoes, mangosteens, melons, papayas (pawpaws), passion fruits, pineapples, pomegranates, pomelos, rambutans, star fruits, sugar cane, and watermelons. You can use tinned varieties to make up a tropical fruit salad.

## Garam masala*

A mixed condiment added to Indian and Malay dishes at the last stage of cooking, or sprinkled on just before serving. Although readily obtainable, I recommend that you make your own. Here are two variations. The first is a basic recipe and the second more aromatic.

> ½ oz (15 g) cumin seeds
> ½ oz (15 g) peppercorns
> ½ oz (15 g) cloves
> ½ oz (15 g) cardamom seeds (weigh after removing from pods)

Roast the spices individually in a frying pan without oil. Cool, grind to a fine powder, and store in an airtight jar.

> ½ oz (15 g) cumin seeds
> ½ oz (15 g) black cumin seeds
> ½ oz (15 g) cloves
> ½ oz (15 g) cardamom seeds (weigh after removing from pods)
> 1 oz (25 g) peppercorns
> 2-inch (5-cm) piece cinnamon quill

Roast the spices individually in a frying pan without oil, then cool and grind to a fine powder. Mix in ¼ teaspoon of mace powder and ½ teaspoon of grated nutmeg. Store in an airtight jar.

*Garlic\**   Practically all my recipes include this herb. Fresh
garlic is easily obtainable and keeps for a long time at
room temperature. You can also buy dried minced garlic or garlic
purée in jars and tubes, but use these only if fresh garlic is difficult to
obtain. In Malaysia the garlic cloves are smaller and the peel is
blackish in colour, but I have found that the French variety is
stronger in flavour and definitely easier to peel. Garlic not only adds
flavour to dishes but also controls the cholesterol in your body. If
you have earache, believe it or not, a peeled clove of garlic soaked in
warm olive oil and placed in the ear will draw out the pain. Peeled
garlic cloves can be frozen whole, or ground to a paste with oil and
frozen in icetrays. When set, transfer the cubes to a plastic bag and
seal.

*Ginger\**   Fresh green ginger is readily available from Indian
and Chinese grocers, and many supermarkets and
greengrocers now stock it because the demand for it is growing.
Dried ginger powder has been available for some time now, but
should be used only if fresh ginger is difficult to obtain. Fresh
ginger, peeled and cut into small pieces, can be frozen whole or
ground to a paste with oil and frozen in a similar way to garlic.

To use green ginger, scrape off the scaly skin then mince, crush or
pulverize to a paste. In my recipes I have advised you how to prepare
fresh ginger for each dish. When only the juice is called for, pound
some ginger and then extract the juice by squeezing.

I always keep a bottle of the cheapest dry sherry, to which I have
added crushed ginger, and this comes very handy for Chinese
dishes.

Ginger also has a medicinal value. If you preserve sliced ginger in
lemon juice or brine, a slice or two will help when you have eaten too
much. Preserved ginger in attractive jars is easily available; this can
be used medicinally and it also tastes delicious when added to fresh
fruit salads. In Malaysia there are two further varieties of ginger –
Lengkuas and Laos. These are not very strong in flavour but have a
high medicinal value. Fresh Lengkuas and Laos are obtainable from
Chinese grocers.

*Hei-ko*
*(Shrimp paste)*
Similar to blacan but milder in taste.
Available in jars from Chinese grocers;
keeps indefinitely. Use in small
quantities.

*Laurel leaves*    Well known to Indians. Obtained from a perennial aromatic plant. Also produces camphor, which is used by Indians in temples. It is said to have purifying elements, and when soaked in water acts as an antiseptic. The Hindus worship this plant because of its versatility. It has a slightly pungent taste and is used to flavour curries. Use sweet basil or bay leaves as a substitute.

*Lemon grass*    Fresh lemon grass is obtainable from Chinese grocers. Roots easily when placed in water, and multiplies very fast when planted. Favoured mostly by the Malays. Use only the white bulbous part, unless otherwise specified. Usually bruised and used whole in curries, but discard before serving. Also available in powder form, called *sereh* powder. Use 1 teaspoon of this in place of 1 lemon grass stalk. When neither is available, use lemon balm or lemon rind. Fresh lemon grass stalks can be frozen.

*Lime*    The juice of this citrus fruit is used as a souring agent. Whole limes are also used to make pickle. Lemon juice can be used as a substitute, but choose lemons with thin skins for pickling.

*Monosodium glutamate**    White crystals sold under the name MSG, and used mainly by the Chinese. Although it has no taste of its own, it is said to bring out flavour. Also sold under the names of Ve-tsin and Aji-no-moto.

*Mushrooms, straw and oyster*    Available only in tins from Chinese grocers.

*Mustard seeds**    Used mainly by the Indians. This is the black variety, which is more pungent than the yellow. In powdered form it is blended with other spices to make curry powder. Used whole for 'final fry' (*tarka*) (see page 30).

*Mustard green*   A variety of spinach with distinctive yellow flowers. Obtainable fresh from Chinese grocers. I often buy more than I need, and freeze it. To do this, blanch it in boiling water for 1 minute, immediately cool in iced water, thoroughly drain, then freeze in suitable portions.

*Noodles**   See page 28.

*Onions*   In Malaysia the red onions known as Bombay onions are widely used. These are stronger in flavour than ordinary onions, and are often the size of shallots. It is not often possible to obtain these, so use small ordinary onions which are firm. Avoid the large Spanish variety as they contain a lot of fluid.

Deep-fried onion flakes are also very popular as a garnish. Make up a batch as follows and store them in airtight jars. Use firm onions and slice them finely. Heat some oil in a wok, and deep-fry on medium heat until the onions are brown and crisp, taking care not to burn them. Have a newspaper handy on which you can quickly place the browned onions after you remove them from the oil. Allow them to drain well, changing the newspaper once or twice. When completely cool, store in airtight jars.

*Onion seeds*   Available only from Indian grocers. Mainly used in vegetarian cooking by the Indians. They have a very delicious and distinct flavour, and keep indefinitely.

*Oyster sauce**   A blend of oysters and soya sauce. If difficult to obtain, use plum sauce, which is more common and also cheaper. Keeps indefinitely.

*Palm sugar*   Also known as *jaggery*. Made from coconut palms. Substitute raw sugar crystals or dark brown sugar. Alternatively, a blend of maple syrup and treacle can be used. If you are using a substitute, test the sweetness as you may need to increase or decrease the quantity.

*Peanuts**   Raw peanuts are generally used. Roasted peanuts are suitable, but be careful when adding salt.

*Peanut oil*    In Malaysia this is the most widely used oil, but a good quality vegetable oil can be substituted.

*Plum sauce**    A combination of plums, sugar and spices. Readily available, keeps indefinitely. Can be used as a substitute for oyster sauce if you are on a tight budget.

*Prawns, dried*    Small prawns, salted and dried in the sun. Readily obtainable from Chinese grocers and some non-vegetarian Indian grocers. Will keep indefinitely in airtight jars. To use, soak in water to soften. The soaking water can be strained and used. Some recipes call for powdered dried prawns, in which case do not soak.

*Rice**    See pages 26–8.

*Saffron**    Pronounced 'zafran' in the East.
The world's most expensive spice. This is understandable when you realize that it requires nearly 100,000 crocus blossoms, picked by hand, to produce a pound of saffron. The saffron comes from the stigmas, which are also removed by hand. Each crocus has only three stigmas. Once native only to Southern Europe and Asia, the saffron crocus is now widely cultivated in Mexico and California. To use, soak a few strands in a little warm milk or water. Powdered saffron can be used for colouring, but use only authentic saffron strands when it is the flavour that is required. The Indians use saffron in curries and rice dishes, but mostly in sweet dishes. Never use turmeric as a substitute, either for flavouring or colouring.

*Salted vegetables*    Also known as Hum Choy. Used mainly in Chinese cooking. Available in tins. To use, drain and soak in fresh water, rinsing two or three times to remove excess salt.

*Sambal**    A combination of chillies and spices. See pages 104–5. Served by the Malays as an accompaniment, as the Indians would serve pickles. Ready-made sambals are available from Chinese and Indian grocers and some supermarkets. Supermarkets usually sell only 'Sambal Olek', which can also be used when a recipe calls for ground chillies. Almost all sambals keep indefinitely.

## Sesame oil*

Oil extracted from toasted sesame seeds. Usually added just before serving or otherwise as specified. It has a nutty flavour and enhances any dish. Used mostly by the Chinese.

## Screwpine leaves

From the *Pandanus* family. Sharp sword-like leaves used to flavour rice and puddings. The green essence drawn from the leaves also acts as a colouring agent. Very popular in Malay cooking, but regrettably there is no substitute. Fresh leaves are available from Chinese grocers; these freeze well, but make sure you seal them tightly as they have an overpowering aroma. The artificial essence is available in Malaysia and is sometimes obtainable here. It is a clear essence, so green food colouring would have to be added to provide the colour.

## Shark's fin

Highly prized ingredient for a gourmet soup. It has a glutinous texture, and in its original form requires a great deal of preparation. A semi-processed variety, which needs a much shorter cooking time, is available in tins from Chinese grocers.

## Soya beancurd

A highly nutritious ingredient, widely used by the Malays and the Chinese. Available in squares, with a creamy, custard-like texture. Can be stored in the refrigerator for 3 or 4 days if immersed in water, which should be changed daily.

Today a 'long-life' beancurd called *tofu* is sold in cartons and is obtainable from Chinese grocers and some healthfood shops. I always collect a few extra cartons when I venture into London on a shopping spree, but do check with your local healthfood shops. Deep-fried beancurd is also available. This is sold in tiny squares which are hollow inside. Ideal for soups and vegetable dishes, plain or stuffed. Freezes well.

Dried beancurd sheets are also obtainable, and these keep indefinitely in a dry place. Before using, the sheets must be soaked until soft. They can be used in soups and stir-fried vegetable dishes, and also to wrap meat or fish before steaming.

*Soya beans, fermented*    Also known as *taucheo*.
Available in tins and jars from
Chinese grocers and some supermarkets. Can be used whole or
coarsely crushed. These beans are black and heavily salted, so you
should rinse them before using and be careful not to over-salt
any dish they are being added to. They keep indefinitely in the
refrigerator.

*Soya sauce**    Two varieties are used in this book: light soya
sauce and thick soya sauce. Use light soya
sauce where flavouring is required but where the dish needs to
retain a delicate colour. Soya sauce is now widely sold under
different brand names and may vary in strength. Varieties not sold
under a genuine oriental label tend to be more salty. (See page 116.)
All varieties keep indefinitely.

*Star anise*    A star-shaped pod with 6 or 8 segments, each
containing a seed. Obtained from an evergreen
tree of the magnolia family, native to China. Imparts a delightful
flavour and aroma and is now widely used all over Malaysia.

*Tamarind*    An acid-tasting fruit, shaped like a broad bean
with a half-moon curl. When green it has a sharp
taste like a gooseberry. The pods are allowed to mature on the tree
until the flesh turns dark brown and soft and the skin becomes
brittle. They are then shelled and sometimes seeded, and sold in
packets which could very easily be mistaken for dates. To use, soak a
small fistful in 3 fl oz (85 ml) of hot water until pulpy and then
vigorously squeeze out the juice through a fine sieve or a piece of
muslin. If a recipe calls for a larger quantity of tamarind juice, adjust
the quantities accordingly.

Concentrated tamarind is now available from Chinese and Indian
grocers. Follow the same method but use only 1 teaspoon of the
concentrated pulp. Lemon juice or vinegar in roughly the same
proportions can be used as a substitute, although these will not
provide the laxative and cooling properties which tamarind has.
Tamarind is used in curries, pickles and chutneys and also in
refreshing drinks.

*Turmeric\** An aromatic root belonging to the ginger family. Contains a bright yellow dye with a slightly pungent flavour. Also adds colour to curries. In Malaysia fresh turmeric (*manjal*) is used, but powdered turmeric and dried roots are widely available. Use in moderation, and never substitute turmeric for saffron.

*Wontan skins* Small square sheets rolled from egg noodle dough. Available in packets from Chinese grocers. They freeze well.

# Glossary

| | Malay | Chinese | Tamil | Hindi |
|---|---|---|---|---|
| **Meat and Poultry** | | | | |
| Beef | Daging Lembu | Ngau yoke | Mattu erachi | Gai ka gosht |
| Brains | Otak | Nao | Moolai | Bheja |
| Chicken | Ayam | Kai | Koli | Murgh |
| Duck | Itik | Ngap | Vatthu | Baduk |
| Egg | Telur | Tan | Muttai | Anda |
| Kidney | Buah pinggang | Yew | Pukkam | Gurda |
| Lamb | Daging anak kambing | Yeong yoke | Attu erachi | Bakri ka gosht |
| Liver | Limpa | Chee yuen | Eeral | Kaleji |
| Minced meat | Daging cincang | — | Kotthu erachi | Kheema |
| Pork | Daging babi | Chee yoke | Pandi erachi | Dukar ka gosht |
| Quail | Burung puyuh | Um chun | Kadai | Bateir |
| Quail's egg | Burung puyuh telur | Um chun tan | Kadai muttai | Bateir ka anda |
| Sausage, Chinese | Daging babi cincang | Larp cheong | — | — |

|  | Malay | Chinese | Tamil | Hindi |
|---|---|---|---|---|
| **Seafood** | | | | |
| Abalone | Trepang | Pow yee | Nethali | — |
| Anchovy, dried | Ikan bilis | Kong yee chye | Nethilipudi | — |
| Cockles | Kerang | See hum | Matti | — |
| Crab | Ketam | Hai | Nandu | Khekda |
| Cuttlefish/squid | Sotong | Yee | Sotong | — |
| Dried fish | Ikan kering | Hum yee | Karavadu | Sukhi macchli |
| Fish, general | Ikan | Yu | Meen | Macchli |
| Pomfret | Bawal | Chong yee | Vowal | Pomfret |
| Prawns/shrimps | Udang | Har | Eral | Jinga |
| **Vegetables** | | | | |
| Bamboo shoots | Rebung | Chuk sun | Mungil thuilr | Banska ankur |
| Beansprouts | Taugeh | Nga choi | Paitha mulai | — |
| Aubergine/ egg plant | Terung | Ai kwa | Katherikai | Baigan |
| Cabbage, Chinese | Kubis panjang | Choy sum/ Pak choy | — | — |
| Celery | Daun seladeri | Kan choy | — | — |
| Chillies, green | Cabai hijau | Cheng lat chew | Parachai milahai | Hari mirch |
| Chillies, red | Cabai merah | Hoong lat chew | Sovapu milahai | Lal mirch |
| Dried mushrooms | Cendawan kering | Tung ku | Kalanvathal | — |
| Drumstick | Kelur | — | Murunggakai | Sekta |
| Ladies' fingers/okra | Sejenis tumbuhan | Yeong kok tau | Vendaikai | Bhendi |
| Marrow/ bottle-gourd | Sejenis labu | — | Churaikai | Kaddu |
| Mustard green | Sayur bunga | Pak choy sum | — | — |
| Onion | Bawang | Yang tsung | Vengayam | Piyaz |
| Radish | Sejenis lobak | Lo pak | Mullangai | Mooli |
| Snake-gourd | Ular labu | Sei kwa | Pudalankai | Chichinda |
| Snow peas/ mange tout | Kacang salji | Ho lan tau | Pattani | Mattar |
| Spring onions | Daun bawang | Chung | Vengaya kuruthu | Hari piyaz |
| Spinach | Bayam | Heen choy | Pasala keerai | Palak |

| | *Malay* | *Chinese* | *Tamil* | *Hindi* |
|---|---|---|---|---|
| Sweet potato | Keledek | Fan see | Sakaravali kenanguu | Rataloo |
| Turnip | Ubi sengkuang | Sahkot | Moolangai | Mooli |
| Water convolvulus | Kangkong | Oong choy | — | — |

*Fruits*

| | *Malay* | *Chinese* | *Tamil* | *Hindi* |
|---|---|---|---|---|
| Apricot | Buah aprikot | Hung toh | Chakkara-badami | Jardaloo |
| Banana 1 | Pisang | Ley | Vazhaikai | Kela |
| Banana 2 | Pisang raja | Kung chew | Sovapu vazhaikai | Lal kela |
| Coconut | Kelapa | Yeh | Thengai | Nariyel |
| Date | Pohon kurma | Hoong choh | Pericham-palam | Khajoor |
| Durian | Durian | Low lin | Durian | — |
| Guava | Jambu batu | Kai see kor | Koyya phazam | Amrud |
| Jackfruit | Cempedak | Chempelut | Palapalam | Kathial |
| Lime | Limau | Shin kum | Elumichai-palam | Nimbu |
| Longan | Longan | Loongan | Longan | — |
| Lychee | Laici | Lai chee | Lychee | Lichi |
| Mango | Mangga | Moong khor | Manggai | Aamb |
| Mangosteen | Manggis | San cheok | Manggis | Mangosteen |
| Melon | Temikai | Team kwa | Thapusini | Tarbuza |
| Papaya/pawpaw | Betik | Mok kwa | Pappali-palam | Papita |
| Passion fruit | Bush mankisa | Passion fruit | — | — |
| Pineapple | Nanas | Wong lai | Anaaspalam | Ananas |
| Pomelo | Pomelo | Pomelo | — | — |
| Pomegranate | Buah delima | Sek low | Medulam-pazam | Anar |
| Rambutan | Rambutan | Hoong mo tan | Rambutan | — |
| Watermelon | Semangka | Sai kwa | Mulanpalam | Kalingar |

*Spices and Herbs*

| | *Malay* | *Chinese* | *Tamil* | *Hindi* |
|---|---|---|---|---|
| Asafoetida | — | — | Perungayam | Hing |
| Almond | Badam | Hung ngan | Badam kottai | Badam |

|  | Malay | Chinese | Tamil | Hindi |
|---|---|---|---|---|
| Aniseed | Jintan manis | Yau kok | Perum-jeerakam | Sonf |
| Basil | Kemangi | — | Thulasi | Tulsi |
| Bay leaf/laurel | Daun bay | Yee kwai see yip | Levanga elai | Tejpatta |
| Candlenut | Buah keras | — | Sathi kai | — |
| Cardamom | Buah pelega | Wok lok wuat | Elakai | Elaichi |
| Chillies, dried | Lada kering | Lat chew khon | Kanjal milai | Sukhi mirch |
| Cinnamon | Kayu manis | Mook kwai pei | Lavangga-pattai | Dalchini |
| Clove | Bunga cengkih | Ting leong | Lavangam kerambu | Lavang |
| Coriander leaves | Daun ketumbar | Yim sai | Malli kolunthu | Kotmir |
| Coriander seed | Ketumbar | Yim sai mai | Kothamalli-virai | Dhaniya |
| Cumin | Jintan putih | Chou kok | Jeerakam | Zeera |
| Curry leaves | Daun kai pla | — | Karuveppillai | Kadipatha |
| Fennel | Adas | Siew wui heong | Sombu | Sonf |
| Fenugreek | — | — | Vethiam | Methi |
| Five-spice | Serbuk rempah | Wu hsiang fen | — | — |
| Garam masala | Garam kasar | — | Garam masala | Garam masala |
| Garlic | Bawang putih | Suen tau | Poondu | Lasan |
| Ginger | Halia | Keong | Inji | Adrak |
| Lemon grass | Serai | Heong mau | Elembiche pul | — |
| Mace | Bunga pala | Tau khau fah | Jadhipatri | Javanthri |
| Mint | Pudina | — | Pudina kerai | Pudina |
| Mustard seed | Biji sawi | — | Kadagu | Rye |
| Nutmeg | Buah pala | Tau khau | Jadhikai | Jaiphal |
| Onion seed | — | — | Vengai vitthai | Kalonji |
| Screwpine leaf | Daun pandan | — | Cendol ilai | — |
| Pepper, black | Lada hitam | Hu chia | Karupu milaghu | Kali miri |
| Poppy seed | Kas kas | — | Kasakasa | Khus Khus |
| Saffron | Kunyit kering | — | Kunkumapoo | Zafran or kesar |

|  | Malay | Chinese | Tamil | Hindi |
|---|---|---|---|---|
| Salt | Garam | Yim | Uppu | Nimak |
| Sesame seed | Bijan | Chee ma | Ellu | Til |
| Shallots | Bawang | Choong tau chai | Vengayam | Choti piyaz |
| Star anise | Bunga lawang | Pak kok | Perung chiram | — |
| Tamarind | Asam jawa | — | Pulli | Imli |
| Turmeric | Kunyit | Wong keong | Manjal | Haldi |
| Vinegar | Cuka | Choe | Chorukka | Sirka |

## Miscellaneous

|  | Malay | Chinese | Tamil | Hindi |
|---|---|---|---|---|
| Beancurd | Tauhu | Tauhu/Taufu | Tauhu | — |
| Beanpaste | Inti kacang | Tau sah | — | — |
| Blacan | Blacan/Terasi | — | Blacan/Terasi | — |
| Black soya beans | Taucheo | Taucheong | Taucheo | — |
| Chilli sauce | Sos cabai | Lat chew cheong | Sos milahai | — |
| Coconut milk | Santan | — | Thenggai pal | Nariyel ka dudh |
| Fish sauce | — | Yu chiap | — | — |
| Lentil | Sejenis pokok kacang | — | Parappu | Dhal |
| Oyster sauce | Sos tiram | Ho yeow | — | — |
| Peanut | Kacang tanah | Fah sung | Verkadalai | Phalli |
| Plum sauce | Sos sa-jenis | Shin mui cheong | Plum sos | — |
| Rice | Beras | Fan | Arisi | Chawal |
| Rice noodles/ vermicelli | Bee hoon | Mei fun | — | — |
| Rice noodles, flat | Kuih teow beehoon | Cheong fun | — | — |
| Rice noodles, round | Laksa beehoon | Lei fun | — | — |
| Soya sauce, light | Kicap cair | See yeow | Kicap | Soya sauce |
| Soya sauce, thick | Kicap pekat | Hak yeow | Kati kicap | — |
| Semolina | Isi gandum | — | Sannaravai | Suji |
| Sesame oil | Minyak biau | Ma yeow | Nallennai | Til ka tel |

|  | Malay | Chinese | Tamil | Hindi |
|---|---|---|---|---|
| Shrimp paste | Petis | Hei ko | — | — |
| Sugar | Gula | Tong | Sarkarai | Chinni |
| Sugar, palm | Gula melaka | — | Vellam | Goodh |
| Sugar, rock | Gula batu | — | Kalkandu | Misri |
| Wheatflour | Terigu | — | Godumai mavu | Gehu ka atta |
| Yellow noodles (egg) | Mee | Mee | — | — |

# 2.

# *Malay Cuisine*

*Introduction*     There are two main groups in Islam, the Shias and the Sunnis. The Sunnis are the majority and the Malays are orthodox Sunnis. Meals are always taken after prayers, which are at five specific times, *waktu semba-hayang*, at dawn, at noon, in the afternoon, at sunset and at nightfall, and these times are calculated according to the position of the sun.

Although the Muslim year is divided into twelve months, it loses eleven days per year due to the cycle of the sun and the moon. Each Muslim month has a religious event. The Muslims' New Year is not a joyous occasion – it commences with Muharram, when Imam Husain, grandson of Mohammed the Prophet (Peace be on Him), fought the Jehad or holy war, and lost most of his family. During this month there are no social events and meals are very simple.

The third month, that of Rabi-Il-Awal, contains the Prophet's (Peace be on Him) birthday. This occurs on the twelfth day of the month and is a day of general rejoicing and celebration after special prayers.

The next most important month is Ramadan, the ninth month, when Muslims fast for thirty days. No food or drink is taken from about 4 a.m. until the sun has completely set. At the end of the thirty days the great *kenduri* (feast) of Hari Raya Puasa is celebrated, when exotic foods are prepared. After this, 'open house' is declared and guests of all nationalities come to wish the Malays 'Selamat Hari Raya'. Guests are served special *kuihs* (cakes) and other delicacies, along with delicious non-alcoholic drinks. This is the most colourful event in Malaysia.

The last month of the year is also a rejoicing month. Many Malays go on *haj*, holy pilgrimage, to Mecca, and there are great celebrations when they return. The men then prefix their names with the title of *haji* and the women with *hajjah*. Goats are sacrificed, and the meat is distributed among those who have not been on *haj*.

When visiting a Malay, the visitor bows and lifts the right hand to the forehead, saying *'Assalam alaikum'* (Peace be with you). The host replies *'Valaikum salaam'* (And with you). If the visitor is invited in, he removes his footwear outside before entering the house. Even before the guests are seated comfortably, there is a bustle to prepare a meal or a snack and drinks. The visitor is obliged to accept, even if he only takes a token amount.

Family meals generally consist of one meat or fish dish, one or two vegetables, rice and perhaps a soup. Desserts are not generally served except on special occasions, and the popular sweets of the Malays are generally eaten as a snack. On festive occasions a Malay menu could consist of 8–14 dishes.

The ancient tradition of the men and women dining separately is dying, but the *adat*, table manners, are still preserved. Malays generally eat with the fingers of their right hand only. Before any meal commences, the youngest member passes salt around and a pinch is placed on the tongue to refresh the mouth. During Ramadan, the fast of each day is broken by taking a pinch of salt and perhaps a date. No one rushes to gobble food.

Because of the religious restrictions (see page 16), you will not find any pork recipes in this section.

Malay *makan* (food) is prepared with love and care, but traditional Malay food can be found only in private homes. I have attempted to bring you some of these delicacies, and I would like to wish you *'Selamat makan dan selamat menjam selur'* – happy dining and hearty appetite.

# Soups and Starters

## Mutton Soup
Serves 4–6
### Sop Kambing

A delicious soup, ideal for a cold winter's evening.

2 tablespoons vegetable oil
1 thumbsize piece fresh ginger, finely crushed
1 piece mace
4 bay leaves
½ lb (225 g) mutton *or* lean lamb, cut into small pieces
2½ pints (1·5 litres) water
2 spring onions, finely chopped
1 teaspoon five-spice powder
1 teaspoon sugar
salt and pepper to taste
few fresh coriander leaves, chopped
1 onion, finely sliced and deep-fried until brown and crisp

Heat the oil in a large pan and fry the ginger, mace and bay leaves. Add the meat and brown evenly. Add all the remaining ingredients, and simmer for about 1–1½ hours or until the meat is tender. Discard the mace and bay leaves. Serve hot, adding a few drops of lemon juice if you like.

## Spicy Chicken soup
Serves 6–8
### Soto Ayam

Soups are very popular in Malaysia, and the Malays generally serve them with the main meal. Alternatively you can convert a soup into a meal in itself by adding noodles to it. To this soup you can add scalded rice vermicelli, hard-boiled quail's eggs and tailed beansprouts.

6 pints (3.6 litres) water
4 lb (1·8 kg) chicken, cleaned and jointed
2 tablespoons cooking oil
2 medium carrots, boiled and mashed
salt and pepper to taste
1 large onion, finely sliced and deep-fried, for garnishing
2 spring onions, finely chopped, for garnishing
lemon wedges

*Ingredients to be ground together*
2 tablespoons black peppercorns
1 piece blacan, stock cube size
1½ teaspoons turmeric powder
8 shallots *or* 2 medium onions
1 thumbsize piece fresh ginger
4 cloves garlic
5 candlenuts *or* 10 almonds
1 stalk lemon grass (use white part only)

Bring the water to the boil and simmer the chicken till cooked. Remove the chicken from the pan and shred the meat. Strain the stock and keep it on a gentle simmer. Heat the oil in a frying pan and fry the ground ingredients until fragrant. Add to the stock with the mashed carrots and shredded chicken. Cook for 5 more minutes. Check the seasoning. Serve hot, with deep-fried onion flakes, spring onion and lemon wedges.

## Acidy Prawn Soup

*Serves 6–8*

### Tom Yam Kung

This dish was introduced to me by my English brother-in-law after his recent visit to Terengganu. It is of Thai origin but popular in Terengganu, which is fairly close to the Thai border.

1 tablespoon sesame oil
2 lb (900 g) raw prawns, shelled and deveined (keep heads and shells for stock)
2 pints (1·2 litres) water
salt to taste
2 stalks lemon grass *or* thinly peeled rind of 1 lemon

3 fresh red chillies, seeded and sliced (reserve 1 for garnish)
1 tablespoon fish sauce *or* light soya sauce
juice of 1 lemon
few fresh coriander leaves, finely chopped
4 spring onions, finely chopped

Heat the sesame oil in a large pan and fry the prawn heads and shells till they turn pink. Add the water, salt, lemon grass or lemon rind and 2 of the chillies. Bring to the boil and simmer for 30 minutes. Strain the stock and return to the boil. Add the prawns, fish sauce and lemon juice, and simmer till the prawns are cooked. Adjust the seasoning and add more lemon juice if necessary. Serve hot, garnished with coriander leaves, spring onions and chillies. This soup should have a distinctive lemony taste, so correct before serving if necessary.

## Soupy Noodles, Malay style        Serves 6–8
### Mee Sup Masakan

3 tablespoons cooking oil
6 cloves garlic, crushed
4 medium onions, finely sliced (deep-fry 2 until crisp and set aside)
3 pints (1·8 litres) chicken stock
salt to taste
1 lb (450 g) tender beef, cut into thin slices
8 oz (225 g) fish balls (see pages 117–18)
8 oz (225 g) prawns, shelled, deveined and seasoned with salt and pepper
1 lb (450 g) egg noodles, cooked according to instructions on the packet
8 oz (225 g) beansprouts, tailed
4 oz (100 g) sayur bunga (flower spinach) *or* Chinese cabbage, finely
   shredded and blanched for 1 minute
sliced chillies
2 thin omelettes made from 4 eggs, rolled and thinly sliced
2 oz (50 g) celery tops, chopped (optional)

Heat the oil and brown the garlic and the raw onion. Reduce the heat and stir in the stock. Season to taste and add the beef. Bring to the boil and simmer till the beef is tender. Add the fish balls and prawns and continue to simmer till they are cooked. Remove the meat, fish balls and prawns from the soup and set aside on a warm dish. Continue simmering the soup.

To serve, fill individual bowls with helpings of noodles, bean-sprouts, beef, prawns, fish balls and spinach or Chinese cabbage. Pour the hot soup over, and garnish with chillies, omelette slices, celery tops and deep-fried onions. Serve hot and immediately, or the noodles will turn soggy.

## Easy-to-make Satay with Sauce and Accompaniments

*Serves 4–6*

Watching the hawker prepare satay, I felt I could never achieve this dish except in the summer when I could use the barbecue. Here is a very simple method which does not require a barbecue or skewers.

### Satay

8 oz (225 g) each of lean beef, skinned chicken meat and lamb, cut into bitesize pieces
4 dessertspoons vegetable oil

*Marinade*
2 teaspoons five-spice powder
1 teaspoon sugar
1 teaspoon lemon juice
1 thumbsize piece fresh ginger, finely crushed
salt to taste
6 fl oz (175 ml) thick coconut milk

Mix together the marinade ingredients. Add the meats and marinade for 1 hour. Heat the oil in a wok, add the meats and stir well. Cover and allow to simmer till the meats are cooked. Put the pieces of meat in a shallow ovenproof dish, and place under a preheated grill to brown them a little before serving.

### Satay Sauce

5 dried chillies, seeded and soaked in water
1 stalk serai (use white part only)

½-inch (1-cm) piece blacan
1 tablespoon vegetable oil
2 oz (50 g) salted peanuts, coarsely pounded
6 fl oz (175 ml) thick coconut milk
juice of 4 lemons
2 tablespoons sugar
pinch of salt

Drain the chillies, and pound them with the serai and blacan. Heat the oil and fry the pounded ingredients well. Add the remaining ingredients and stir well. Cook on a low heat until the sauce is thick.

## Pressed rice squares

2 cups long-grain rice, washed and drained
3 cups water
1 teaspoon salt

Mix all the ingredients together in a large pan and bring to the boil, then reduce the heat, cover the pan and cook till all the water is absorbed. Place the cooked rice in a greased baking dish and spread it out evenly with the help of some foil. Put some weights on the foil and press down the rice. Leave to cool, then run a wet knife along the walls of the tin to loosen the rice. Turn out on to a chopping board and cut the rice into squares, wetting the blade after each cut to prevent the rice sticking.

To serve satay, place the pieces of meat and the rice squares on a large platter and garnish with chunky pieces of onions, cucumber and pineapple. Serve the sauce in a separate bowl.

# Poultry and Egg Dishes

## Crispy Chicken of Pinang
### Pinang Ayam

*Serves 4–6*

Ideal as a finger snack for a cocktail party.

10 chicken drumsticks, any excess fat removed
10 chicken wings, only tips removed
oil for deep-frying
lemon wedges

*Marinade*
2 teaspoons chilli powder
1½ teaspoons salt
1 tablespoon sugar
1 teaspoon turmeric powder
2 candlenuts *or* 6 almonds, ground
2 inches (5 cm) fresh ginger, ground
2 stalks lemon grass (use white part only)

Mix together all the marinade ingredients and marinate the chicken for 2–3 hours or longer if possible. Heat the oil in a wok, deep-fry the chicken pieces for 5 minutes, then remove the chicken from the oil. Reheat the oil until it starts smoking and fry the chicken again till very crisp and golden brown.

Serve with lemon wedges.

## Chicken with Condensed Tomato Soup
### Ayam Curry

*Serves 4–6*

The Malays have taken to using tomatoes a great deal. Many dishes now include tomato ketchup, but try this one with condensed tomato soup. Serve with white rice, or if you have time try it with thick pancakes.

3 dessertspoons vegetable oil
1 onion, finely chopped
1 inch (2·5 cm) fresh ginger, finely minced
4 cloves garlic, finely minced
3 teaspoons curry powder, mixed with a little water
1½ lb (675 g) meaty chicken pieces
3 oz (75 g) condensed tomato soup
½ lb (225 g) button mushrooms, left whole
salt to taste
6 fl oz (175 ml) water

Heat the oil in a large pan and brown the onions. Add the ginger and garlic and fry for 1–2 minutes. Reduce the heat, add the curry powder paste and fry till the oil rises. Add the chicken pieces and fry well till all the pieces are covered with the curry sauce. Cover and simmer till the chicken is almost done. Stir occasionally, adding a few drops of water to prevent the chicken burning. Add the condensed soup, mushrooms, salt and half the water. Mix well and simmer for a few minutes. If the gravy is too thick, add the remaining water and simmer for 1–2 more minutes. Serve hot.

## Easy pancakes

1½ cups ready dry pancake mixture
1 large egg
3 fl oz (85 ml) evaporated milk
3 fl oz (85 ml) water
butter or margarine for frying

Put all the ingredients except the butter in a bowl and mix with an electric whisk until smooth. Heat a griddle and put a little butter to grease. Pour on a ladle of the batter, but do not spread too wide as the pancakes should be fairly thick. Cook on both sides. To keep the pancakes warm, wrap in a linen napkin.

## Spicy Grilled Chicken                    *Serves 4–6*
### Ayam Makanan Panggang

This is authentically an Indonesian dish, but it is highly favoured by the Malays and reached Malaysia with migration a few generations ago. It is delicious when cooked on a barbecue, but if you cannot wait for the summer months, try cooking it under the grill as I did.

3 lb (1·3 kg) chicken, halved lengthwise
salt and pepper
6 fl oz (175 ml) thick coconut milk
juice of 1 lemon

*Ingredients to be ground together*
2 cloves garlic
1 fresh red chilli, seeded
1 inch (2·5 cm) fresh ginger
4 candlenuts *or* 8 almonds
1 teaspoon white pepper
1 piece blacan, stock cube size

Rub the chicken with salt and pepper and brown it on both sides under a high preheated grill. Keep warm. In a wok or pan fry the ground ingredients for 2–3 minutes. Add the coconut milk, bring to the boil and simmer till the gravy is thick. Remove from the heat and add the lemon juice. Pour this mixture over the chicken and grill under a low heat, turning occasionally to cook the chicken evenly. Baste regularly with the mixture. When cooked, place the chicken on a serving dish and pour the remaining mixture over. Garnish with tomato, cucumber and lemon slices.

## Chicken Cooked with Red Chillies
### Cabai Merah Ayam

*Serves 4–6*

3 tablespoons butter
1 tablespoon vegetable oil
1 large onion, finely chopped
2 cloves garlic, finely minced
1 thumbsize piece fresh ginger, finely minced
1 teaspoon salt
8 chicken drumsticks or thighs, skinned
½ teaspoon turmeric powder
6 fresh red chillies, one reserved whole to make a chilli flower (see page 34), the remainder seeded and crushed
¼ pint (150 ml) water
juice of 1 lemon

Heat the butter and oil and fry the onion, garlic and ginger until the onions are soft. Add the salt and chicken pieces and brown evenly. Stir in the turmeric powder and the crushed chillies and mix well. Add the water and lemon juice, stir well and continue to simmer till the chicken is tender. Garnish with the chilli flower and serve hot with boiled rice. This dish should be dry, so if there is excess water you should increase the heat during the final stages of cooking.

## Mild Chicken Curry
### Opor Ayam

*Serves 4–6*

Although a mild curry, this has a strong aroma and a pleasant taste. Delicious when served with Roti Canai (see page 102) and Kacang Buncis Goreng (see page 87).

2 tablespoons coriander powder
1 dessertspoon cumin powder
1 teaspoon five-spice powder
1 teaspoon turmeric powder
½ teaspoon freshly ground black pepper
1 teaspoon salt
3 lb (1·3 kg) chicken, jointed to make 8–12 pieces
4 dessertspoons ghee *or* vegetable oil
4 ripe tomatoes, finely chopped
12 fl oz (350 ml) thick coconut milk

*Ingredients to be ground together*
2 cloves garlic
1 thumbsize piece fresh ginger
2 onions
1 stalk lemon grass (use white part only)
6 candlenuts *or* 12 almonds
6 dessertspoons desiccated coconut, dry-roasted to a deep brown

Mix together the first six ingredients and rub well into the chicken pieces. Set aside for 1 hour. Heat the ghee in a large heavy pan and fry the ground ingredients. When the oil separates, add the chicken pieces and fry till all the pieces are evenly coloured. Add the tomatoes and coconut milk and bring to the boil, stirring occasionally. Season to taste. Reduce the heat and allow the chicken to simmer uncovered till cooked. The gravy should be fairly thick. Serve hot.

## Spicy Shredded Chicken
### Ayam Sambal

*Serves 4–6*

One Christmas I gave a cocktail party and served this sambal in vol-au-vent cases. You could use it as a sandwich filler, with slices of cucumber, or make open sandwiches, garnishing the bread or toast first with a crisp piece of lettuce leaf.

4 breast pieces of chicken, skinned and finely sliced
2 oz (50 g) creamed coconut
6 fl oz (175 ml) water
4 tablespoons vegetable oil
1 onion, finely chopped
½ teaspoon light soya sauce
4 tablespoons lemon juice
½ teaspoon salt

*Ingredients to be ground together*
2 tablespoons coriander leaves
1 inch (2·5 cm) fresh ginger
½ teaspoon five-spice powder
1 stalk lemon grass (use white part only)
10 dried red chillies, soaked for 5 minutes (seeded for milder flavour)

Put the chicken, coconut cream and water into a pan and bring to the boil, then reduce the heat and cook till the chicken is tender. Heat the oil in a separate pan and fry the onions till brown and crisp. Add the ground ingredients and fry for 2–3 minutes. Mix together the soya sauce, lemon juice and salt and add to the pan with the chicken and stock. Stir-fry on a high heat till the chicken is dry. Check the seasoning. Serve hot with rice and a salad or as suggested above.

# Spicy Duck
## Itik Rempah

*Serves 4–6*

I enjoy this dish – the duck is skinned and the excess fat is removed, so though spicy it is not too heavy to digest.

juice of 3 lemons
½ teaspoon pepper
2 tablespoons light soya sauce
1 tablespoon dry white wine *or* dry sherry
2 tablespoons sugar
3 lb (1·3 kg) duckling, skinned and jointed, excess fat removed
4 tablespoons vegetable oil
2 onions, finely sliced

*Ingredients to be ground together*
1 stalk lemon grass *or* 4 strips lemon rind
1 teaspoon turmeric powder
10 dried red chillies (seeded for milder flavour)
2 fresh red chillies (seeded for milder flavour)
piece blacan, stock cube size
2 cloves garlic

Mix the first five ingredients together and marinade the duck for 2–3 hours or longer if possible. Heat the oil in a large heavy pan and fry the onion slices till brown. Add the ground ingredients and a few drops of water, and fry till the water disappears and the oil separates. Add the duck without the marinade, and stir well on a high heat for about 10 minutes. If it begins to stick to the pan, slowly add the marinade. Reduce the heat and simmer till the duck is tender and the gravy fairly thick. Serve with rice and a vegetable curry or salad.

# Malay Egg Curry
## Rendang Telur

*Serves 4–6*

6 large eggs, hard-boiled and shelled
4 tablespoons vegetable oil
1 large onion, finely sliced
3 oz (75 g) creamed coconut, dissolved in ½ pint (300 ml) hot water

1 stalk lemon grass, bruised

*Ingredients to be ground together*
6 fresh red chillies *or* 12 large dry red chillies, soaked in water
1 inch (2·5 cm) fresh ginger
3 cloves garlic
½ teaspoon turmeric powder
1 teaspoon salt

Heat the oil and fry the onions till soft. Add the ground ingredients and fry for 1–2 minutes. Add the remaining ingredients except the eggs, and bring to the boil. Reduce the heat and simmer for about 15 minutes. Pierce a sharp knife through each egg without cutting the egg into two. Place the eggs in the sauce and simmer till the sauce is thick. Test for seasoning. Discard the lemon grass before serving. Serve hot with Nasi Beriyani and Acar Timun (see pages 92, 90).

## Spicy Eggs
### Telur Masakan

Serves 4–6

*Telur* means 'egg' and *masakan* translated means 'is it possible?' Yes it is possible, and eggs have always made an economical and hearty meal.

2 tablespoons vegetable oil
2 onions, finely sliced
6 large eggs, hard-boiled, shelled, and fried whole in a little oil
1 teaspoon salt
1 dessertspoon vinegar
½ teaspoon sugar

*Ingredients to be ground together*
2 cloves garlic
6 fresh red chillies (seeded for milder flavour)
½ teaspoon turmeric powder

Heat the oil and fry the onions till brown and crisp. Reduce the heat, add the ground ingredients and sprinkle on a few drops of water. Fry until the oil separates. Add the eggs and the remaining ingredients and stir well to coat the eggs evenly. Simmer for 5 minutes. Serve hot with plain boiled rice and Salad in Coconut Milk (see page 91).

# Meat and Offal Dishes

## Stewed Mutton
## Kambing Rebusan

Serves 4–6

The Malays use tomato sauce and evaporated milk generously, and here is a delicious way they prepare mutton.

1 lb (450 g) mutton *or* lean lamb, cut into bitesize pieces
4 oz (100 g) ghee *or* unsalted butter
½ pint (300 ml) warm water
2 onions, sliced, deep-fried and drained
6 oz (175 g) tomato ketchup
4 fl oz (110 ml) evaporated milk

*Ingredients to be ground together*
6 cloves garlic
1 thumbsize piece fresh ginger
2 green chillies
½ teaspoon turmeric
1½ teaspoons salt
2 teaspoons cumin powder
2 teaspoons pepper
1 tablespoon sugar

Mix the meat with the ground ingredients and allow to stand for 1 hour. Heat the ghee or butter in a heavy pan and brown the meat evenly. Reduce the heat and add the water. Simmer for 15 minutes. Add the browned onions and tomato ketchup, and simmer till the meat is nearly tender. Add the milk, stirring well, and adjust the seasoning. Simmer till the meat is cooked and the gravy is nice and thick. Serve with Nasi Kunyit and Acar Timun (see pages 95, 90).

## Tender Meat with Vegetables                    Serves 4–6
### Daging Masak Sayur

If you have had a hard day and cannot face preparing three or four dishes, try this recipe, serving it with plain boiled rice or even French bread.

2 lb (900 g) mutton *or* lean lamb *or* beef, cut into bitesize pieces
1 pint (600 ml) boiling water
3 tablespoons cooking oil
2 onions, finely sliced
1 large carrot, thickly diced
1 lb (450 g) potatoes, peeled and halved
6 shallots *or* very small onions peeled and left whole
4 oz (100 g) frozen peas
4 oz (100 g) tomato purée
6 tablespoons tomato ketchup
6 eggs, hard-boiled and shelled
4 spring onions, finely chopped, for garnish

*Ingredients to be ground together*
3 green chillies (seeded for milder flavour)
5 cloves garlic
1 inch (2·5 cm) fresh ginger
1 tablespoon cumin powder
1 teaspoon coriander powder
½ teaspoon turmeric
2 teaspoons five-spice powder
1 teaspoon salt

Boil the meat in the water till tender, then strain and reserve the stock. In a deep pan heat the oil and fry the onion slices till brown and crisp. Add the ground ingredients, and stir-fry till the oil separates. Add the meat and stir so that it is well coated. Add the stock and the remaining ingredients except the eggs and spring onion. Bring to the boil, then reduce the heat, cover the pan and simmer until the vegetables are done. Add hot water if it gets too dry. Check the seasoning, then add the eggs and stir well. Garnish with the chopped spring onions, and serve hot.

## Lamb Curry
### Kari Kambing

*Serves 4–6*

In this recipe you will notice that I have used curry powder. There is a wide range now available, and you can choose a mild, medium or hot flavour to suit your taste.

2 oz (50 g) ghee *or* unsalted butter, *or* 4 tablespoons vegetable oil
1 large onion, finely sliced
1 inch (2·5 cm) fresh ginger, finely minced
6 cloves garlic, finely minced
4 tablespoons curry powder
½ teaspoon turmeric powder
½ teaspoon chilli powder (optional)
salt to taste
2 lb (900 g) boned shoulder of lamb, cut into bitesize pieces
4 oz (100 g) creamed coconut, soaked in ¾ pint (450 ml) hot water
1 teaspoon five-spice powder
2 tablespoons almond flakes for garnishing

Heat the ghee in a large heavy pan. Add the onion and brown evenly. Add the ginger and garlic and fry till the raw smell begins to disappear. Mix the curry powder and turmeric to a paste with a little water, reduce the heat, and add to the pan with the chilli powder and salt. Fry well till the oil rises above the spices, then add the lamb, stirring well. Cover the pan and allow the lamb to cook for 10 minutes. Add the coconut milk and five-spice powder, cover the pan again, and cook till the lamb is tender and the gravy is fairly thick. Adjust the seasoning. Garnish with almond flakes, and serve hot with plain boiled rice or Roti Canai (see page 102).

## Tender Beef in Aromatic Gravy
### Daging Lembu Rendang

*Serves 4–6*

One of the classic Malay dishes. The Malays cook this as a dark, dry dish, but I enjoy it with a thick gravy.

4 tablespoons vegetable oil *or* ghee
1 teaspoon chilli powder

2 lb (900 g) tender beef, cut in thin slices
1½ teaspoons salt
¾ pint (450 ml) thick coconut milk
5 tablespoons desiccated coconut, dry-roasted to a deep brown and finely
   ground
juice of 1 lemon

*Ingredients to be ground together*
2 fresh red chillies (seeded for milder flavour)
1 stalk lemon grass (use white part only)
1 teaspoon turmeric
3 inches (8 cm) fresh ginger
3 cloves garlic
2 large onions *or* 10 small Bombay onions

Heat the oil or ghee and fry the ground ingredients and the chilli powder until fragrant. Add the beef and salt and fry well for 5 minutes on medium heat. Add the coconut milk and bring to the boil, stirring constantly to prevent curdling. Reduce the heat and simmer uncovered until the beef is tender. During the last 10 minutes add the ground coconut and stir well. The gravy should be thick. Serve hot, stirring in the lemon juice just before serving. Serve with Nasi Goreng (see page 92).

## Beef Braised in Soya Sauce          *Serves 4–6*
## Memasak Daging Lembu

Here is a dish which shows the Chinese influence on Malay cooking.

2 tablespoons thick soya sauce
1 tablespoon brown sugar
2 lb (900 g) braising beef, cut into thin slices
2 tablespoons sesame oil
1 tablespoon vegetable oil
2 onions, finely sliced
1 thumbsize piece fresh ginger, sliced thinly
2 cloves garlic, finely crushed
1 tablespoon tomato purée, mixed with 4 fl oz (110 ml) hot water
2 cloves

½ teaspoon grated nutmeg
salt and pepper to taste

Mix together the soya sauce and sugar, and marinade the beef slices for 1 hour. Heat both oils in a wok and fry the onions, ginger and garlic until the onions are transparent. Add the beef and stir-fry on a high heat until the beef is evenly browned. Reduce the heat, add the remaining ingredients, and continue to stir-fry until the beef is tender. As you have thinly sliced and marinaded the beef this should not take more than 10–15 minutes. Season to taste, and serve hot with boiled rice or noodles.


## Beef with Sweet Desiccated Coconut     *Serves 4–6*
## Serunding Daging Lembu

Serunding is the mixture of grated coconut, sugar and spices. When the dish is ready the coconut should be moist and chewy. Serunding is often served as an accompaniment, in which case follow the recipe below but omit the beef and reduce the stock to 6 fl oz (175 ml).

2 lb (900 g) tender beef, cut into thin slices
6 tablespoons vegetable oil
2 bay leaves
4 tablespoons dark brown sugar
salt to taste
1 lb (450 g) desiccated coconut, dry-roasted till crumbly and brown

*Ingredients to be ground together*
4 tablespoons coriander powder
½ teaspoon aniseed powder
1 stalk lemon grass (use white part only)
1 thumbsize piece fresh ginger
2 onions
10 dried red chillies, soaked for 5 minutes
1 teaspoon turmeric powder

Boil the beef in 2 pints (1·2 litres) of water for 1 hour. Drain, reserving the stock. Heat the oil and fry the ground ingredients until fragrant. Add the bay leaves, sugar and salt and fry for 2–3 minutes. Add the beef and stir well. Add the browned coconut and the reserved stock, and bring to the boil, then reduce the heat and simmer for 20 minutes. Serve hot with rice noodles or plain boiled rice.

## Beef Patties                                    *Serves 4–6*
### Bergedel

These are ideal to serve with drinks at a cocktail party. They also make a good starter, or an accompaniment to dishes such as Soto Ayam with Noodles (see page 54).

12 oz (350 g) lean minced beef
5 large potatoes, boiled, peeled and mashed
2 tablespoons cornflour
2 eggs, separated
¼ teaspoon mustard powder
2 medium onions, finely chopped
2 spring onions, finely chopped
a few sprigs fresh coriander, finely chopped
salt and pepper to taste
oil for deep-frying

Mix together all the ingredients except the egg whites and oil. Using your hands, make even balls of the mixture then flatten them lightly. Beat the egg whites lightly. Heat the oil on a medium heat, dip the patties in egg white and deep-fry until each side is golden brown. Drain on kitchen paper. Serve hot as an accompaniment or cold as a snack.

## Dry Liver Curry                                 *Serves 6–8*
### Rendang Limpa

Offal is more popularly used in the East than in the West, although I remember that not too long ago fried liver and devilled kidneys were served for breakfast in England. I use ox liver, as I have found that this does not become as tough and dry as other kinds.

2 tablespoons vegetable oil
2 onions, finely sliced
1½ lb (675 g) ox liver, thickly sliced and washed twice in salted water to remove any excess blood
3 oz (75 g) creamed coconut, soaked in ½ pint (300 ml) hot water
1 cup desiccated coconut, dry-roasted to a deep brown and ground to a paste
lemon juice to taste

*Ingredients to be finely ground together*
1 stalk lemon grass (use white part only)
1 thumbsize piece fresh ginger
6–8 dried red chillies (seeded for milder flavour)
1 teaspoon turmeric powder
1 teaspoon coriander powder
1 teaspoon five-spice powder
1 teaspoon salt

Heat the oil and fry the onions till golden brown. Add the ground ingredients and fry till the raw smell disappears and the oil separates. Add the liver and stir the spices well into all the liver pieces. Add the coconut milk, reduce the heat and simmer till the liver is cooked and the gravy is thick. Five minutes before removing from the heat, add the ground desiccated coconut. Serve hot, sprinkled with lemon juice.

# Seafood Dishes

## Fish Stewed in Coconut
### Ikan Bawal Rebusan

*Serves 4–6*

3 white pomfrets, cleaned and cut into 2-inch (5-cm) slices or 8 pieces of
    small halibut, 2 inches (5 cm) thick
1½ teaspoons salt
5 oz (150 g) creamed coconut, soaked in 12 oz (350 ml) boiling water but
    not stirred
5 tablespoons cooking oil
1 large onion, finely chopped
juice of 2 lemons
2 teaspoons sugar
chopped fresh coriander leaves and lemon wedges for garnish

*Ingredients to be ground together*
1 thumbsize piece fresh ginger
1 teaspoon chilli powder or to taste
½-inch (1·2-cm) cube blacan

Place the fish in a large pan and sprinkle with a little salt. Gently
pour on the top half of the coconut water, and simmer till the fish is
cooked. Remove to a serving dish and keep warm. Heat the oil in
another pan and fry the onion till fairly dark brown. Add the ground
ingredients and fry till the oil separates. Add the remaining coconut
milk, lemon juice and sugar and simmer, stirring constantly, till the
sauce is thick. Pour the sauce over the fish and garnish with chopped
coriander and lemon wedges. Serve hot with boiled rice and a
vegetable dish.

## Hot Spicy Fish
### Hot Ikan Sambal

*Serves 4–6*

4 tablespoons vegetable oil
1 lb (450 g) firm white fish fillets, dried well and rubbed with salt

2 tablespoons tamarind juice (see page 44)
salt to taste
9 fl oz (260 ml) thick coconut milk

*Ingredients to be ground together*
12 dried red chillies (seeded for milder flavour)
6 candlenuts *or* 12 almonds
2 inches (5 cm) fresh ginger
5 shallots *or* 2 small onions
1 piece blacan, stock cube size

Heat the oil in a wok or large pan and fry the fish pieces until evenly browned on both sides. Remove and keep warm. In the same oil fry the ground ingredients until fragrant. Add the tamarind juice and salt and half the coconut milk. Bring to the boil. Reduce the heat, return the fish pieces to the pan, and cook for 10 minutes, gradually adding the remaining coconut milk. Cook uncovered till the fish is done and the sauce is thick. Serve hot with plain boiled rice.

## Fish Wrapped in Foil
### Otak-Otak

*Serves 6*

This is a very popular Malay fish dish. It is traditionally steamed in banana leaves, but steaming in foil will not impair the flavour.

1½ lb (675 g) firm white fish, skinned, boned and coarsely chopped
5 eggs, well beaten
3 spring onions, finely chopped
4 cloves garlic, finely crushed
2 inches (5 cm) fresh ginger, finely crushed
1 stalk lemon grass (white part only), finely crushed, *or* grated rind of ¼
  lemon
¼ teaspoon turmeric powder
½ teaspoon chilli powder
1 teaspoon cumin powder
1 tablespoon coriander powder
1½ teaspoons salt
1 oz (25 g) creamed coconut, dissolved in 4 fl oz (110 ml) water, *or* 6 fl oz
  (175 ml) fresh single cream
6 pieces of foil, measuring 12 × 8 inches (30 × 20 cm), lightly greased

Mix all the ingredients with your hands, making sure that the spices are evenly blended into the fish. Divide the mixture into 6 portions. Place a portion on the centre of each piece of foil, then wrap the sides over and seal the two open ends. Place in a steamer and steam on a high heat for 30–40 minutes. Serve hot or cold.

## Fish Head Curry
### Ikan Kepala Kari

*Serves 4*

Fish heads are very popular in Malaysia for curries and soups. In fact, it sometimes costs more to buy just the heads of certain fish. I use salmon heads and, if you ask him, your fishmonger may keep some by for you. During the winter months the heads are smaller, but in the summer two heads should be ample for 4 persons.

5 tablespoons oil
4 small salmon heads, gills, fins and any scales removed
4 oz (100 g) okra, washed, dried and fried whole in a little oil
2 tablespoons tomato purée
9 fl oz (260 ml) thick coconut milk
juice of 1 lemon
salt to taste

*Ingredients to be finely ground together*
2 small onions
2 cloves garlic
1 inch (2·5 cm) fresh ginger
1 stalk lemon grass (use white part only)
4 fresh red chillies (seeded for milder flavour)
*3 tablespoons vindaloo curry paste

Heat the oil and fry the ground ingredients on a medium heat until the oil separates. Add the fish heads and stir well, coating them well with the sauce. Add the remaining ingredients and stir well. Slowly bring to the boil and cook gently until the heads are done. Serve hot with plain boiled rice and a vegetable dish.

* Various curry pastes can be bought. Vindaloo paste is hot, but you can choose a milder flavour if you prefer.

# Fresh Prawns and Dried Anchovies in a Rich Chilli Sauce
*Serves 4–6*

## Udang and Ikan Bilis Sambal

1 large onion, sliced
1 piece blacan, stock cube size, dry-roasted
½ teaspoon chilli powder
½ teaspoon turmeric powder
3 cloves garlic, finely minced
4 red chillies, seeded and ground
2 tablespoons tomato purée
2 teaspoons sugar
1 teaspoon salt
8 oz (225 g) large prawns, shelled and deveined
4 oz (100 g) dried anchovies, split and deep-fried till crisp, then drained

In a wok heat 4 tablespoons of the oil used to deep-fry the anchovies and fry the onions until soft. Add the blacan and when it is completely soft add the chilli and turmeric, first mixed to a paste with a little water, and the remaining ingredients, except the prawns and anchovies. When the oil rises above the spices, add the prawns and stir-fry until they turn pink. (If using cooked prawns this will require only 2–3 minutes.) Add the anchovies and mix well. Serve hot with boiled rice and a vegetable dish.

# Fresh Squid in a Dark Sauce
*Serves 4–6*

## Sotong Masak Hitam

My sons' favourite dish. The main work involved in the preparation of this dish is cleaning the squid. It is easier to do this under a running tap. Remove the ink sac and skin and cut off the head. Remove the flat transparent bone and thoroughly rinse the inside. Do not discard the heads, as they are edible once cleaned thoroughly.

2 tablespoons brown sugar
1 teaspoon salt

2 teaspoons thick soya sauce
1 tablespoon tomato purée
juice of 1 lemon
2 tablespoons vegetable oil
1 lb (450 g) fresh squid, cleaned, boiled in salt water for 5 minutes and
    thickly sliced

*Ingredients to be ground together*
2 fresh red chillies
2 cloves garlic
1 thumbsize piece fresh ginger
1 piece blacan, stock cube size

Mix together the sugar, salt, soya sauce, tomato purée and lemon
juice and set aside. Heat the oil and fry the ground ingredients until
the oil separates. Add the squid and stir-fry for 2 minutes. Increase
the heat, add the soya sauce mixture, and stir-fry for 5 minutes.
Serve hot with plain boiled rice and stir-fried Sayur Bunga (see page
84).

## Crab Curry
*Ketam Kari*

Serves 4–6

Since crabs are available in abundance, the Malaysians have many
recipes for them – this is one of their favourites.

4 tablespoons cooking oil
1 pint (600 ml) thick coconut milk
6 medium crabs, cleaned and cut into quarters (do not dislodge any roe, as
    it is delicious in the curry)
salt

*Ingredients to be ground together*
3 dried chillies (seeded for milder flavour)
3 fresh red chillies (seeded for milder flavour)
2 stalks lemon grass (use white part only)
1 thumbsize piece fresh ginger
4 cloves garlic
½ teaspoon turmeric powder
1 large onion

Heat the oil in a large heavy pan and fry the ground ingredients until fragrant. Pour in half the coconut milk and bring to the boil. Add the crabs, the remaining coconut milk and the salt. Allow the crabs to simmer gently, uncovered, until the sauce is reduced by half. Serve as a main course with rice or as a starter.

## Roe Pâté
### Ikan Telur Sambal

*Serves 4–6*

This is a simple and delicious sandwich filling and will keep in an airtight container in the refrigerator for 2–3 weeks. It can also be used as a filling for vol-au-vents, or on open sandwiches.

4 tablespoons vegetable oil
½ lb (225 g) roe, chopped (the tinned variety is best)
2 teaspoons lemon juice

*Ingredients to be ground together*
3 dry red chillies, soaked and seeded
1 small onion
4 almonds
½ teaspoon turmeric powder
1 teaspoon sugar
salt to taste

Heat half the oil in a wok or pan and fry the roe till brown. Remove to a bowl and mash till smooth. Heat the remaining oil and fry the ground ingredients till fragrant. Pour over the roe and mix well. Add the lemon juice and mix again. Store in the refrigerator.

## Whitebait Fritters
### Fresh Ikan Bilis Goreng

*Serves 4–6*

A delightful snack or starter. If you are planning a coffee party, why not try this dish? The fritters can be prepared a little while in advance, and kept warm on a hot plate.

2 oz (50 g) self-raising flour, blended to a smooth paste with a little water
1 dessertspoon cornflour
1 egg, beaten
1 fresh red chilli, finely chopped
1 onion, coarsely chopped
4 spring onions, coarsely chopped
a few sprigs fresh coriander leaves, chopped
salt and pepper
4 oz (100 g) whitebait, washed, cleaned and drained
oil for frying
½ cucumber, sliced

Mix together all the ingredients except the fish, the oil and the cucumber. When a smooth paste has formed, add the fish and stir well. Heat the oil in a wok. Pour in 2 dessertspoons of the mixture and flatten to form a pancake. Fry until evenly brown on both sides. Serve hot with slices of cucumber and a chilli sauce of your choice.

# Vegetable Dishes

## Malay Vegetable and Fruit Salad
Serves 4–6
*Rojak*

Each state in Malaysia makes its own version of Rojak, but this is a hawker's version which I enjoyed eating on the beautiful island of Penang.

5 oz (150 g) sweet potato, boiled, peeled and sliced
½ cucumber, sliced
½ fresh pineapple, sliced *or* 8 oz (225 g) tinned pineapple, well drained
1 turnip, sliced (when not in season use radish)
2 fresh mangoes, sliced (optional)
6 oz (175 g) Chinese cabbage *or* mustard green, parboiled in salted water
4 oz (100 g) beansprouts, tailed
8 fried beancurd cakes, cut in half diagonally
1 piece soft beancurd, chilled first, fried, and cut into cubes

*Sauce ingredients*
4 fresh red chillies
½-inch (1·2-cm) piece blacan
* 2 teaspoons sugar crystals, boiled in 3 tablespoons water until dissolved, and cooled
3 oz (75 g) roasted peanuts, ground coarsely in a coffee grinder
juice of 2 lemons
1 tablespoon tamarind juice (see page 44)
salt to taste

To make the sauce, pound the chillies and blacan with a pestle and mortar, then combine with all the other sauce ingredients in a mixing bowl. Pour into a small sauce bowl, and either arrange the vegetables and fruits around it, or toss all together before serving.

* If you find sugar crystals difficult to obtain, use peanut brittle instead of the sugar and peanuts. Pound enough to make 1 cup.

## *Malay Vegetable Salad*                              *Serves 4–6*
### *Gadoh-Gadoh*

Like Rojak (above), this can be served as a starter, a snack or an accompaniment to a main course.

12 pieces fried beancurd, halved diagonally
4 oz (100 g) beansprouts, tailed and washed
4 oz (100 g) whole frozen beans, cooked in salted water
1 large potato, boiled, peeled and sliced
½ cucumber, unpeeled and cut into matchstick size strips
4 cabbage leaves, shredded and blanched for 1 minute
3 eggs, hard-boiled and cut into quarters
2 crisp lettuce leaves, shredded and soaked in cold sugar water for 5
  minutes

*Sauce ingredients*
1 thumbsize piece fresh ginger
2 cloves garlic
1 stalk lemon grass
4 fresh red chillies
1 onion
1 piece blacan, stock cube size
3 tablespoons oil
2 cups salted peanuts, ground coarsely
1 teaspoon salt
5 tablespoons sugar
juice of 1 lemon
9 fl oz (260 ml) thick coconut milk

Arrange all the vegetables on a large oval platter, separating each variety with shredded lettuce leaves and leaving an empty space in the centre.

To prepare the sauce, first pound together the ginger, garlic, lemon grass, chillies, onion and blacan. Heat the oil and fry the pounded ingredients till the oil separates. Add the remaining ingredients and simmer till the sauce is thick. (For a milder sauce, seed the chillies and increase the sugar and lemon juice.) Place the sauce in a bowl in the centre of the vegetables. You can let the guests help themselves from the platter or serve it as a tossed salad.

## *Beansprouts with Salted Fish*
### *Taugeh*

*Serves 4–6*

This is a pleasant and economical dish to accompany any curry or noodle dish. Salted fish is obtainable from Chinese grocers and some non-vegetarian Indian grocers, or you can substitute Bombay Duck, which is now sold in many supermarkets.

2 tablespoons oil
4 cloves garlic, finely crushed
4 oz (100 g) salted fish, soaked for 5 minutes in warm water and thinly
    sliced (if using Bombay Duck, do not soak)
1 lb (450 g) beansprouts, tailed, washed and well drained
2 spring onions, cut in 1-inch (2·5-cm) lengths
salt and pepper to taste

Heat the oil in a wok and fry garlic until golden. Add the salted fish and fry till crisp. Increase the heat and add the beansprouts and spring onion. Stir-fry for 2–3 minutes, then check the seasoning and serve hot.

## *Malay Style Vegetable Curry*
### *Lontong*

*Serves 4–6*

1 tablespoon oil
1 pint (600 ml) thick coconut milk, mixed with 1 teaspoon salt
6 fried beancurd, diagonally halved
7 oz (200 g) each of the following:
    long beans, halved
    white cabbage, coarsely cut
    tinned bamboo shoots, drained and sliced
    okra, tops cut sparingly and left whole

*Ingredients to be finely ground together*
3 red chillies (seeded for milder flavour)
2 teaspoons coriander powder
1 stalk lemon grass (use white part only)
6 candlenuts *or* 12 almonds

1 inch (2·5 cm) fresh ginger
1 piece blacan, stock cube size
1 small onion

Fry the ground ingredients in the oil until the oil separates and bubbles. Stir in half the coconut milk and gently bring to the boil. Add all the vegetables and the beancurd and cook for 10 minutes. Add the remaining coconut milk and continue to cook, uncovered, till all the vegetables are done. Check the seasoning. Serve hot. You can garnish with some cooked shelled or unshelled prawns or quartered hard-boiled eggs.

## Mustard Green with Hot Sauce    Serves 4–6
### Sayur Bunga with Sambal

In Malaysia, Kang Kong (water convolvulus) is the cheapest variety of spinach, but I have replaced this with mustard green. You can use ordinary spinach if you find difficulty in obtaining the other two.

4 tablespoons oil
2 oz (50 g) dried prawns, pounded coarsely
salt to taste
1 lb (450 g) mustard green, washed and cut into 2-inch (5-cm) lengths

*Ingredients to be ground together*
3 dried red chillies
3 fresh red or green chillies
6 almonds
2 small onions
1 piece blacan, stock cube size

Heat the oil and fry the ground ingredients well. Add the prawns and salt and fry for 2–3 minutes. Increase the heat, add the mustard green, and stir-fry for 3–4 minutes. If you like the mustard green softer, cook a few minutes longer. Serve hot.

# Savoury Okra
*Serves 4–6*

## Kacang Bhendi

Okra is commonly known in the East as 'ladies' fingers'. This vegetable has a sticky consistency, and if you do not like that you can deep-fry the okra whole before putting in the spices and other ingredients.

4 tablespoons oil
1 onion, finely sliced
2 large tomatoes, finely chopped
1 lb (450 g) okra, washed and drained, tops cut sparingly and cut into
    1-inch (2·5-cm) pieces
1 tablespoon chopped fresh coriander

*Ingredients to be ground together*
2 fresh red chillies (seeded for milder flavour)
2 fresh green chillies (seeded for milder flavour)
½ teaspoon turmeric powder
1 thumbsize piece fresh ginger
2 cloves garlic
½ teaspoon salt

Heat the oil in a wok or large frying pan with a lid, and fry the onions till brown. Add the ground ingredients. Stir-fry for 2 minutes. Add the tomatoes and cook, covered, for 2–3 minutes. Add the okra and stir-fry on a high heat for 2–3 minutes. Reduce the heat, cover the wok, and simmer till the okra is done. Young, tender okra should take about 5–7 minutes, but allow 10 minutes for larger ones. The okra should be soft but not broken. Adjust the seasoning, and garnish with fresh coriander leaves.

# Bean Curd with Straw Mushrooms
*Serves 4–6*

## Tauhu Goreng Lagi Cendawan Jerami

In Malaysia there are a variety of beancurds, but in England I have found only two – soft white cakes and deep-fried squares. In this recipe I have used the soft cake, and a word of warning – be very gentle. Straw mushrooms are available only in tins. You can use tiny fresh button mushrooms instead.

½ teaspoon chilli powder
4 teaspoons tomato purée
6 dessertspoons vegetable oil
2 cloves garlic, finely chopped
2 teaspoons fresh ginger, finely crushed
5 spring onions, white stalks chopped finely, green kept for garnish
salt and pepper
15 oz (425 g) tinned straw mushrooms, drained
4 squares chilled soft beancurd, each cut into 9 pieces and fried in a little
   oil until light brown on all sides

Mix the chilli powder and tomato purée to a paste with 4 tablespoons of water. Heat the oil in a wok or large saucepan and fry the garlic and ginger till fragrant. Add the chopped spring onions, chilli paste, salt and pepper and stir well. Add the mushrooms, mix well, and simmer for 2–3 minutes. Finally add the fried beancurd cubes and stir gently so that they are covered with the sauce. Serve hot, garnished with the green part of the spring onions.

   You can elaborate on this dish by adding 4 oz (100 g) of parboiled and drained chicken livers when you add the chilli paste.


## Malay Style Mixed Vegetables
### Sayur Lodeh

Serves 4–6

*Sayur* means vegetables and *lodeh* means cooked until very soft. The Chinese keep their vegetables crisp, but this dish is more like a vegetable stew.

3 tablespoons vegetable oil
2 onions, finely sliced
1 teaspoon crushed fresh ginger
8 cloves garlic, finely crushed
2 fresh red chillies, seeded and finely chopped
6 oz (175 g) crisp white cabbage, cut into 2-inch (5-cm) lengths
6 oz (175 g) cauliflower, cut into small florets
2 carrots, peeled and cut into thin slices
6 oz (175 g) whole French beans, cut into 1-inch (2·5-cm) lengths

1 red and 1 green chilli, seeded and cut in half lengthwise
a few fresh coriander leaves, chopped
6 curry leaves *or* 2 bay leaves
½ teaspoon turmeric powder
1 teaspoon salt
½ pint (300 ml) thick coconut milk

Heat the oil and fry the onions, ginger, garlic and chopped red chillies till fragrant. Add the cabbage, cauliflower, carrots, beans, halved chillies, coriander and curry leaves, turmeric and salt, and stir-fry for 2 minutes. Add the coconut milk and bring to the boil, stirring constantly. Reduce the heat and simmer uncovered until the vegetables are soft but not broken.

If you are not a strict vegetarian you can add shelled cooked prawns 2 or 3 minutes before removing from the heat. If you prefer a milder taste, use only one chopped chilli and omit the halved ones.


## *Fried Long Beans*   Serves 4–6
### *Kacang Buncis Goreng*

The long beans in Malaysia are sometimes over a foot long, so the name is apt. They can occasionally be found in Chinese grocery shops, but you can use whole French or runner beans, fresh or frozen. If you are using frozen beans you will find it easier to chop them finely while they are still slightly frozen.

3 tablespoons vegetable oil
2 oz (50 g) dried prawns, soaked in water for 5 minutes, drained, and water reserved
1 lb (450 g) long beans, finely chopped
1 teaspoon salt

*Ingredients to be ground together*
2 fresh red chillies (seeded for milder flavour)
½ teaspoon turmeric powder
1 piece blacan, stock cube size
1 stalk lemon grass (use white part only)
3 candlenuts *or* 6 almonds
1 teaspoon sugar

Heat the oil in a wok and fry the soaked prawns until crisp. Add the ground ingredients and fry till the oil separates. Add the chopped beans, 2 tablespoons of the prawn water and the salt. Stir well. Reduce the heat, cover the wok, and allow the beans to cook for 2–3 minutes, or a little longer if you prefer them softer. Serve hot as an accompaniment.

## *Rich Potato Curry* (OVEN)
### *Ubi Kentang Kari*

Serves 4–6

Most people take the potato for granted. I am sure that vegetarians will approve of this dish and consider it a feast.

1 teaspoon chilli powder
½ teaspoon turmeric powder
1 teaspoon salt
4 tablespoons vegetable oil
1 teaspoon crushed fresh ginger
1 clove garlic, finely crushed
1 teaspoon fenugreek seeds, dry-roasted and ground finely
3 oz (75 g) sesame seeds, dry-roasted and ground finely
2 oz (50 g) creamed coconut, soaked in 4 oz (110 ml) hot water
1 large green pepper, seeded and thickly sliced
1 large red pepper, seeded and thickly sliced
a few fresh coriander leaves, chopped
4 large potatoes, boiled, peeled and cut into cubes

Mix the chilli, turmeric and salt to a paste with a little water. Heat the oil in a wok or large pan and fry the ginger and garlic until golden brown. Reduce the heat and add the chilli mixture, sesame and fenugreek and stir well. Pour in the coconut milk and bring to the boil, stirring constantly. Add the sliced peppers and coriander leaves, and simmer for 2–3 minutes. Add the potatoes and stir gently to coat them with the sauce. Simmer gently until the sauce is thick, taking care the potatoes do not break up.

Here is a hint for non-vegetarians. You can serve this with a fish or meat curry, and as an accompaniment, serve crisp deep-fried dried anchovies with a sprinkling of chilli powder.

# Malay Mixed Vegetable Pickle
## Acar

This can be made up in large quantities and stored in airtight jars in the refrigerator, where it will keep crisp for a considerable time. Serve cold as an accompaniment.

1 pint (600 ml) pickling vinegar
1 unpeeled cucumber, cut into strips 2 × 1 inches
3 large carrots, peeled and cut into strips 2 × 1 inches
½ lb (225 g) white cabbage, cut into 2-inch (5-cm) lengths
1 cauliflower, cut into small florets
3 red and 3 green chillies, seeded and halved lengthwise
9 oz (250 g) demerara sugar
10 oz (275 g) salted peanuts, coarsely ground in a coffee grinder
10 oz (275 g) sesame seeds, deep-fried until golden and drained
1½ teaspoons turmeric powder
3 tablespoons chilli powder
6 fl oz (175 ml) vegetable oil
5 cloves garlic, finely minced
salt to taste

Bring the vinegar to the boil in a large pan, and scald the vegetables one variety at a time for about 1 minute. Remove each vegetable with a deep sieve, shaking out as much of the vinegar as possible. (The used vinegar can be cooled, strained, bottled, stored in the refrigerator and used for cooking.) When all the vegetables have been scalded and well drained, place them in a large bowl. Add the sugar, peanuts and sesame seeds and toss well. Set aside. Mix the turmeric and chilli powder to a paste with a little water. Heat all the oil in a pan and fry the garlic over a medium heat until fragrant. Add the chilli mixture and salt and fry well. Remove from the heat and allow to cool. When completely cool, add to the vegetables and toss well again. Set aside, preferably overnight, before serving.

## Cucumber Pickle
### Acar Timun

Like the last recipe, this stores well in an airtight jar in the refrigerator. It makes a lovely accompaniment for curries and rice.

1 tablespoon vegetable oil
1 tablespoon mustard seeds
1 teaspoon turmeric powder
3 teaspoons salt
2 large cucumbers, cut in 2-inch (5-cm) lengths, seeds removed but unpeeled
½ lb (225 g) fresh French beans, cut in 2-inch (5-cm) lengths
10 fresh red chillies, seeded and halved lengthwise
30 shallots, peeled and left whole
4 tablespoons sugar
6 fl oz (175 ml) white vinegar
5 oz (150 g) salted peanuts

Heat the oil in a large pan and fry the mustard seeds till they begin to pop. Reduce the heat and add the turmeric, the salt and the vegetables. Stir-fry for 2–3 minutes. Add the remaining ingredients and bring to a quick boil. Remove from the heat and cool completely before putting into airtight jars.

## Pineapple with Seasoned Dried Anchovies
### Sambal Nanas

Serves 4–6

2 tablespoons oil
2 oz (50 g) dried anchovies, split and deep-fried until crisp
1 medium-sized fresh pineapple, cut into rings and halved, *or* 1 large tin sliced pineapple, very well drained

*Ingredients to be finely ground together*
1 inch (2.5 cm) fresh ginger
1 large onion

4 cloves garlic
6 dried chillies, seeded, soaked in water for 5 minutes and drained

Fry the ground ingredients in the oil until the raw smell disappears. Add the fried anchovies and stir well. Gently fold in the pineapple slices and cook for 5–10 minutes. (If you are using tinned pineapple, reduce the cooking time to 1–2 minutes.) Serve warm as an accompaniment to a main course, or on a bed of shredded Iceberg lettuce as a starter.

## Salad in Coconut Milk          *Serves 4–6*
### Salad in Santan

If you are planning a menu which includes hot curries, this salad will help temper down the chillies.

1 fresh pineapple, thinly sliced, *or* 1 large tin sliced pineapple, very well
   drained
½ cucumber, thinly sliced
1 large onion, cut in thin rings
1 fresh red chilli, seeded and cut into thin rings
salt to taste
a few fresh coriander leaves
juice of ½ lemon
9 fl oz (260 ml) thick coconut milk

Put all the ingredients, except the coconut milk, in a large bowl, mix thoroughly, and chill. Before serving pour the coconut milk over the salad and mix with a wooden spoon. Serve chilled.

# Rice, Noodles and Bread Dishes

### Spiced Yellow Rice
### Nasi Beriyani

*Serves 4–6*

The Malay *beriyani* is cooked in a different way from the Indian *biryani* (see page 242).

3 tablespoons ghee *or* unsalted butter
1-inch (2·5-cm) fresh ginger, finely minced
3 cloves garlic, finely minced
1 chicken breast, skinned and cut into very thin slices
2 cups long-grain *or* Basmati rice, washed and drained
3 cups hot water
1 stalk lemon grass
½ teaspoon garam masala
¼ teaspoon saffron powder mixed with 1 tablespoon warm water
1 teaspoon salt
1 onion, finely sliced and deep-fried till crisp and brown

Heat the ghee and fry the ginger, garlic and chicken for 5 minutes. Add the rice and fry for a further 2–3 minutes. Add the hot water, lemon grass, garam masala, saffron and salt. Bring to the boil. Reduce the heat as low as possible and cover the pan. Check after 15 minutes – if all the water has been absorbed, remove from the heat and gently loosen the rice grains. Cover the pan again and leave for 5 minutes. Serve hot, garnished with the browned onions.

### Malay Fried Rice
### Nasi Goreng

*Serves 4–6*

This dish can be served on its own with a chilli sauce, or accompanied by a meat or fish curry and a vegetable dish.

4 cups long-grain rice
6 cups water

1 teaspoon butter
4 tablespoons oil
6 oz (175 g) cooked prawns
6 oz (175 g) cooked chicken meat, diced
8 oz (225 g) long beans, diced
salt and pepper
¼ teaspoon monosodium glutamate
3 eggs, made into a thin omelette, rolled and thinly sliced
4 oz (100 g) crisp lettuce, finely shredded
1 large onion, sliced and deep-fried until brown and crisp

*Ingredients to be ground together (preferably in an electric blender)*
4 cloves garlic
1 small onion
3 red chillies (seeded for milder flavour)
1 piece blacan, stock cube size
2 oz (50 g) dried prawns, soaked for 5 minutes and drained

For best results, cook the rice a day ahead. Put the rice, water and butter in a large pan, and bring to the boil. Reduce the heat to low, cover the pan, and cook till the rice is fluffy. Heat the oil in a wok and fry the ground ingredients until the oil separates. Add the prawns, chicken, beans, salt and pepper, and stir-fry for 2–3 minutes. Reduce the heat. Add the rice and monosodium glutamate, and toss the mixture using two wooden flat spoons. When the rice is thoroughly heated it is ready to serve, garnished with the omelette, lettuce and onion flakes.

## Rice Served with a Spicy Squid and Prawn Curry

*Serves 4–6*

### Nasi Lemak

In Malaysia this dish is very popular for breakfast or as a light snack. Hawkers sell it in small portions wrapped in banana leaves. My family enjoys this dish immensely, and I serve it as a main course. Serve with a light soup and with fresh pineapple slices brushed with a chilli flower dipped in soya sauce.

*Ingredients for rice*
2 cups long-grain rice, washed thoroughly and drained

3 cups thin coconut milk
1 pandan (screwpine) leaf, tied in a knot (optional)
½ teaspoon salt
1 teaspoon butter *or* margarine

*Ingredients for curry*
4 fresh red chillies, seeded
½ teaspoon turmeric powder
1 piece blacan, stock cube size
1 thumbsize piece fresh ginger
3 cloves garlic
2 candlenuts *or* 5 almonds
½ teaspoon salt
2 teaspoons sugar
4 tablespoons vegetable oil
1 large onion, thickly sliced
8 oz (225 g) squid, cleaned, boiled in salted water for 5 minutes and thinly
   sliced
12–15 large raw prawns, shelled and deveined *or* 6 oz (175 g) large shelled
   cooked prawns
2 tablespoons tomato purée

*Ingredients for garnish*
2 oz (50 g) dried anchovies, deep-fried until crisp and drained
2 hard-boiled eggs, quartered
8 oz (225 g) mustard green *or* spinach, cut into large pieces and blanched
   for 1 minute in boiling water
a few thick cucumber slices

Place all the ingredients for the rice in a large pan and bring to the
boil. Reduce the heat, cover the pan and cook till the rice is fluffy.
Discard the pandan leaf before serving.

To prepare the curry, first put the chillies, turmeric, blacan,
ginger, garlic, nuts, salt and sugar into an electric blender. Add a
little oil and blend until finely ground. Heat the oil in a wok and fry
the onion until slightly brown. Add the ground ingredients and fry
till the oil separates. Add the squid and prawns and stir-fry for 2–3
minutes or until the prawns turn pink. Add the tomato purée and
fry for 2 more minutes.

To serve *Nasi Lemak*, arrange the rice on a platter, with the fried
anchovies, hard-boiled eggs, blanched greens and cucumber slices
placed round it in groups. Serve the curry in a separate dish.

# Scented Fried Rice
## Nasi Minyak

*Serves 4–6*

Nasi Minyak is usually served by the Malays with meat and vegetable dishes on festive occasions.

2 tablespoons ghee *or* unsalted butter
1 large onion, finely sliced
2 cloves garlic, finely minced
½ teaspoon turmeric powder
½ teaspoon five-spice powder
½ teaspoon salt
2 cups long-grain rice, washed, soaked for 1 hour in water and drained
3 cups water
2 hard-boiled eggs, halved
2 tablespoons almond flakes

Heat the ghee in a deep pan and fry the onion, garlic, turmeric, five-spice powder and salt. Add the drained rice and fry for 2–3 minutes. Pour in the water and bring to the boil, stirring occasionally. Cover the pan and allow the rice to cook on the lowest possible heat till all the liquid has been absorbed and the rice grains are fluffy. Leave to rest, covered, for 5 minutes before loosening the grains. Serve hot, garnished with egg halves and almond flakes.


# Glutinous Yellow Rice
## Nasi Kunyit

*Serves 4–6*

This dish can be prepared a day ahead and packed into a wet mould. If you want to serve it hot, steam it in the mould for 5–8 minutes before serving. Turn out of the mould and garnish with slices of cucumber.

3 cups glutinous rice (pudding rice), washed and drained
2 tablespoons turmeric powder
2–3 pandan (screwpine) leaves, tied in a knot (optional)
2 oz (50 g) creamed coconut, soaked in ½ pint (300 ml) hot water
1 teaspoon salt

Mix the rice with the turmeric and allow it to stand for about 45 minutes. Pour on enough water to cover the rice, and leave overnight. Next day, drain the rice and steam it in a deep bowl in boiling water for 5 minutes. Loosen the grains, push in the pandan leaves and mix in the coconut milk and salt. Steam till the rice is fully cooked. Serve hot or cold.

## Vegetarian Fried Noodles
### Sayur Mee Goreng

*Serves 4–6*

This can be served with any curry instead of rice.

1 teaspoon chilli powder
1 teaspoon turmeric powder
4 tablespoons vegetable oil
1 large onion, finely sliced
1 piece blacan, stock cube size
2 fresh red chillies, finely sliced
salt to taste
1 tablespoon light soya sauce
2 large potatoes, peeled, boiled, cut into small pieces and mixed with ½ teaspoon chilli powder and ¼ teaspoon turmeric powder
6 pieces fried beancurd, sliced
½ lb (225 g) beansprouts, tailed and washed
1 lb (450 g) fresh thick egg noodles (if using dried noodles, follow the instructions on the packet)
2 eggs, beaten

Mix the chilli powder and turmeric to a paste with a little water. Heat the oil in a wok and fry the onion until soft. Reduce the heat and add the blacan, chilli mixture, red chillies, salt and soya sauce. Fry for 2–3 minutes. Add the potatoes and stir-fry for 2 minutes. Add the beansprouts, beancurd slices and noodles, and gently stir-fry until the noodles are evenly coated. Make a well in the centre of the noodles, add a little more oil, and pour in the beaten eggs. When they start to set, mix in the noodles and fry well till the eggs are cooked. Serve hot.

# Spaghetti with a Fish Sauce
*Serves 4–6*
## Easy Laksa

The story behind this dish is like Mother Hubbard's bare cupboard. Once after a hectic day in the office I found I had only some spaghetti, a tin of mackerel and some salad. Now we have this dish quite often, as it is so delicious.

8 oz (225 g) spaghetti, boiled until soft and drained
14 oz (400 g) tinned mackerel in tomato sauce
2 tablespoons curry powder
salt to taste
onion, cucumber, tomato and lettuce to garnish

Empty the mackerel into a pan and mash it with a fork. Mix in the curry powder and salt and bring to the boil. To serve, put some spaghetti into each person's bowl, pour the fish sauce over, and garnish with onion, cucumber, tomato and lettuce.

# Egg Noodles in Sweet Potato Gravy
*Serves 4–6*
## Mee Rebus

The first time I tried this dish was at a little Malay stall, and immediately I knew I had to find out how it was prepared. After several attempts and mistakes I found this method.

4 tablespoons vegetable oil
4 chicken breasts, thinly sliced
2 pints (1·2 litres) chicken stock
2 large sweet potatoes, boiled, peeled and mashed
1 lb (450 g) fresh thick egg noodles, scalded in boiling water and run under cold water (if using dry noodles, follow the cooking instructions on the packet)

*Ingredients to be finely ground*
10 large dried red chillies, seeded
6 candlenuts *or* 12 almonds
1 onion
1 thumbsize piece fresh ginger

1½ tablespoons coriander powder
½ teaspoon turmeric powder
1 tablespoon fermented soya beans

*Garnish*
4 hard-boiled eggs, cut into quarters
4 fresh red chillies, seeded and cut into thin strips
2 beancurd cakes, deep-fried until brown and cut into small cubes
6 stalks spring onion, finely chopped
½ lb (225 g) beansprouts, tailed
2 lemons, cut into wedges

Prepare the ingredients for the garnish first, and lay them out decoratively on a large platter. Heat the oil and fry the ground ingredients until fragrant. Add the chicken and fry well. Add the stock, and simmer for 10 minutes. Gradually add the mashed sweet potato and stir till the gravy is smooth. To serve, put some noodles into a deep bowl for each person, cover the noodles with a portion of chicken and gravy, and top with a little of each of the garnishing ingredients.

## Savoury Rice Vermicelli
### Mee Siam

*Serves 4–6*

6 tablespoons vegetable oil
1 large onion, finely sliced
20 large dried red chillies (all or half seeded for mild or moderately hot flavour), finely ground
3 tablespoons black fermented soya beans, coarsely crushed
4 cloves garlic, finely minced
2 tablespoons light soya sauce
8 oz (225 g) shelled cooked prawns
6 fried beancurd cakes, cut into slices
10 oz (275 g) beansprouts, tailed and washed
1 lb (450 g) rice vermicelli, soaked in warm water until soft, then put in a colander under running cold water and drained well
2 fresh red chillies, seeded and finely sliced
1 large onion, finely sliced and deep-fried until crisp and brown
2 hard-boiled eggs, cut into wedges
1 lemon, cut into wedges

Heat the oil in a wok on a medium heat and fry the raw onion slices and ground chillies until the onions are soft. Add the fermented beans, garlic and soya sauce and stir-fry for 1–2 minutes. Add the prawns, beancurd cake and beansprouts, and stir-fry for 2–3 minutes. Remove half the mixture from the wok and set aside. To the remaining half add half the rice vermicelli and fry, stirring gently, until evenly heated. Repeat the procedure to fry the rest of the vermicelli. Serve hot, garnished with fresh chillies, fried onion, eggs and lemon wedges. Serve with any of the sauces on pages 104–5. (I have suggested you fry vermicelli in two batches as it is very delicate.)

## Fish Balls with Rice Vermicelli in a Sour Gravy
Serves 4–6

### Assam Ikan Bulu Meehoon

Fish balls were introduced by the Chinese, and the Malays have naturally adapted to using them in their cooking. In this recipe I am again using curry paste, which can be purchased from supermarkets and from Indian or Chinese grocers. Purchase a brand that suits your taste in chilli.

4 tablespoons vegetable oil
1 tablespoon tomato purée
juice of 2 lemons
1 pint (600 ml) water
2 stalks lemon grass
3 fresh red chillies, seeded and sliced lengthwise
1 teaspoon salt
3 tablespoons sugar
1 teaspoon monosodium glutamate (optional)
4 oz (100 g) okra, washed and left whole
24 fish balls, left whole (see pages 117–18)
12 oz (350 g) rice vermicelli, soaked in warm water until soft, then put in a colander under running cold water and drained well
a few fresh coriander leaves, chopped

*Ingredients to be ground together*
2 small onions
2 pieces blacan, stock cube size
3 tablespoons curry paste

Heat the oil in a pan and fry the pounded ingredients until the oil separates. Mix together the tomato purée, lemon juice and water, add to the pan with the lemon grass, chillies, salt, sugar and monosodium glutamate, and bring to the boil. Add the okra and simmer for 2 minutes, then add the fish balls and simmer for 10 minutes more. Season to taste. To serve, place the vermicelli in individual bowls, place some fish balls and okra on top, pour the gravy over to cover the vermicelli and garnish with chopped fresh coriander.

# Fried Sandwiches with a Savoury Fish Filling
*Makes 8*

## Ikan Roti Goreng

If you are bored with those plain sandwiches try this version. It has always been a success with my family and friends.

*Filling ingredients*
½ teaspoon curry powder
¼ teaspoon chilli powder
2 teaspoons vegetable oil
1 onion, finely chopped
4 oz (100 g) mackerel in tomato sauce, mashed with a fork
salt to taste

Mix the curry powder and chilli to a paste with a little water. Heat the oil and fry the onions till soft. Reduce the heat, add the curry paste, and fry well. Add the mashed mackerel, stir well, and simmer for 5 minutes. Season to taste and leave to cool.

*Sandwich ingredients*
1 egg, lightly beaten
6 fl oz (175 ml) milk
salt to taste
16 slices sandwich bread, crusts removed and buttered thinly on one side
margarine for frying

Mix together the egg, milk and salt. Spread the mackerel mixture evenly on 8 slices of bread, and cover with the remaining slices, sealing the edges with drops of the egg mixture. Cut into rectangles. Brush each sandwich on both sides with the egg mixture and fry each side until golden brown. Serve while the sandwiches are crisp and hot.

N.B. If you have an electric sandwich toaster, you can seal each sandwich by buttering both sides of the bread, but do not brush with the egg mixture.

## Three Layered Sandwich
### Tiga Lapis Sandwich

*Serves 4–6*

During the summer months one is often hunting for new ideas when fêtes, garden parties and coffee mornings are in full swing. The prawn filling can be prepared a day in advance.

2 tablespoons margarine
8 oz (225 g) cooked prawns, shelled and coarsely chopped
1 stalk lemon grass, bruised
16 very thin slices cucumber
16 slices sandwich bread, 8 buttered on one side, 8 buttered on both sides
lettuce leaves
4 spring onions, finely chopped

*Ingredients to be ground together*
1 large onion
2 cloves garlic
½ teaspoon chilli powder
3 candlenuts *or* 6 almonds
1 tablespoon tomato purée
½ teaspoon sugar
salt to taste

Heat the margarine in a pan and fry the ground ingredients. Add the prawns and lemon grass and simmer till dry. Season to taste. Discard the lemon grass and allow the mixture to cool.

On a single buttered slice of bread spread some of the prawn mixture. Place a double buttered slice on top and put on 4 slices of cucumber. Next another double buttered slice, spread with more of the prawn mixture. Finally, top with a single buttered slice to complete the sandwich. Make the rest of the sandwiches in the same way. Cover them with a damp cloth and put a weight on top for 15 minutes. Remove the crusts just before serving, and cut each sandwich into 3 pieces. Place them on a large platter, and garnish with lettuce leaves and chopped spring onion.

## Thick Pancakes
### Roti Canai

*Serves 4–6*

The Malay section would be incomplete without this delicious bread. It is an excellent accompaniment to most curries.

1 lb 5 oz (600 g) strong plain flour
1 teaspoon salt
2 tablespoons sugar
very cold water
12 oz (350 g) melted ghee *or* unsalted butter

Sift the flour and salt into a large bowl and add the sugar. Make a well and add sufficient water to make a pliable dough. Knead the dough well, cover with a damp cloth, and stand the bowl in a warm place for 6 hours.

Add 2 oz of melted ghee and knead it into the dough till the dough has an elastic feel. Divide the dough into 6 or 8 pieces and roll each into a ball with your hands. Flatten one ball of dough at a time and roll into a thin circle. Spread with 1 teaspoon of ghee and fold over the edges to make a square. Sprinkle with a little flour and roll out lightly to the size of a saucer.

Heat a non-stick frying pan or griddle. Pour in 1 teaspoon of ghee and cook one pancake till golden, then lift it, pour in another teaspoon of ghee, and replace the pancake the other way up. When the second side is nearly done, crush the sides to release steam and give it a flaky effect. Repeat till all the pancakes are cooked. Serve hot. (To keep them warm, wrap them in a linen kitchen towel.)

## Lacy Pancakes
*Roti Kirai*

1 lb 5 oz (600 g) plain flour
1 teaspoon salt
2 pints (1·2 litres) thin coconut milk
¼ teaspoon saffron
4 lightly beaten eggs
ghee *or* unsalted butter for frying

Sift the flour and salt into a large bowl and make a well. Add half the coconut milk and mix to a smooth consistency with an electric whisk. Add all the other ingredients and whisk until there are no lumps. Heat a flat-bottomed wok or a griddle and add ½ teaspoon of ghee. When the ghee has melted, add a ladle of batter. Swivel the wok to spread the batter thinly, leaving a few holes. Cook on one side only. Remove and fold into four, the cooked side outermost. When folded the pancakes look like open lacy hand fans. Serve hot with curries. (To keep them warm, wrap them in a linen kitchen towel.)

# Condiments

## Hot Chilli Sauce
### Chilli Sambal

4 dessertspoons vegetable oil
2 onions
10 fresh red chillies
1 teaspoon sugar
½ teaspoon salt
juice of 1 lemon

Put the onions and chillies in an electric blender with a little oil and blend until smooth. Heat the oil in a pan and fry the onion and chilli mixture till the oil separates. Add the sugar, salt and lemon juice. Remove from the heat, cool completely, and store in an airtight jar. This sauce will keep for up to 6 months and is handy to have.

## Coconut and Chilli Sauce
### Fried Coconut Sambal

This can be made in advance and served with most Malay dishes as an accompaniment.

6 dessertspoons vegetable oil
4 oz (100 g) raw peanuts, unskinned
4 fresh red chillies, finely sliced (seeded for milder flavour)
2 onions, finely chopped
4 dessertspoons dried prawns, soaked in hot water, drained and ground
1 stalk lemon grass, finely chopped (use white part only)
10 oz (275 g) desiccated coconut
salt to taste

Heat the oil in a heavy pan and fry the peanuts till brown. Remove and drain on kitchen paper. In the same oil fry the chillies and onions. When the onions are golden in colour add the ground dried prawns and stir well. Add the lemon grass and desiccated coconut and season to taste. Continue to cook, stirring constantly, till the coconut is evenly golden brown. Fold in the fried peanuts. Cool completely and store in an airtight jar.

## Prawn Paste Chilli Sauce
### Sambal Blacan

8 fresh red chillies
1 piece blacan, stock cube size, dry-roasted till soft
juice of ½ lemon
1 teaspoon grated lemon rind

Pound the chillies and blacan to a coarse consistency. Mix in the lemon juice. Serve in a small bowl, garnished with grated lemon rind.

## Tomato Sambal
### Sambal Buah Tomat

4 tablespoons oil
2 fresh red chillies, coarsely pounded
1 piece blacan, stock cube size, dry-roasted
1 teaspoon salt
1 tablespoon sugar
4 large red firm tomatoes, cut into tiny cubes
1 onion, sliced finely and deep-fried till crisp

Heat the oil and fry the chillies, blacan, salt and sugar. When the blacan has become a smooth paste, add the tomatoes and stir-fry on a high heat for 1 minute. Crush the fried onions with your fingers and add to the pan. Stir-fry for a further minute. Remove from the heat and cool. It will keep in an airtight jar in the refrigerator for a few weeks.

# Sweets and Drinks

## Pineapple Syrup
### Nanas Sirap

This makes a refreshing drink.

6 fl oz (175 ml) water
6 oz (175 g) sugar
6 cloves
1 inch (2·5 cm) cinnamon quill
1 fresh ripe pineapple, finely blended in a liquidizer

Combine the water, sugar, cloves and cinnamon quill in a heavy pan and place on a low heat until the sugar has dissolved. Add the pineapple, raise the heat to medium, and cook for 15–20 minutes. Strain, cool and bottle. Dilute in water to taste.

N.B. If you prefer a chunky drink, remove the cloves and cinnamon quill and do not strain.

## Ice and Nut Drink                    Serves 4–6
### Ice Kacang

1 oz (25 g) cooked red kidney beans *or* tinned kidney beans, drained
5 oz (150 g) Liang Fen jelly (black seaweed jelly), cut into small cubes
4 oz (100 g) drained sweet corn
½ pint (300 ml) sweet coconut milk (this is available in tins, or you can follow one of the methods on pages 24–5 and sweeten to taste)
12 fl oz (350 ml) evaporated milk
2 oz (50 g) cendol (optional) (see page 112)
2 tablespoons dark brown sugar, dissolved in 3 fl oz (85 ml) boiling water and cooled
finely crushed ice

Mix all the ingredients together and chill. Top with crushed ice just before serving. For a more decorative effect, make ice cubes with water and some strawberry or raspberry syrup. When set, crush and store in the freezer till required.

## Lychee Pudding

Serves 4–6

a 1-oz packet gelatine
6 tablespoons sugar
1 small tin evaporated milk
2 eggs, beaten
a few drops red food colouring
1 large tin lychees

Prepare the gelatine according to the instructions on the packet, using lychee syrup and water to make up the required quantity of liquid. Add the sugar, evaporated milk, eggs and colouring. Whisk until smooth. In individual wet moulds place a few lychees, reserving 6 for garnish, and pour the gelatine mixture over slowly. Cool and leave in the refrigerator to set. To serve, remove from moulds and top each with a lychee.

## Steamed Banana with Coconut Sauce
Serves 4–6

### Pisang Besriam

6 green bananas (*pisang rajah*) if available, *or* not too ripe ordinary
    bananas
4 heaped teaspoons green pea flour (hoen kee)
4 oz (100 g) creamed coconut, dissolved until smooth in ½ pint (300 ml)
    hot water
5 tablespoons sugar
a few drops pandan essence (optional)
a few drops green food colouring

Peel the bananas and steam them whole, allowing 10 minutes if using *pisang rajah*, but only 5 minutes if using ordinary bananas. Cool and arrange in a deep serving dish. Blend the flour to a smooth paste with 1–2 tablespoons of coconut milk. Put the remaining coconut milk, sugar, pandan essence and colouring in a pan and gently bring to the boil. Gradually add the green pea flour mixture, stirring constantly until the sauce thickens. Serve the bananas with the sauce poured over them.

If you find it difficult to obtain green pea flour you can use cornflour instead, but when blending to a paste you must make sure the coconut milk is completely cooled.

## Jackfruit Custard
### Pudding Chempedak

*Serves 4–6*

14 oz (400 g) jackfruit, drained and finely chopped (save the syrup for the recipe below)
2 oz (50 g) soft brown sugar
4 oz (100 g) creamed coconut, diluted in 9 fl oz (260 ml) hot water and cooled
a few drops pandan essence (optional)
dash of mace powder
2 tablespoons butter
pinch of salt
4 eggs, lightly beaten

Boil the jackfruit with the sugar for a few minutes, then reduce the heat and add the coconut milk, pandan essence, mace, butter and salt. Simmer for a few minutes, then remove from the heat, add the eggs, and mix well. Pour into a wet mould. Cool and leave to set in the refrigerator. To serve, remove from the mould and cut in slices.

### To use the jackfruit syrup

a 1-oz packet gelatine
a few drops vanilla essence
sugar to taste
mandarin segments to decorate

Prepare the gelatine according to the instructions on the packet, using jackfruit syrup and water to make up the required quantity of liquid. Add vanilla essence and sugar to taste. Cool and pour into wet moulds, cool and leave to set. To serve, remove from the moulds and decorate with mandarin segments.

# Jelly Drink
## Agar-agar Minuman

*Serves 4–6*

Agar-agar is the local gelatine in Malaysia and is also called 'seaweed jelly' or China grass. You can substitute ordinary gelatine powder.

*Jelly ingredients*
¼ oz (7 g) agar-agar, soaked overnight and drained
1½ pint (900 ml) water
8 oz (225 g) sugar
a few drops vanilla essence
red, yellow and green colouring

*Drink ingredients*
a 15-oz (425-g) tin evaporated milk
½ pint (300 ml) milk
½ teaspoon cinnamon powder
½ teaspoon grated nutmeg
3 oz (75 g) rock sugar *or* 5 oz (150 g) golden syrup
crushed ice for decoration

Boil the agar-agar in the water until dissolved, then add the sugar and simmer till that has dissolved. Add the vanilla essence. Strain into 3 bowls and colour one red, one yellow and one green. Cool and leave to set. When set, coarsely break up the jelly and mix the colours together. Keep chilled. Heat the evaporated milk, milk, spices and sugar till all the sugar has dissolved, then strain and chill.

To serve, place portions of the jelly in individual bowls, pour on a generous helping of the milk mixture, and top with crushed ice.

# Banana Fritters
## Goreng Pisang

*Makes 12*

Delicious as a snack, especially when you get one of those sudden peckish moments.

6 fairly green bananas, cut into half lengthwise (use *pisang rajah* if
  available)
oil for deep-frying

*Batter*
3 oz (75 g) self-raising flour
3 tablespoons rice flour
pinch of salt
water

Sift together the flour, rice flour and salt and mix with some water to make a smooth batter, thick enough to coat the back of a wooden spoon. Heat the oil in a wok until nearly smoking. Dip the bananas in the batter and fry a few pieces at a time until golden brown on both sides. Drain on kitchen paper and serve hot.

You can substitute 2 sweet potatoes, boiled, peeled and sliced thinly, for the banana.


## Sago Pudding
### Gula Melaka

Serves 4–6

Gula Melaka is the name of the palm sugar required for this recipe, but I find that soft brown sugar combined with treacle and fresh ginger makes an excellent substitute.

12 fl oz (350 ml) water
8 tablespoons soft brown sugar
1 tablespoon treacle
2 thin slices fresh ginger
a few drops of pandan essence (optional)
5 oz (150 g) sago, washed and soaked in 2 pints (1·2 litres) water
12 fl oz (350 ml) thick coconut milk with a pinch of salt

Boil together the water, sugar, treacle, ginger and essence until the sugar has dissolved. Strain, and cool completely. Bring the sago and water to the boil and cook till the sago is soft and transparent. Remove from the heat, drain in a sieve, and pour cold water over it to remove excess starch. Divide the sago among individual serving bowls and chill. To serve, pour on first coconut milk and then the syrup, according to taste.

# Baked Coconut Custard
## Buah Kelapa Bengka

*Serves 4–6*

A favourite local *kuih* (cake). Delicious served cold or warm.

1 bunch pandan (screwpine) leaves, finely chopped
4 eggs
pinch of salt
½ teaspoon grated nutmeg
1 pint (600 ml) thick coconut milk
8 tablespoons sugar, or to taste
4 tablespoons self-raising flour, sifted
icing sugar for decoration
melted butter

Put all the ingredients except the icing sugar and butter in a large bowl, and whisk with an electric whisk until smooth. Strain the mixture into a greased baking dish, and bake on the centre shelf of a pre-heated oven at 325°F (170°C) until firm and golden brown. When still hot, brush a little melted butter over the top and sprinkle with some icing sugar. Serve warm or cold, cut in slices.

# Bread Pudding with Coconut Milk
## Roti Pudding

*Serves 4–6*

The Muslims are very partial to bread pudding. In this section I have used coconut milk, and in the Indian section marzipan.

6 thick slices stale bread, crusts removed
12 fl oz (350 ml) thick coconut milk
2 eggs, beaten
2 tablespoons melted butter
8 tablespoons sugar
1 tablespoon sultanas
2 teaspoons finely grated orange peel
pinch of salt
½ teaspoon grated nutmeg
a few drops vanilla essence

12 red glacé cherries, halved
2 tablespoons almond flakes

In a large bowl, soak the bread in the coconut milk. Mix together all the other ingredients except the cherries and almond flakes. Pour over the bread and mix gently with a fork. At this stage the bread will break up. Grease a deep square tin and pour the mixture into it, spreading it out evenly. Decorate with the cherries and almond flakes. Bake on the centre shelf of the oven at 350°F/180°C for 1 hour or till set. Serve warm or cold with whipped cream.

## Cendol                                             *Serves 4–6*

Cendol is the name given both to the flour threads, and to this refreshing drink. You can use the threads in my recipe for Ice Kacang (see page 106).

4 oz green pea flour
1¼ pints (750 ml) water
a few drops green food colouring
½ lb (225 g) palm sugar *or* soft brown sugar
6 tablespoons granulated sugar
¾ pint (450 ml) water
3 pandan (screwpine) leaves *or* a few drops pandan essence
1 pint (600 ml) thick coconut milk *or* evaporated milk, thoroughly chilled

Mix the flour, 1¼ pints of water and the green colouring. Stir well and cook on a low heat, stirring constantly. Cook till the mixture thickens and boils, then remove from the heat. Place a sieve with large holes over a basin of cold water, and push the flour mixture through the holes into the water. When the threads have cooled, drain them and chill in the refrigerator.

In a separate pan dissolve the palm sugar and granulated sugar in ¾ pint of water. Add the pandan leaves and bring the syrup to the boil. Strain the syrup and cool.

To serve, mix the flour threads and coconut milk and add enough syrup to sweeten. Top with crushed ice.

# 3.
# Chinese Cuisine

# *Introduction*
There are no religious restrictions on food as far as the Chinese are concerned (except perhaps for those who have adopted Islam). Some Chinese in Malaysia still follow Confucianism and Taoism, but Buddhism dominates. Like the Muslim calendar, the Chinese calendar is also based on the cycle of the sun and the moon, but they have adopted a theory which allows the dates of their feasts and festivals to alter only slightly within a month every year.

Although there are several festivals and feasts, the Chinese New Year is by far the most important for the Chinese in Malaysia. The entire household is cleaned, new clothes are made, and special dinners are prepared – these sometimes consist of between 10 and 20 dishes. Presents are bought and offerings made in temples. The houses are decorated with strips of red paper with inscriptions of good wealth, fortune and happiness. Red is used because it is said to drive evil spirits away. Red packets containing money (*ang pow*) are given to children, friends and visitors of all nationalities. Elaborate meals are cooked and traditional cakes and biscuits served, and celebrations can go on for up to five days. Oranges are sent out as gifts for good luck.

The Chinese generally eat their meals at round tables, and each diner is provided with a rice-bowl, a sauce dish, a pair of chopsticks, a porcelain spoon (although plastic is becoming more popular) and a teacup. Each diner helps himself to the food with his chopsticks and spoon, putting it into his individual rice-bowl, not directly into the mouth as this is impolite. The meal generally ends with a soup, and Chinese tea is drunk during the meal.

For special occasions each dish is served individually. Bones and other inedible items should be placed in the saucer on which the rice-bowl rests, and when you have finished you should place your spoon in the rice-bowl with the chopsticks placed over the bowl. When large groups are being entertained, the host knows his guests have been satisfied and happy if the table is cluttered and messy but all the food is consumed.

The Chinese breakfast usually consists of noodles with soup, or a rice porridge, or *dim sum* (dumplings). Lunch is usually very simple, and if you are dining alone it could just be one main dish with a soup. There are no teatime rules, but there is always room for one of the many delicious steamed cakes and a refreshing drink.

Family meals usually consist of a meat or fish dish, a vegetable dish, rice or noodles and a soup. The Chinese generally eat their dinner before 7 p.m. – later a light supper is taken, which is usually bought from stalls or hawkers.

The Chinese always cut their ingredients uniformly, usually into bitesize pieces as these are easier to handle with chopsticks. When planning a Chinese meal for, say, 4–6 persons, do not increase the quantities of ingredients but allow one dish per person – this way you will have a wider variety on the table. Make sure you do not choose too many stir-fry dishes which have to be served immediately. Plan well so that you can enjoy the meal with your guests instead of rushing to and from the kitchen.

I have already explained Soya Sauce on page 44, but since in this section it is used a great deal a further hint may be useful. On an oriental label, light soya sauce is called 'Superior Soy' and thick soya sauce is called 'Soy Superior'. A little confusing – so study the label carefully.

Most of the recipes I have included in this section are the ones I have enjoyed on my several visits to Malaysia, so *'Cheng sik'* – happy dining.

# Soups

## Duck Soup with Salted Vegetables    Serves 4–6

1 tablespoon vegetable oil
1 thumbsize piece fresh ginger, crushed
½ duck, cut into large pieces and excess fat removed
2 pints (1·2 litres) water
8 oz (225 g) tinned salted vegetables (*Hum Choy*), soaked in cold water for
    1–2 hours
½ teaspoon monosodium glutamate *or* Ve-tsin
pinch of sugar
freshly ground black pepper
salt to taste
2 tomatoes, halved
1 medium onion, sliced and deep-fried until brown and crisp

Heat the oil in a large pan and fry the ginger for 1–2 minutes. Add
the duck pieces and fry till evenly brown. Pour in the water and add
the salted vegetables. Bring to the boil. Reduce the heat and simmer
till the duck is tender. Add the remaining ingredients except the
onion flakes and simmer for a further 10 minutes. Serve hot,
garnished with onion flakes.

## Beancurd and Fish Ball Soup    Serves 4–6

Fish balls and fishcakes are obtainable from Chinese supermarkets,
but you can make your own. Make a larger quantity than you need,
as they freeze well and are very handy for quick meals. I suggest you
use coley.

1 tablespoon vegetable oil
2 cloves garlic, finely crushed
1 pint (600 ml) chicken stock
1½ teaspoons salt
freshly ground pepper
4 pieces soft beancurd, each cut into 12 cubes

4 spring onions, finely chopped
18 fish balls, bought or home made (see below)

*Fish ball ingredients*
8 oz (225 g) skinned white fish, coarsely minced
½ teaspoon salt
¼ teaspoon white pepper
pinch of caster sugar
2 teaspoons cornflour

First make the fish balls if you are not using ready-made ones. Using your hands, mix together all the ingredients. Shape into firm balls the size of a small walnut, and leave them in cold salted water until required.

Heat the oil in a large pan and fry the garlic until golden. Pour in the stock and bring to the boil. Add the drained fish balls and simmer for 10 minutes. Add the remaining ingredients, except the spring onions, and continue to simmer gently for a further 10 minutes. Do not stir vigorously or you will break the beancurd cubes. Add the spring onions a minute before removing from the heat. Serve hot.

N.B. To make fish cakes, use the same ingredients as for the fish balls but shape the mixture into two or three tight blocks. Coat the blocks in beaten egg and flour and fry them till golden brown on all sides. Cut into thin slices and add to soups and fried noodles or use as a garnish to vegetable dishes.

## Hot and Sour Soup                          *Serves 4–6*

This recipe is from the Szechuan cuisine, which uses hot spices.

2 pints (1·2 litres) chicken stock
6 oz (175 g) chicken meat, thinly sliced
6 oz (175 g) pork, thinly sliced
1 oz (25 g) dried prawns, soaked and drained
2 beancurd cakes, cut in small cubes
2 oz (50 g) dried Chinese mushrooms, soaked, caps cut in thin strips
3 oz (75 g) tinned bamboo shoots, cut in thin strips
2 tablespoons light soya sauce
2 tablespoons vinegar
1½ teaspoons salt
1½ teaspoons freshly ground black pepper

2 teaspoons cornflour, mixed with 1 tablespoon water
3 eggs, beaten
spring onions, coriander leaves and green chillies, chopped, for garnish
lemon juice (optional)

Heat the stock and add the chicken, pork and prawns. Simmer for 5 minutes. Add the beancurd, mushrooms, bamboo shoots, soya sauce, vinegar, salt and pepper, and cook for a further 3–5 minutes. Add the cornflour paste and gently pour in the egg in a thin stream, stirring continuously until the egg is set. Serve, garnished with spring onion, coriander leaves and chillies. If you wish you can increase the amount of pepper, and add lemon juice to suit your taste.

## Dumpling Soup
## (Fried Wontan Soup)
*Serves 4–6*

Frozen wontans are obtainable in Chinese supermarkets, and you can also buy the skins if you wish to make your own. They freeze well and are always handy – they can be used for soups and noodles or even just fried and served with chilli sauce as a snack.

20 wontan skins
oil for deep-frying
1 teaspoon sesame oil
1 clove garlic, finely minced
4 cups chicken stock
salt and pepper to taste
a few stalks mustard green *or* spinach, cut into 2-inch (5-cm) lengths
2 spring onions, chopped
chopped coriander leaves

*Filling ingredients*
4 oz (100 g) fresh prawns
4 oz (100 g) pork with a little fat
6 water chestnuts
2 spring onions
½ teaspoon minced ginger
½ teaspoon light soya sauce
½ teaspoon salt
¼ teaspoon sugar

1 teaspoon cornflour
pepper
1 egg yolk

Blend together all the filling ingredients, adding more cornflour if the mixture is too liquid. Fill each wontan skin with 1 teaspoon of the mixture and seal securely. Deep-fry until golden brown, and drain.

Heat the sesame oil, and when it starts to smoke fry the garlic until brown. Add the stock, salt and pepper and the greens and bring to the boil. Add the wontans and bring to the boil again. Serve hot.

To make this into a complete meal instead of a starter, add some cooked egg noodles, beansprouts and Chinese cabbage.

Instead of deep-frying the wontans you can drop them into boiling water until the skins are soft, then drain and add them to the soup.


## Mixed Vegetable Soup                    *Serves 4–6*

If you are planning a menu with fried or dry dishes, serve this as an accompaniment for the diners to sip while eating the main course.

2 oz (50 g) pork fat, cut into small cubes
1 inch (2·5 cm) fresh ginger, finely crushed
4 oz (100 g) Chinese cabbage, coarsely cut
1 carrot, finely cut in julienne strips
4 tender celery stalks, cut in julienne strips
¾ pint (450 ml) chicken stock
1 tablespoon light soya sauce
salt and pepper to taste
pinch of sugar
1 teaspoon cornflour, mixed with 2 teaspoons water
1 teaspoon sesame oil

Heat the pork fat in a heavy pan until the oil separates and the pork bits have burnt. Discard the burnt bits. Add the ginger and vegetables and stir-fry for 1–2 minutes. Add the remaining ingredients, except the cornflour and sesame oil. Bring to the boil and simmer till the vegetables are tender, but do not overcook. Stir in the cornflour paste to thicken. Adjust the seasoning if necessary, and serve hot with a sprinkling of sesame oil.

## Pork Soup with Chinese Herbs
### Bah Kuk Tea

*Serves 4–6*

This is served from late evening until the early hours of morning, and is said to help avoid hangovers. It also serves as breakfast for the early morning shift labourers. Bah Kuk Tea spices are obtainable in Chinese supermarkets and medicine shops. They come packed in sachets like *bouquet garni*.

2 lb (900 g) meaty spare ribs, cut in large pieces
2½ pints (1·5 litres) water
1½ tablespoons thick soya sauce
1½ tablespoons light soya sauce
salt to taste
10 peppercorns
5 cloves garlic, crushed
1 packet Bah Kuk Tea spices

Put all the ingredients in a pan, bring to the boil, and simmer till the meat is tender, removing any froth as it forms. Remove the meat from the pan, put it into a serving bowl, and strain the stock over it. Serve hot with plain boiled rice.

The traditional accompaniment to this soup is strong Chinese tea. The tea is put into a jug, and boiling water is added, stirred then poured away – this process is repeated three times and the tea is drunk after the third infusion.

## Chicken Porridge

*Serves 4–6*

This dish can be made with a variety of meat and fish. You can also use dried duck, shredded dried fish, or even Chinese sausage, cut into thin diagonal slices. It is an ideal and economical dish for a cold winter's evening, or for a quick light supper or snack.

2 pints (1·2 litres) water
½ lb (225 g) chicken meat, thinly sliced
1 inch (2·5 cm) fresh ginger, finely crushed
salt and fresh ground pepper to taste
pinch of sugar

12 oz (350 g) glutinous rice
1 onion, finely sliced and deep-fried till brown and crisp
3 spring onions, finely chopped

Bring the water to the boil. Add the chicken, ginger, salt, pepper and sugar, and simmer for 15 minutes. Remove the chicken from the stock, add the rice, and bring to the boil again. Reduce the heat, cover the pan, and simmer till the rice is soft. Add a little more hot water, if necessary, to give a creamy consistency. Return the chicken to the pan and cook for 5–10 minutes longer. Garnish with onion flakes and chopped spring onions, and serve hot. As an accompaniment, serve finely chopped red or green chillies soaked in soya sauce.

# Poultry Dishes

## Chicken and Pineapple Salad

*Serves 4–6*

Try this elaborate salad if you are entertaining during the summer, especially if you are aiming to impress your guests.

2 chicken breasts, boned and skinned
salt and pepper
2 bay leaves
2 medium sized ripe pineapples
4 stalks celery, cut in ½-inch (1-cm) pieces
2 oz salted peanuts
2 firm bananas, cut into slices diagonally and sprinkled with lemon juice
¼ cup fruit chutney
¾ cup salad cream
2 teaspoons curry powder
1 small tin mandarin segments, drained
4 tablespoons desiccated coconut

Put the chicken breasts in a pan with water, salt, pepper and 2 bay leaves. Bring to the boil then simmer till the chicken is tender. Drain, cool, and cut the meat into cubes. Cut the pineapples in half. Scoop out the flesh and cut it into cubes, keeping the shells intact. Dry the shells on kitchen paper. In a large bowl combine the chicken, pineapple, celery, half the peanuts and three-quarters of the bananas. Keep chilled. Mix together the chutney, salad cream and curry powder to make a dressing. Before serving, drain any liquid from the chicken mixture, add the salad dressing, and toss well. Spoon the chicken mixture into the pineapple shells. Garnish with mandarin segments, the remaining peanuts and banana slices, and sprinkle with desiccated coconut. Top with a sprig of fresh mint – or even better, a tropical flower such as magnolia or hibiscus, the national flowers of Malaysia.

## Fried Sesame Chicken, Szechuan Style

*Serves 4–6*

Sesame seeds and chicken are a delicious combination, and this dish makes an excellent accompaniment with most rice and noodle dishes.

3 chicken breasts, cut into bitesize pieces
2 spring onions, finely chopped
½ teaspoon minced fresh ginger
¼ teaspoon five-spice powder
5 tablespoons light soya sauce
1 tablespoon rice wine *or* dry sherry
1 tablespoon cornflour
2 tablespoons sesame seeds
½ teaspoon salt
¼ teaspoon ground black pepper
1 egg, beaten
oil for deep-frying
2 tablespoons sesame oil
1 tablespoon light soya sauce

Put the chicken in a bowl with all the other ingredients except the frying oil, sesame oil and the tablespoon of soya sauce. Stir well, and leave for 2 hours. Heat the oil and deep-fry the chicken pieces for about 3 minutes, then lower the heat to medium and continue to fry until the chicken is golden brown. Drain and place on a serving dish. Put the sesame oil and remaining soya sauce in a pan, heat through, and pour over the chicken. Serve hot, garnished with slices of cucumber and tomato.

## Chicken in Black Soya Sauce

*Serves 4–6*

This dish is served cold. In restaurants it is served on its own, or in a mixed barbecue platter with roast duck and roast pork.

4 chicken quarters, about 3 lb (1·3 kg)
1 teaspoon salt
¼ teaspoon pepper

2 teaspoons finely minced fresh ginger
1 tablespoon sesame oil
3 cloves garlic, crushed
1 tablespoon sugar
6 fl oz (175 ml) thick soya sauce
12 fl oz (350 ml) water

Put the chicken, salt, pepper and ginger in a bowl, mix well, and leave in a cool place for 1 hour. Heat the oil and fry the garlic till fragrant. Add the sugar and allow to burn. Add the soya sauce and stir well. Put the chicken pieces in the pan and coat the pieces evenly with soya sauce. Add the water and bring to the boil, then lower the heat, cover the pan, and simmer till the chicken is tender. Remove the chicken from the pan and leave to cool. Cut into bitesize pieces and garnish with lettuce leaves, spring onions and pineapple slices. Serve with the gravy in a separate bowl, and with plain boiled rice.

## Crispy Five-Spice Chicken, Cantonese Style

Serves 4–6

For this dish you will need patience and 24 hours, but it will be worth it.

1 whole 3 lb (1·3 kg) chicken
1½ tablespoons honey *or* golden syrup
1 tablespoon vinegar
1 tablespoon rice wine *or* dry sherry
1 tablespoon salt
½ teaspoon five-spice powder
oil for deep-frying
lemon slices

Bring plenty of water to boil in a large pan, and blanch the chicken for 5 minutes. Remove the chicken from the pan and place on a wire rack to dry overnight. Mix the honey, vinegar and rice wine and rub this mixture all over the chicken skin. Rub the inside of the chicken with the salt and five-spice powder. Heat the oil in a wok and deep-fry the chicken on a low heat for 20 minutes, then raise the heat and continue deep-frying for a further 5 minutes, or until the chicken skin is crisp and golden. Drain and cut into pieces. Serve garnished with lemon slices.

## Sweet and Sour Chicken Wings          Serves 4–6

½ teaspoon salt
pepper
2 cloves garlic, finely minced
¼ teaspoon monosodium glutamate
8 chicken wings, jointed in two with the tips left on
5 tablespoons cornflour
oil for deep-frying
julienne strips of cucumber, spring onion and carrot for garnish

*Sauce ingredients*
1 tablespoon tomato ketchup
½ teaspoon Worcestershire sauce
1 teaspoon sugar
1 teaspoon light soya sauce
1 teaspoon sesame oil
¼ teaspoon vinegar

Mix together the salt, pepper, garlic and monosodium glutamate, and marinade the chicken in this mixture for 1 hour. Put the cornflour in a plastic bag, add the chicken pieces, and shake to coat the chicken. Heat the oil in a wok and deep-fry the chicken until cooked and crisp. Bring all the sauce ingredients to the boil, add the chicken, and stir to coat all the pieces with the sauce. Remove the chicken to a warmed serving dish and garnish with the cucumber, spring onion and carrot. Serve the sauce in a separate bowl. For individual serving make small moulds of cooked plain white rice, top with pieces of chicken, and surround with garnish. Serve sweet and sour sauce and chilli sauce in separate bowls.

# Satin Chicken, Cantonese Style       *Serves 4–6*

a 3 lb (1·3 kg) chicken, cut into small pieces
3 tablespoons vegetable oil
1 medium onion, finely sliced
2 cloves garlic, crushed
6 dried Chinese mushrooms, soaked till soft then caps thinly sliced
½ oz (15 g) black fungus, soaked in warm water for 20 minutes and halved
2 spring onions, chopped
1 fresh red chilli, thinly sliced

*Marinade ingredients*
2 teaspoons light soya sauce
2 teaspoons thick soya sauce
2 tablespoons oyster *or* plum sauce
1 teaspoon sesame oil
1 tablespoon dry sherry
salt to taste
4 teaspoons sugar
3 teaspoons cornflour
1 teaspoon monosodium glutamate *or* Chinese powder (Wei Fen)

Mix together the marinade ingredients, add the chicken pieces, and leave for 30 minutes. Heat the oil in a pan or wok and fry the onion and garlic until golden. Add the chicken and stir-fry for 5 minutes. Add the mushrooms and black fungus and simmer till the chicken is tender. Garnish with the spring onion and chilli, and serve hot with white rice. (Black fungus or *nori* is a dark purple seaweed sold in dried sheets.)

# Spicy Lemon Chicken       *Serves 4–6*

This is a *nonya* (Straits Chinese) style dish with a beautiful blend of Chinese and Malay spices.

oil for deep-frying
a 3 lb (1·3 kg) chicken, cut into 8 pieces with any excess fat removed
juice of 6 lemons, strained
1 tablespoon sugar

½ teaspoon salt
2 tablespoons light soya sauce
cucumber and lemon slices for garnish

*Ingredients to be ground together*
2 onions, diced
5 fresh red chillies
5 dried red chillies, soaked and seeded
6 cloves garlic
1 stalk lemon grass

Heat the oil and deep-fry the chicken pieces until golden brown on all sides. Drain and keep warm. Pour away most of the oil, leaving about 4 tablespoons in the pan. Fry the ground ingredients until fragrant, then stir in the lemon juice, sugar, salt and soya sauce. Add the chicken, stir well, and cook till the chicken is tender. Serve hot or cold, garnished with cucumber and lemon slices.


## Nonya Chicken with Dried Red Chillies

*Serves 4–6*

I am partial to the *nonya* cuisine – the blend of spices is fascinating, and being an Indian, I prefer dishes that have a bite to them.

1 dessertspoon thick soya sauce
1 teaspoon sugar
½ chicken stock cube, crumbled
salt and pepper to taste
2 lb (900 g) boned chicken, cut in bitesize pieces
2 tablespoons sesame oil
2 tablespoons vegetable oil
8 large dried red chillies, soaked for 5 minutes (seeded for milder flavour)
10 cloves garlic, crushed
1 thumbsize piece fresh ginger, finely sliced
1 dessertspoon fermented soya beans, coarsely ground
a few spring onions, cut in 1-inch (2·5-cm) lengths
a few fresh coriander leaves

Mix together the soya sauce, sugar, stock cube, salt and pepper, and marinade the chicken for 1 hour. Heat the sesame and vegetable oils in a large pan and fry the dried chillies till crisp. Remove and drain on kitchen paper. Add the garlic, ginger and fermented soya beans to the pan, and when fragrant add the chicken with its marinade. Stir, cover the pan, and simmer till the chicken is tender. Add the fried chillies and the spring onion, and fry for another minute. There should be no liquid sauce but the chicken should be moist. Garnish with coriander leaves.

## Chicken Rice                                             *Serves 4*

On every visit to Malaysia I have tasted Chicken Rice at various different stalls. I thought I would never be able to achieve the correct flavour, but at last I succeeded. My family thoroughly enjoy this dish. It makes a complete meal when served with a light soup and followed by a salad of fresh or tinned tropical fruits.

4 chicken quarters, excess fat removed
salt
2 cups long-grain rice, washed and drained
2 dessertspoons oil
2 cloves garlic, finely minced
1 inch (2·5 cm) fresh ginger, finely minced
1 dessertspoon thick soya sauce
1 dessertspoon oyster *or* plum sauce
1 teaspoon honey
salt and pepper
1 teaspoon sugar
pinch of cinnamon
pinch of powdered cloves
1 large onion, thinly sliced, deep-fried and drained
chopped spring onion for garnish

Rub the chicken with salt and put it in a steamer. Steam over plenty of water till three-quarters done, then remove and keep warm. Measure 3½ cups of the stock from the steamer, add the rice, and bring to the boil. Reduce the heat as low as possible, cover the pan, and simmer till the rice is cooked and fluffy. While the rice is cooking, heat the oil in a wok and fry the garlic and ginger till brown. Mix together the soya sauce, oyster or plum sauce, honey, salt, pepper, sugar, cinnamon and cloves, add to the pan and bring to the boil. Add the chicken quarters and stir well to coat with sauce. Stir-fry till the chicken is cooked.

Each person is served with some rice garnished with fried onions, a quarter of chicken and a further garnish of chopped spring onion. Serve with chilli sauce, and a plate of hard-boiled eggs, cucumber, onion, tomato and carrots cut in slices. If there is any remaining stock, bring it to the boil, check the seasoning and sprinkle it with spring onions and chopped coriander leaves. Serve with the meal for diners to sip.

## Chicken Livers with Beancurd and Snow Peas
*Serves 4–6*

A hotch-potch dish, with a distinctive Chinese and Malay mix. Delicious.

6 tablespoons vegetable oil
2 cloves garlic, finely minced
2 teaspoons finely minced fresh ginger
8 oz (225 g) chicken livers, cut in large pieces
¼ teaspoon chilli powder
4 tablespoons tomato purée
1 tablespoon water
salt and pepper to taste
8 oz (225 g) snow peas, stringed and blanched for 1 minute in boiling
  water
2 squares beancurd, fried until golden and cut into cubes
5 stalks spring onion, chopped
a few fresh coriander leaves
2 fresh chillies, finely sliced

Heat the oil in a wok or large frying pan and fry the garlic and ginger until fragrant. Add the chicken livers and stir-fry until evenly browned. Mix together the chilli powder, tomato purée and water and add to the pan with the salt and pepper, stirring well. Add the snow peas, beancurd and onions and gently fold into the sauce. Serve hot, garnished with the coriander leaves and sliced chillies. You can increase the chilli powder if you prefer a hotter taste.

# Braised Quails with Chinese Broccoli, Hunanese Style

*Serves 4*

The Hunanese were known as 'China's sorrow' because of their ecological misfortunes – their dishes consisted of almost anything edible, and they added spices to make the food palatable. In Malaysia, however, they have no difficulty obtaining ingredients, though they still use spices out of habit.

4 dressed quails
6 tablespoons sesame oil
12 fl oz (350 ml) water
8 oz (225 g) Chinese broccoli, cut into large pieces
salt
1 teaspoon sugar

*Marinade*
5 tablespoons light soya sauce
1 tablespoon dry sherry
1 teaspoon minced fresh ginger
2 spring onions, finely chopped
pepper and salt
½ teaspoon sugar

Mix together the marinade ingredients and rub into the quails. Leave to stand for 1 hour, then remove the quails from the marinade and fry them in 5 tablespoons of the sesame oil until lightly brown. Place the quails in a clay pot or a heavy casserole, and add the marinade and the water. Cover and cook on a low heat till the quails are done. While the quails are cooking, prepare the broccoli. Heat the remaining tablespoon of sesame oil and stir-fry the broccoli, adding the salt and 1 teaspoon of sugar. When the stalks are tender, transfer the broccoli to a warmed serving platter. Place the cooked quails on top and pour the sauce over them. Serve hot.

# Crispy Szechuan Duck

*Serves 4–6*

a 4 lb (1·8 kg) duck, thoroughly dried
1 tablespoon thick soya sauce
oil for deep-frying

*Marinade*
5 spring onions, finely chopped
1 thumbsize piece fresh ginger, finely minced
1 tablespoon dry sherry
3 tablespoons salt
2 teaspoons freshly ground pepper
¼ teaspoon five-spice powder

Mix together all the marinade ingredients. Rub well into the duck inside and outside and leave for 1 hour. Steam the duck for 2 hours, making sure there is always sufficient water in the steamer. Remove and cool.

Either slit the duck in half or leave it whole, rub soya sauce all over the skin, and deep-fry in hot oil until the duck is crispy. Drain it on kitchen paper, leave to cool and cut it into bitesize pieces. Garnish with cucumber and pineapple slices, and serve with plain rice, noodles, chilli sauce and a soup.

# Braised Spiced Duck, Nonya (Straits Chinese) Style

*Serves 4–6*

An elegant dish, prepared usually during the Chinese New Year. I served it one Christmas as a change from the traditional roast turkey.

4 tablespoons sesame oil
1 thumbsize piece fresh ginger, finely crushed
2 cloves garlic, finely crushed
a 4 lb (1·8 kg) duck, cut in half lengthwise
4 tablespoons thick soya sauce
1 teaspoon five-spice powder
4 tablespoons coriander powder
1 teaspoon dark brown sugar

8 tinned water chestnuts
salt and pepper to taste
2 spring onions, chopped
2 chilli flowers (see page 34)

Heat the oil in a large heavy pan, and when nearly smoking fry the ginger and garlic. Lower the heat, add the duck and brown it on all sides. Add all remaining ingredients, except the spring onion and chilli flowers, and pour in enough water to cover the duck. Simmer till the duck is tender, then remove it to a serving plate and keep it warm. Continue to simmer the sauce till it is reduced by half, then pour it over the duck. Garnish with the spring onion and chilli flowers, and serve hot.

## Sweet Duck, Straits Chinese Style    *Serves 4–6*

We often associate duck with Peking and Cantonese roasts. When I tried this recipe I found it had some Portuguese influence, which in Malaysia is still prominent in the state of Malacca.

a 4 lb (1·8 kg) duckling, split in half lengthwise
1 pint (600 ml) water
1 star anise
1 inch (2 cm) cinnamon quill
4 cloves
2 teaspoons five-spice powder
4 fl oz (110 ml) vinegar
1 oz (25 g) sugar
salt and pepper
1 clove garlic, crushed
oil for basting

Place all the ingredients except the oil in a large pan and bring to the boil. Reduce the heat and cook for 30 minutes with the pan covered, then remove the lid and cook till all the liquid has been absorbed. Remove the duck from the pan and grill under a moderate heat, basting with oil, until the skin is crisp. Cut into bitesize pieces and pour over any juices that have collected in the grill pan. Garnish with shredded lettuce, chilled cucumber and lemon slices.

# Meat and Offal Dishes

## Pork Cooked Twice

*Serves 4–6*

2 lb (900 g) belly of pork, boned, skinned and cut in 2-inch (5-cm) thick
  slices
4 tablespoons dry white wine
4 tablespoons water
salt to taste
4 tablespoons vegetable oil
2 cloves garlic, finely crushed
3 spring onions, finely chopped
1 large green and 1 large red pepper, cut in bitesize pieces

*Seasoning mixture*
1 tablespoon black fermented soya beans, crushed
2 tablespoons soya bean paste (yellow variety)
1 tablespoon thick soya sauce
1 teaspoon sugar
pinch of salt
1 teaspoon sesame oil

Place the pork, wine, water and salt in a large heavy pan and bring to
the boil. Lower the heat and simmer till the pork is nearly tender,
increasing the heat for the last 10 minutes to reduce excess liquid. In
a separate pan or wok heat the oil and fry the garlic till golden, then
add half the spring onion and stir-fry for 1 minute. Add the
seasoning mixture, stirring well, then add the pork and its juices and
stir-fry on a medium heat until the pork pieces are evenly coated.
Check for salt. Finally add the peppers, gently folding them into the
pork, and stir-fry for 1–2 minutes. Garnish with the remaining
spring onion, and serve hot, with boiled rice.

## Pork Steaks, Cantonese Style

*Serves 4–6*

1 lb (450 g) pork loin, cut into ¼-inch thick slices and lightly beaten
5 tablespoons cooking oil

3 tablespoons sesame oil
1 onion, finely sliced
1 fresh red chilli, seeded and thinly sliced
2 spring onions, finely chopped

*Marinade*
2 tablespoons sugar
2 tablespoons thick soya sauce
1 tablespoon rice wine *or* dry sherry
2 tablespoons cornflour
pinch of monosodium glutamate

*Seasoning mixture*
2 tablespoons tomato ketchup
1 tablespoon chilli sauce (optional)
1 tablespoon sugar
2 tablespoons light soya sauce
3 tablespoons water

Mix together the marinade ingredients, add the pork slices, and leave to stand for 30 minutes. Heat the cooking oil and fry the pork slices with their marinade on both sides until light brown. Remove from the pan and keep warm. Heat the sesame oil and fry the onion until soft. Add the seasoning mixture and bring to the boil. Return the pork slices to the pan and coat evenly with sauce, then cover the pan and simmer till the pork is tender. Serve hot, garnished with the chilli slices and spring onion.

## Steamed Pork ribs with Fermented Beans, Cantonese Style

*Serves 4–6*

* 1 lb (450 g) belly of pork with bones, cut into 2-inch (5-cm) pieces, skin removed
2 tablespoons fermented black beans, coarsely chopped
2 cloves garlic, finely minced
2 inches (5 cm) fresh ginger, finely minced
1 teaspoon cornflour
1 red chilli, chopped

* Prepared pork ribs can be bought at some supermarkets, but if you have difficulty in obtaining them, ask your butcher to cut them for you.

2 spring onions, finely chopped (reserve one for garnish)
1 teaspoon dry sherry
2 tablespoons plum *or* oyster sauce
2 teaspoons sugar

Put all the ingredients in an oven-proof dish. Stir well, rubbing the mixture thoroughly into the pork, then leave to marinade for 3–4 hours. Place the dish in a steamer and steam for 1 hour or until the pork is tender. Serve hot garnished with the reserved spring onion.

## Pork Balls and Chinese Cabbage Casserole

*Serves 4*

oil for deep-frying
5 tablespoons sesame oil
8 leaves Chinese cabbage, cut into 2-inch (5-cm) pieces
1½ cups chicken stock
1 tablespoon light soya sauce
½ teaspoon cornflour
1 teaspoon dry sherry

*Pork ball ingredients*
1 lb (450 g) lean minced pork
2 spring onions, finely chopped
1 teaspoon dry sherry
½ inch (1 cm) fresh ginger, finely chopped
½ teaspoon salt
1 tablespoon cornflour
pepper
1 egg, beaten

Mix together the pork ball ingredients. Knead well by hand and make into 4 large or 8 small balls. Deep-fry on a high heat till crisp on all sides. Drain and keep warm. Heat the sesame oil and stir-fry the cabbage leaves until tender. Line a heavy casserole with half the leaves. Place the fried pork balls on the cabbage and cover with the remaining cabbage leaves. Mix together the stock, soya sauce, cornflour and sherry, and pour over the cabbage, together with any remaining sesame oil. Bring to the boil, then reduce the heat, cover the casserole and cook slowly for about 1 hour. Serve hot with rice or boiled noodles.

# Crispy Pork, Peking Style

*Serves 4–6*

The Pekinese roast poultry and meat in a variety of styles. This dish is often found in restaurants, but it is very easy and can be prepared at home.

3 lb (1·3 kg) hand of pork, boned but skin left on
2 inches (5 cm) cinnamon quill
1 star anise
5 peppercorns
salt
4 tablespoons honey

Make diagonal gashes in the pork skin and tie the meat if necessary. Put it in a large pan with the spices and salt to taste, and cover with water. Bring to the boil, then lower the heat and cook till the pork is tender. Pre-heat the oven to its maximum setting. Remove the pork from the liquid, place it on a roasting tray, and pat it dry with kitchen paper. Generously rub the whole joint with salt and honey. Place on the centre shelf of the oven, and roast till skin forms a crackling. To serve, cut in slices and pour over any juices collected on the roasting tray. The stock can be used to make a soup or to boil rice to accompany the pork. Serve with a hot chilli sauce and a vegetable dish.

# Roast Pork in White Wine, Peking Style

*Serves 4–6*

If you are planning to serve roast pork but want something a little different from your usual style, try this recipe.

4 lb (1·8 kg) shoulder pork, skin left on
2 tablespoons vinegar
oil for basting

*Marinade*
1 teaspoon five-spice powder
6 tablespoons rice wine *or* any dry white wine
1 tablespoon finely minced garlic

1 piece salted beancurd, finely mashed
salt and pepper to taste

Rub the skin of the pork with the vinegar. Mix together the marinade ingredients, add the pork, and leave for 1 hour. Pre-heat the oven to 350°F/180°C and roast the pork on the centre shelf, basting with oil occasionally, till it is cooked and the skin is golden and crisp. To serve, cut in slices and garnish with cucumber and tomato.

## *Pork Dumplings*
*Shao Mai*

*Serves 4–6*

In Chinatowns all over the world *dim sum* (dumplings) dishes have become well known. I have chosen this recipe as it is my son Kevin's favourite.

½ lb (225 g) minced pork
2 oz (50 g) fresh prawns, minced
4 Chinese mushrooms, soaked until soft, then finely chopped
1 small carrot, grated (reserve a little for garnish)
2 spring onions, finely chopped
½ teaspoon salt
1 teaspoon sugar
¼ teaspoon pepper
1 teaspoon sesame oil
1 tablespoon rice wine *or* dry sherry
2 tablespoons cornflour
30 wontan skins

In a large bowl knead all the ingredients except the wontan skins until smooth. Divide into 30 portions. Place a wontan skin on a loose fist, put a portion of filling in the centre, and gently push into the hole of the fist to make a bag. Bring the edges together and gently seal. Garnish the tops with the reserved grated carrot. When all the skins have been filled, place the dumplings 1–2 inches apart in a greased steamer tray and steam for 8–10 minutes. Serve hot with chilli sauce.

You can garnish the tops with chopped ham, chopped Chinese mushroom, crabmeat or even coriander leaves and chillies.

## Tender Fried Beef, Szechuan Style

*Serves 4–6*

1 lb (450 g) tender beef, thinly sliced
2 tablespoons vegetable oil
2 tablespoons sesame oil
2 oz (50 g) fresh ginger, thinly sliced
3 cloves garlic, finely minced
½ red pepper, cut in large slices
½ green pepper, cut in large slices
¼ cup water
2 tablespoons thick soya sauce
1 tablespoon sugar
2 tablespoons plum *or* oyster sauce
5 spring onions, cut into 2-inch (5-cm) lengths

*Marinade*
½ teaspoon bicarbonate of soda
½ teaspoon salt
dash of pepper
1 egg white
1 tablespoon cornflour

Mix together the marinade ingredients, add the beef, and leave for 1 hour. Heat the oils in a wok and fry ginger and garlic until fragrant. Add the beef and stir-fry on a medium heat till it is evenly brown. Mix together the water, soya sauce, sugar and plum sauce and add to the pan with the pepper slices. Bring to the boil. Add the spring onions and fry well for 2–3 minutes. The beef will cook very fast as it has been thinly sliced. Do not overcook the pepper. Serve hot with rice.

## Ginger Beef Steaks

*Serves 4–6*

1 lb (450 g) thin tenderized prime beef steaks
2 teaspoons sesame oil
2 tablespoons vegetable oil
2 whole fresh red chillies
2 spring onions, chopped
a few sprigs parsley, chopped

*Marinade*
½ teaspoon mustard
3 tablespoons ginger juice (grate fresh ginger and squeeze out juice)
4 tablespoons dry sherry
1 tablespoon cornflour
2 teaspoons thick soya sauce
2 teaspoons oyster sauce
salt and pepper to taste

Mix the marinade ingredients till smooth. Add the beef steaks and leave in a cool place to marinade for 2 hours. Heat the oils in a wok or large heavy frying pan and fry the steaks, with their marinade, for 3 minutes on each side. Serve hot, garnished with the chillies, spring onions and parsley.

## Hot and Spicy Beef, Straits Chinese Style

*Serves 4–6*

2 tablespoons thick soya sauce
3 cloves garlic, finely minced
1 stalk lemon grass, finely minced
2 skinned tomatoes, finely chopped
3 tablespoons tomato ketchup
1 teaspoon salt
1 teaspoon sugar
1¼ lb (550 g) pot roast beef
oil for deep-frying
3 fresh red chillies, chopped (seeded for milder flavour)
juice of 2 lemons
a little grated lemon rind

Mix together the soya sauce, garlic, lemon grass, tomatoes, ketchup, salt and sugar, and put in a large pan with the beef. Add enough water to cover the beef, bring to the boil, then reduce the heat, cover the pan and simmer till the beef is tender. Remove the meat from the pan and simmer the stock to reduce it. Heat the oil in a wok and fry the beef until crisp on all sides. Drain, cut into slices, and keep warm. To the reduced stock add the chillies and lemon juice. Pour this sauce over the beef slices, garnish with grated lemon rind and serve hot.

# Stir-fried Mixed Meat, Cantonese Style

*Serves 4–6*

2 chicken gizzards
2 squid
1 teaspoon sugar
1 tablespoon light soya sauce
1 tablespoon cornflour
dash of pepper
½ teaspoon salt
1 teaspoon monosodium glutamate (optional)
3 tablespoons sesame oil
1 teaspoon vegetable oil
1 inch (2·5 cm) fresh ginger, cut in thin slices
1 red chilli, seeded and finely sliced
3 oz (75 g) chicken meat, thinly sliced
3 oz (75 g) lean pork, thinly sliced
2 oz (50 g) fresh prawns, shelled and deveined
2 oz (50 g) pork liver, thinly sliced
12 straw mushrooms
1 green pepper, cut in large pieces

Halve the chicken gizzards and make criss-cross cuts without cutting them right through. Flatten the squid bodies and make criss-cross cuts half-way through, then cut them into bitesize pieces. Mix the sugar, soya sauce, cornflour, pepper, salt and monosodium glutamate to a paste.

Heat the oils in a wok and fry the ginger and chilli slices for a few seconds. Add the chicken, pork, gizzards, prawns, squid, liver and mushrooms, and stir-fry for 2–3 minutes. The prawns should turn pink and the gizzards and squid should curl. Add the green pepper and the soya sauce mixture and bring to a quick boil, stirring constantly. Serve hot, on a bed of boiled noodles with beansprouts.

## Chinese Roast Pork
### Char Siew

*Serves 4–6*

I always keep portions of this in my freezer as it is so useful – you can serve it with stir-fried noodles or a quick fried rice, or even use it thinly sliced in soups or as a garnish for vegetable dishes. For barbecued spare-ribs, use the same marinade and cook either under the grill or over charcoal.

2 lb (900 g) tender loin pork
4 tablespoons oil
2 tablespoons honey
½ teaspoon Chinese red colouring *or* cochineal

*Marinade*
3 oz (75 g) sugar
1 oz (25 g) red beancurd paste
1 teaspoon five-spice powder
4 tablespoons sweet sherry
1 teaspoon salt
1 tablespoon ginger paste (see page 39)
1 tablespoon garlic paste (see page 39)
1 tablespoon thick soya sauce

Dry the pork with kitchen paper and prick all over with a fork. Mix together the marinade ingredients and rub well into the pork. Leave to marinade for about 4 hours, turning the pork occasionally. Pre-heat the oven to 400°F/200°C. Place the pork on a rack in a baking tray, brush with oil, and roast for 5 minutes on each side, then reduce the oven temperature to 300°F/150°C and roast till the pork is tender, brushing with oil to prevent it drying. Five minutes before removing the pork from the oven, mix the honey and red colouring and brush it all over the meat ensuring that the oven temperature remains at 300°F/150°C. Remove the joint from the oven, slice thinly, and serve hot or cold. The marinade mixture can be heated in a pan with 1 tablespoon of sesame oil and poured over the pork slices. Serve with rice or noodles and a chilli sauce.

## Pork Liver with Assorted Vegetables    Serves 4–6

1 teaspoon thick soya sauce
1½ teaspoons salt
dash of pepper
½ teaspoon vinegar
1 teaspoon rice wine *or* dry sherry
1 teaspoon cornflour
4 tablespoons sesame oil
1 inch (2·5 cm) fresh ginger, finely sliced
5 cloves garlic, finely minced
14 oz (400 g) pork liver, cut in ¼-inch (6-mm) thick slices
4 oz (100 g) snow peas, stringed and blanched for 1 minute in boiling
   water
4 oz (100 g) carrot, sliced and blanched for 1 minute in boiling water
6 oz (175 g) green pepper, sliced
a few spring onions, cut in 1-inch (2·5-cm) lengths

Mix together the soya sauce, salt, pepper, vinegar, wine and
cornflour. Heat the sesame oil until smoking and fry the ginger and
garlic for a few seconds. Add the liver and stir-fry for 30 seconds.
Add the snow peas, carrot, green pepper and spring onions, then the
soya sauce mixture, and stir-fry for a further 1–2 minutes. Serve
hot. Take care not to overcook the liver, or it will get hard and dry.

# Seafood Dishes

## Prawns in Honey
*Serves 4–6*

1 lb (450 g) large prawns, shelled and deveined, tails left intact
1 oz (25 g) unsalted butter
1 honeydew melon, cut in 4–6 slices

*Marinade*
2 cloves garlic, crushed
2 inches (5 cm) fresh ginger, thinly sliced
2 tablespoons honey
6 tablespoons light soya sauce
2 tablespoons dry sherry
2 tablespoons sesame oil

Mix together the marinade ingredients, add the prawns, and leave overnight. Heat the butter and sauté the drained prawns until they turn pink and curl. Serve with slices of melon. The marinade mixture can be heated and served separately as a dipping sauce.

## Fried Prawns with Chinese Sausages
*Makes 16*

½ teaspoon salt
½ teaspoon sugar
2 tablespoons cornflour
1 egg white (size 3)
16 large prawns, shelled and deveined, tails left intact
2 Chinese sausages, steamed and cut into 16 equal pieces
oil for deep-frying

Mix the salt, sugar, cornflour and egg white, and soak the prawns in this mixture for 25 minutes. Roll each prawn round a piece of sausage and secure with a toothpick if necessary. Heat the oil, and when it is hot fry a few prawns at a time until golden brown. Serve hot, with grated carrots, blanched beansprouts and a hot chilli sauce.

# Cold Aspic Prawns

Makes 4–6

1 sachet gelatine
chicken stock
4 oz (50 g) large prawns, shelled and deveined
1 small red pepper, diced
3 oz (75 g) petit pois, boiled for 3 minutes with a pinch of salt and drained
1 tablespoon sesame oil
pinch of salt
dash of pepper
tomato and cucumber slices for garnishing

Prepare the gelatine according to the packet instructions, using cold chicken stock instead of water. Keep warm. Boil the prawns for 2–3 minutes and drain. (If you are using cooked prawns this will not be necessary.) Wet 4–6 individual moulds and arrange the prawns, red pepper and petit pois in each one. Add the sesame oil, salt and pepper to the prepared gelatine and carefully pour into the moulds. Cool, then chill in the refrigerator. Unmould and garnish with slices of tomato and cucumber.

# Prawn Balls

Serves 4–6

a 12 oz (350 g) tin sweet corn, drained
1 lb (450 g) cooked prawns
2 eggs (size 2)
1 tablespoon plain flour
2 tablespoons cornflour
2 spring onions, finely chopped
salt and pepper to taste
oil for deep-frying

Blend the corn and the prawns in a blender for 1 minute on full speed. Add all the other ingredients except the oil, and mix well with a spoon. Heat the oil and deep-fry tablespoonfuls of the mixture, a few at a time, till golden. Serve hot with a green salad and chilli sauce.

If you are having a drinks party, put the prawn balls on cocktail sticks and arrange them round a small bowl of chilli sauce. Pass them around, allowing each guest to dip in the sauce according to individual taste.

## Chilli Prawns                                    *Serves 4–6*

Large raw prawns are obtainable frozen from most Chinese super-markets. They are grey in colour. Sometimes your fishmonger may order them specially for you, but you will have to buy a large quantity. You can also try this recipe with crab claws.

1 lb (450 g) large raw prawns
4 cloves garlic
4 fresh red chillies
1 inch (2·5 cm) fresh ginger
4 fl oz (110 ml) tomato ketchup
4 fl oz (110 ml) water
2 dessertspoons white vinegar
2 dessertspoons sugar
1½ teaspoons cornflour
salt and pepper to taste
4 tablespoons oil

Wash the prawns thoroughly, keeping them whole. Trim the whiskers but keep the shells on. Crush the garlic, chillies and ginger together finely. Mix together the tomato ketchup, water, vinegar, sugar and cornflour.

   Heat the oil in a wok and fry the garlic mixture until fragrant. Add the prawns, salt and pepper and stir-fry for 2–3 minutes. Pour in the tomato sauce mixture and cook, covered, on a high heat until the prawns turn pink – about 10 minutes. Serve hot as a starter, or with boiled rice or stir-fried noodles.

## King Prawns Baked in Salt, Cantonese Style                           *Serves 4–6*

In Malaysia fresh prawns of all sizes are available in abundance. Large raw prawns are available in Chinese supermarkets (see previous recipe).

1 lb (450 g) raw king prawns
1 teaspoon rice wine *or* dry sherry
1 tablespoon cornflour
salt and pepper to taste
1 lb (450 g) coarse salt
2 tablespoons lard
a few crisp lettuce leaves

Wash the prawns thoroughly, keeping them whole. Trim the whiskers but keep the shells on. Mix together the wine, cornflour, salt and pepper and marinade the prawns in this mixture. Place the coarse salt in a heavy casserole or clay pot, and heat up to 325°F/170°C. Place the prawns on a piece of greaseproof paper and dab them with lard. Wrap the paper over the prawns to make a packet. When the salt has reached the required temperature, place the packet on it, put the lid on the pot, and bake for 20 minutes. Serve hot on a bed of crisp lettuce with a chilli sauce of your choice.

The salt can be cooled and stored for use again.

## *Fried Pomfret with Hot Bean Paste, Szechuan Style*
*Serves 4–6*

Pomfret is a freshwater fish and is available frozen in Chinese supermarkets. You can substitute whiting, mackerel, bream or sole.

1 tablespoon flour
½ teaspoon salt
2 pomfrets, cleaned and scaled but left whole
1 tablespoon fermented black beans
2 cloves garlic, minced
1 tablespoon chopped ginger
1 cup stock
1 teaspoon light soya sauce
½ teaspoon salt
1 teaspoon rice wine *or* dry sherry
1 teaspoon hot bean paste
1 teaspoon cornflour
oil for deep-frying
1 red chilli, seeded and thinly sliced
2 spring onions, cut into 2-inch (5-cm) lengths

Combine the flour and salt and coat the fish with the mixture. Mix the black beans, garlic and ginger in one bowl and the stock, soya sauce, salt, wine, bean paste and cornflour in another. Heat the oil in a wok and deep-fry the fish until crisp on both sides, then drain and keep warm. Pour off all but 3 tablespoons of the oil, re-heat, and fry the black bean mixture until fragrant. Add the soya sauce mixture and bring to the boil. Pour this sauce over the fish, and garnish with chilli slices and spring onions. Serve with plain boiled rice.

## Sweet and Sour Fish                                    *Serves 4–6*

1 teaspoon salt
1 teaspoon sugar
1 egg white
3 tablespoons cornflour
1 tablespoon water
pepper
2 lb (900 g) halibut *or* cod, cleaned and filleted
3 tablespoons oil
4 spring onions, cut in 1-inch (2·5-cm) lengths (reserve one for garnish)
1 carrot, cut into 1-inch (2·5-cm) julienne strips
1 oz (25 g) green peas
1 fresh red chilli, seeded and cut into 1-inch (2·5-cm) strips
oil for deep-frying
4 oz (100 g) tapioca *or* rice flour, seasoned with salt and pepper

*Sauce ingredients*
juice from an 8 oz (225 g) tin pineapple rings (reserve pineapple for garnish)
4 fl oz (110 ml) tomato ketchup
3 tablespoons cornflour
4 tablespoons water
1 tablespoon vinegar
1 teaspoon sweet chilli sauce
1 teaspoon sugar
salt and pepper to taste

Mix the salt, sugar, egg white, cornflour, water and pepper together and rub this mixture well into the fish pieces. Mix the sauce ingredients together. Heat 3 tablespoons of oil in a large pan and stir-fry the spring onion, carrot, peas and chilli for 2–3 minutes. Add the sauce ingredients and bring to the boil. Keep warm. In a wok heat enough oil to deep-fry the fish pieces. Put the tapioca or rice flour in a plastic bag and add the fish pieces. Seal the bag and shake to coat the fish pieces evenly. Deep-fry the fish until golden and crisp. Drain and place on a serving dish. Garnish with the reserved spring onion and pineapple rings, and pour the hot sweet and sour sauce over the fish just before serving.

## Fish Cake with Chinese Cabbage         *Serves 4–6*

To make fish cakes, see page 118.

½ pint (300 ml) chicken stock
½ teaspoon salt
dash of pepper
½ teaspoon sugar
1 tablespoon dry sherry
2 fl oz (55 ml) evaporated milk
4 tablespoons vegetable oil
8 large Chinese cabbage leaves, cut into 2-inch (5-cm) pieces
8 straw mushrooms *or* dry mushrooms, soaked until soft, stalks removed
    and caps left whole
2 fish cakes, cut into ¼-inch (6 mm) thick squares
2 teaspoons cornflour mixed with 4 teaspoons water
1 tablespoon sesame oil

Mix together the stock, salt, pepper, sugar, sherry and evaporated milk. Heat the vegetable oil in a wok and stir-fry the hard white parts of the cabbage for 2 minutes. Add the mushrooms and the stock mixture and bring to the boil. Add the fish cakes and the remaining cabbage, and cook for a further 3 minutes. Thicken the sauce with the cornflour mixture. Sprinkle with the sesame oil just before serving, and serve hot.

## Steamed Fish                                    *Serves 4–6*

In Malaysia this dish is prepared with whole fish, but you can use steaks or fillets. Any fish can be used, though bass, carp, bream, trout or sole are particularly good.

1 large onion, cut into chunky rings
1 rainbow trout, about 1½ lb (675 g), cleaned, scales removed, rubbed
    generously with salt and rinsed in cold water
4 Chinese dried mushrooms, soaked until soft and caps cut in thin slices
4 spring onions, cut in thin shreds about 1 inch (2·5 cm) long
1 teaspoon sesame oil
2 teaspoons light soya sauce
salt and pepper to taste

*Sauce ingredients*
2 tablespoons cornflour
1 tablespoon light soya sauce
6 tablespoons water
1 tablespoon sesame oil
2 oz (50 g) beef *or* pork, cut into very thin strips
1 thumbsize piece fresh ginger, cut into thin strips

Put a steamer on to boil to collect steam before you start. Put the onion rings in an ovenproof dish which will fit in the steamer, and arrange the fish on top. Cover the fish with the mushrooms and half the spring onions. Pour over 1 teaspoon of sesame oil and the soya sauce, and sprinkle with salt and pepper. Place the dish in the steamer (the water should be boiling vigorously) and steam till the fish is cooked. This should take about 20–30 minutes.

Meanwhile make the sauce. Mix together the cornflour, soya sauce and water. Heat 1 tablespoon of sesame oil in a frying pan, and stir-fry the beef or pork with the ginger strips. When the meat is evenly brown, add the cornflour mixture, bring to the boil, and simmer until you have a thick sauce. Keep warm.

To serve, remove the fish to a warmed serving dish and pour the sauce over it. Garnish with the remaining spring onions and the steamed onion rings, and serve with plain boiled rice.

## Simmered Fish with
## Chinese Broccoli
*Serves 4–6*

12 oz (350 g) white fish fillets, cut into bitesize pieces
4 tablespoons vegetable oil
2 tablespoons shredded fresh ginger
1 lb (450 g) Chinese broccoli, cut into 2-inch (5-cm) lengths (if not
   available, use ordinary broccoli)
½ teaspoon salt
1 teaspoon sugar
1 teaspoon cornflour mixed with 4 tablespoons water

*Marinade*
½ teaspoon salt
dash of pepper
1½ teaspoons sugar
1 teaspoon rice wine *or* dry sherry
1½ teaspoons cornflour

Mix together the marinade ingredients, add the fish pieces, and
leave for 15 minutes. Heat the oil and stir-fry the ginger and
broccoli for 3–4 minutes. Add the salt, sugar and cornflour paste,
and bring to a quick boil. Remove the broccoli to a warmed serving
platter, reserving the sauce in the pan. Reheat the sauce, add the fish
pieces with their marinade, and gently simmer till the fish is cooked.
To serve, place the fish pieces on the broccoli and pour the sauce
over. Serve with plain boiled rice or boiled noodles.

## Squid with Fermented Black Beans   *Serves 4–6*

To make squid curls, clean the squid, removing the tentacles, ink
sac, inner organs and central bone carefully under running water.
Peel the thin outer skin and rinse well. Slit the body and open it out
flat. Score with a lattice pattern, cutting fairly deep but not right
through. Cut the scored body into 1-inch (2.5-cm) squares.

2 tablespoons oil
2 tablespoons sesame oil
1 lb (450 g) squid, cleaned and blanched for 5 minutes in boiling water

1 red pepper, cut into pieces the same size as the squid pieces
2 chopped spring onions for garnish

*Sauce ingredients*
1 tablespoon salted black beans, coarsely chopped
1 teaspoon minced garlic
1 teaspoon shredded fresh ginger
3 tablespoons plum sauce
3 teaspoons sugar
1 teaspoon light soya sauce
1 teaspoon cornflour
salt to taste
1 red chilli, finely sliced

Mix together the sauce ingredients. Heat the oils in a wok, put in the sauce mixture, and bring to the boil. Add the squid and pepper, and stir-fry for 2–3 minutes. Garnish with chopped spring onion and serve hot.

## Abalone with Oyster Mushrooms, Cantonese Style
*Serves 4–6*

This is a luxury dish, ideal for a special cocktail party or as a dinner party *hors d'oeuvre*.

1 large tin abalone, drained and thinly sliced
1 large tin oyster mushrooms, drained and left whole
crisp lettuce leaves, arranged on a serving dish
1 tablespoon cornflour mixed with 1 tablespoon water

*Sauce ingredients*
1 cup stock
1 tablespoon oyster sauce
½ teaspoon sugar
1 teaspoon sesame oil
salt to taste
1 teaspoon rice wine *or* dry sherry
¼ teaspoon ginger powder
dash of pepper

Put the sauce ingredients in a large pan and bring to the boil. Blanch the abalone slices and oyster mushrooms for 2 minutes, and arrange alternately on the bed of lettuce. Thicken the sauce with the cornflour paste and pour over the abalone slices. Serve hot.

## Fried Shark's Fin    *Serves 4–6*

14 oz (400 g) tinned shark's fin, drained and shredded if necessary
3 tablespoons vegetable oil
2 cloves garlic, finely minced
4 oz (100 g) pork, finely shredded
4 oz (100 g) bamboo shoots, finely shredded
3 eggs, lightly beaten with a little pepper
2 spring onions, cut into 1-inch (2·5-cm) lengths
salt to taste
1 teaspoon sesame oil
a few leaves of Iceberg lettuce

Place the drained shark's fin in a pan and cover with water. Bring to the boil, then cover and simmer for 20 minutes. Drain and keep aside. Heat the vegetable oil in a wok and fry the garlic till lightly browned. Add the pork and stir-fry for a few minutes. Add the shark's fin and bamboo shoots and fry for a few more minutes. Make a well and add the beaten eggs, then increase the heat and stir-fry quickly until the eggs have set and coated the other ingredients evenly. Add the spring onions and season with salt. Just before serving, sprinkle with the sesame oil and serve hot on a bed of lettuce.

# Vegetable Dishes

## Braised Monk's Vegetables

Serves 4–6

2 tablespoons light soya sauce
½ teaspoon sugar
½ teaspoon salt
dash of pepper
½ teaspoon sesame oil
½ teaspoon Ve-tsin (optional)
4 tablespoons vegetable oil
1 clove garlic, finely minced
1 carrot, thinly sliced
3 oz (75 g) snow peas (mangetout), stringed
3 oz (75 g) tinned straw mushrooms, drained
3 oz (75 g) sliced bamboo shoots, drained
4 Chinese dried mushrooms, soaked until soft and caps thinly sliced
3 oz (75 g) tinned baby corn, cut in half lengthwise
1 dessertspoon cornflour mixed with 2 tablespoons water
2 spring onions, chopped

Mix together the soya sauce, sugar, salt, pepper, sesame oil and Ve-tsin. Heat the oil in a wok and fry the garlic until light brown. Add the carrots and snow peas and stir-fry for 2–3 minutes. Add the remaining vegetables except the spring onions and fry for a further 2–3 minutes. Add the soya sauce mixture and bring to the boil. Check the seasoning, and thicken with the cornflour paste. Serve hot, garnished with spring onions.

The left-over tinned vegetables can be drained and frozen in an air-tight box and will keep a long time.

## Chinese Cabbage in Oyster Mushroom Sauce

*Serves 4–6*

Serve as a main dish for a vegetarian menu or as an accompaniment with a meat or fish dish. You can use Choy Sum (flower spinach) instead of Chinese cabbage.

salt
1 tablespoon oil
1 lb (450 g) Chinese cabbage, cut into large pieces

*Sauce ingredients*
1 teaspoon oil
3 cloves garlic, crushed
a 14-oz (400 g) tin oyster mushrooms, drained
2 tablespoons oyster *or* plum sauce
½ teaspoon sugar
1 teaspoon sesame oil
2 teaspoons light soya sauce
1 tablespoon cornflour
1 tablespoon water

Fill a large pan with water and bring to the boil. Add salt and 1 tablespoon of oil and keep on the boil. Blanch the cabbage pieces for 1–2 minutes. Then drain and place them on a serving dish. Keep warm. In a wok heat 1 teaspoon of oil and fry the garlic till golden. Add the mushrooms and stir-fry for 2 minutes. Mix together the remaining ingredients, add to the wok, and stir well to coat the mushrooms. Cook till the sauce is thick. Pour hot over the cabbage leaves and serve.

## Chinese Cabbage, Nonya (Straits Chinese) Style

*Serves 4–6*

1 tablespoon light soya sauce
1 teaspoon salt
1 tablespoon sugar
2 tablespoons vinegar
½ teaspoon cornflour

1 tablespoon sesame oil
4 tablespoons vegetable oil
2 cloves garlic, crushed
8 large dried chillies, broken into 1-inch (2·5-cm) pieces
1 dessertspoon shredded ginger
1½ lb (675 g) Chinese cabbage, cut into 2-inch (5-cm) pieces
freshly ground black pepper

Mix together the soya sauce, salt, sugar, vinegar, cornflour and sesame oil. Heat the cooking oil in a wok and fry the garlic till brown. Fry the chillies until brown and the ginger until fragrant. Add the soya sauce mixture and bring to the boil. Add the cabbage and fry for 2–3 minutes. Just before dishing up, sprinkle generously with ground black pepper. Serve hot.


## Bamboo Shoots with Salted Beancurd

*Serves 4–6*

Salted beancurd squares are usually obtainable in tins from Chinese supermarkets, but if you cannot get them, use 1 teaspoon of yellow beancurd paste which can usually be found in large supermarkets.

3 tablespoons vegetable oil
3 tablespoons sesame oil
3 cloves crushed garlic
1 square salted beancurd, mashed
1 lb (450 g) tinned bamboo shoots, cut in julienne strips
4 oz (100 g) shelled prawns
8 oz (225 g) tinned straw mushrooms, drained, *or* tiny fresh button
  mushrooms
salt and pepper to taste
1 onion, sliced, and deep-fried until brown
2 red chillies, seeded and finely sliced

Heat the oils in a wok and fry the garlic and beancurd for 1 minute. Stir in the bamboo shoots, prawns and mushrooms, season with salt and pepper, and stir-fry for 2–3 minutes. Serve hot, garnished with the fried onions and sliced chillies. For a milder flavour, omit the chillies and substitute finely chopped spring onions.

## Fried Beancurd Cakes with Beansprouts

*Serves 4–6*

This is a very simple dish which requires no cooking – it makes a lovely starter or can be served with drinks.

½ lb (225 g) beansprouts, tailed, washed and drained
½ cucumber, half cut into thin rings and the other half into thin strips
salt and pepper to taste
12 pieces fried beancurd cake, cut in half diagonally
2 firm tomatoes, cut into thin rings

*Sauce ingredients (or use a ready-made chilli sauce)*
3 fresh red chillies, finely crushed
2 cloves garlic, finely minced
1½ tablespoons thick soya sauce
juice of 1 lemon
½ teaspoon sugar
4 fl oz (110 ml) hot water
2 oz (50 g) salted peanuts, pounded finely

Season the beansprouts and cucumber strips with salt and pepper. Make a hollow in each piece of beancurd and fill with the seasoned vegetables. Garnish a serving dish with the cucumber and tomato rings and place the filled beancurds in the centre. Mix together the sauce ingredients and serve in a separate bowl. Guests help themselves to a piece of beancurd and pour chilli sauce on to the vegetables according to taste. Serve iced Chinese tea as an accompaniment.

## Mixed Stuffed Vegetables, Cantonese Style

*Serves 4–6*

8 large dried mushrooms, soaked until soft, stalks removed but caps left whole
4 small green peppers, halved and seeded
2 pieces beancurd cake, quartered, a well made in each piece
a few coriander leaves

4 tablespoons light soya sauce
1 teaspoon dry sherry
1 teaspoon sugar
2 tablespoons water

*Stuffing ingredients*
8 oz (225 g) fatty pork, minced
4 oz (100 g) prawns, minced
1 carrot, grated
1 teaspoon sugar
2 teaspoons cornflour
2 teaspoons light soya sauce
1 teaspoon sesame oil
salt and pepper

Mix the stuffing ingredients thoroughly, using your hands, and stuff the mushrooms, green peppers and beancurd cakes, being very gentle when filling the beancurd cakes. Gently push a coriander leaf on to the stuffing. Steam the vegetables, each variety separately, for 5 minutes. Heat together the soya sauce, sherry, sugar and water until the sugar is dissolved. Serve the stuffed vegetables hot, accompanied by the soya sauce in a little bowl and a hot chilli sauce.

## Crisp Chinese Cabbage with a Sweet-sour Flavour, Szechuan Style

*Serves 4–6*

1½ lb (675 g) Chinese cabbage, cut into fine strips
salt
3 fresh red chillies, seeded and cut into thin long strips
thumbsize piece fresh ginger, finely shredded
4 tablespoons sesame oil
8 peppercorns
4 tablespoons sugar
1 tablespoon salt
4 tablespoons vinegar

Wash and drain the cabbage, season with salt, and leave aside for 2 hours. Rinse well and put in a large bowl with the chillies and ginger. Toss well. Heat the sesame oil in a pan and fry the

peppercorns. Add the sugar, salt and vinegar and bring to the boil.
Pour immediately over the cabbage and mix well. Serve chilled.


## Chinese Vegetable and Fruit Salad      Serves 4–6
### Rojak

8 oz (225 g) mustard green *or* spinach, blanched for 1 minute and drained
8 oz (225 g) beansprouts, tailed and blanched for 1 minute and drained
7 oz (200 g) thinly sliced pineapple, fresh or tinned
7 oz (200 g) thinly sliced green mango
4 oz (100 g) papaya, sliced, fresh or tinned
6 fried beancurd cakes, cut in half diagonally
½ cucumber, cubed
4 oz (100 g) turnip, thinly sliced
8 oz (225 g) roasted peanuts, coarsely ground
1½ oz (40 g) roasted sesame seeds
salt to taste
2 oz (50 g) prawn paste (Heiko)
2½ oz (65 g) sugar
2 oz (50 ml) tamarind, soaked in ½ pint (300 ml) hot water, juice squeezed
   and strained
1½ oz (40 g) dried red chillies, ground

In a large bowl toss all the vegetables and fruits with the beancurd,
ground peanuts, sesame seeds and salt. Mix together the prawn
paste, sugar, tamarind juice and dried chillies, add to the vegetables
and fruit, and toss well. Serve chilled.


## Chinese Stuffed Vegetable Fondue      Serves 4
### Yong Tau Foo

This dish is one of my favourite snacks and is commonly available at
stalls in Malaysia. I have found it makes a successful fondue.

4 large ladies' fingers, slit lengthwise, but not right through
1 cucumber, cut in thick diagonal slices with seeds removed
4 large green chillies, slit, but not right through, and seeded

4 large red chillies, slit, but not right through, and seeded
1 long aubergine, cut in thick diagonal slices with a little centre pith
    removed
4 fried beancurd cakes, slit three-quarters through
oil for frying

*Stuffing ingredients*
1 lb (450 g) coley, skinned and boned
1 tablespoon cornflour
½ teaspoon salt
dash of pepper
½ teaspoon sesame oil

*Stock ingredients*
1 pint (600 ml) chicken stock
salt and pepper
1 teaspoon sesame oil
2 spring onions, chopped

Place the stuffing ingredients in a blender and process until well blended. Fill all the vegetables and the beancurd cakes with stuffing and fry until golden brown on each side. Lay out decoratively on a large platter. Bring the stock ingredients to the boil in a fondue pan, and keep hot. Everyone chooses their vegetables and simmers them for 2–3 minutes in the hot stock, dipping them in chilli sauce before eating. End the meal by drinking the stock as soup, either as it is or with some cooked noodles and beansprouts added. If you have any stuffing left over, make fish balls to go with the noodles.

## Beansprout Salad                              Serves 4–6

There's nothing better on a hot day than a crisp salad. This salad can be served as an accompaniment, but will make a light satisfying meal in itself if served with warm French garlic bread and herb butter balls.

12 oz (350 g) red cabbage, washed, dried and finely shredded
6 oz (175 g) beansprouts, tailed, washed and thoroughly drained
4 firm tomatoes, quartered
1 avocado, peeled, stoned and cut into cubes (optional)
1 small tin asparagus heads, drained

1 tablespoon butter
1 teaspoon olive oil
1 clove garlic, minced
2 tablespoons sesame seeds
juice of 1 lemon
1 teaspoon sugar
1 teaspoon mustard
½ teaspoon mild chilli sauce
salt and pepper

Toss all the vegetables in a large bowl and keep aside in a cool place. Heat the butter and olive oil in a frying pan over a medium flame, and fry the garlic and sesame seeds until the sesame seeds are golden brown. Remove from the heat, cool slightly, pour the mixture on to the vegetables and toss well. Mix together the lemon juice, sugar, mustard, chilli sauce, salt and pepper, pour on to the salad and toss again. Seal the bowl with cling-film and chill in the refrigerator before serving.

## Green Cabbage with Chinese Sausage, Cantonese Style

*Serves 4–6*

3 tablespoons oil
2 dark and 2 light Chinese sausages, thinly cut diagonally
5 dried Chinese mushrooms, soaked until soft, stems discarded and caps
   cut in half
1 lb (450 g) green cabbage hearts *or* tender spring greens, cut in 2-inch
   (5-cm) lengths
1 tablespoon soya sauce
1 teaspoon oil
½ teaspoon sugar
6 fl oz (175 ml) chicken stock
1 teaspoon cornflour mixed to a paste with 1 tablespoon water

Heat the 3 tablespoons of oil in a wok and fry the sausage and Chinese mushrooms for 2–3 minutes. Add the cabbage and stir-fry until the leaves are coated with oil. Add the soya sauce mixed with the teaspoon of oil and the sugar, pour in the stock, and bring to the boil. Simmer for a further 2 minutes. Thicken with the cornflour paste and serve hot.

To make this a complete meal, cook 3 cups of rice with 4½ cups of water. When the water has nearly evaporated, place the cabbage and sausage mixture on the top, cover, and cook till all the water has evaporated and the rice is fluffy. Serve hot with a soup and chilli sauce of your choice.

# Rice, Noodles and Bread Dishes

## Spicy Noodles with Seafood
### Laksa

Serves 4–6

Each state in Malaysia has its own version of this dish, but here is my favourite.

1 lb (450 g) rice vermicelli
8 oz (225 g) large fresh prawns, shelled and deveined (reserve shells and heads)
6 tablespoons oil
12 fl oz (350 ml) thick coconut milk
6 fried beancurd cakes, cut in half diagonally
24 fish balls or 2 fish cakes each cut into 12 slices (see pages 117–18)
salt to taste
1 lb (450 g) beansprouts, tailed and washed (blanched and drained if you wish)
½ cucumber, cut in julienne strips
4 spring onions, chopped
lemon wedges

*Ingredients to be ground together*
2 stalks lemon grass (use white part only)
2 cloves garlic
1 inch (2·5 cm) fresh ginger
5 candlenuts or 12 almonds
1 piece blacan, stock cube size
6 dried chillies (seeded for milder flavour)
1 teaspoon turmeric powder
1 large onion

Soak the rice vermicelli in fairly hot water until soft, then drain in a colander and run under cold water. Make a stock by boiling the prawn shells and heads with 1 pint (½ litre) of water, then strain and keep warm. Heat the oil in a large pan and fry the ground ingredients till fragrant. Add the prawn stock and bring to the boil. Reduce the heat and add the coconut milk, stirring constantly to prevent curdling. At simmering point add the prawns, beancurd, fish balls and salt. Simmer until the prawns are done. To serve, place first some beansprouts and then some vermicelli in each bowl. Pour on a generous helping of the hot soup, and garnish with the cucumber, spring onion and lemon.

In some states they add cockles as a garnish. You may do the same if you enjoy the taste.

## Rice Noodles with Mixed Meat
### Cantonese Bee Hoon with Mixed Meat

*Serves 4–6*

1 lb (450 g) fresh round rice noodles
4 tablespoons light soya sauce
4 fl oz (110 ml) water
½ teaspoon chilli sauce
salt to taste
3 tablespoons vegetable oil
2 tablespoons sesame oil
4 cloves garlic, crushed
4 oz (100 g) pork, thinly sliced
4 oz (100 g) shelled prawns
4 oz (100 g) chicken, thinly sliced
2 oz (50 g) pig's liver, thinly sliced
5 oz (150 g) mustard green, cut in 2-inch (5-cm) lengths
5 dried mushrooms, soaked until soft and caps cut in half
2 spring onions, finely chopped

Soak the noodles in hot water to loosen the threads, then drain in a colander and run under cold water. Mix together the soya sauce, water, chilli and salt, and set aside. Heat the oils in a wok and fry garlic until fragrant. Add the pork, prawns, chicken and liver and stir-fry for 3–5 minutes. Add the soya mixture and cook till the meats are done. Add the mustard green and mushrooms and fry for a further 2 minutes, stirring continuously. Add the noodles and fold in gently. Add more soya sauce if necessary. Garnish with the spring onions and serve hot.

## Cantonese Style Roast Duck, Wontan and Noodles
*Duck and Won Tan Lomein*

Serves 4–6

1 lb (450 g) fresh egg noodles
18 wontans (to make your own see page 119)
sesame oil
8 oz (225 g) Szechuan duck (see page 132)
1½ tablespoons light soya sauce
1 dessertspoon dry sherry
salt and pepper to taste
3 tablespoons vegetable oil
8 Cos lettuce leaves, cut in 2-inch (5-cm) lengths
2 spring onions, cut in 2-inch (5-cm) lengths
1 tablespoon cornflour mixed with 2 tablespoons water
a few fresh coriander leaves, chopped
2 chilli flowers (see page 34)

Soak the noodles in hot water to loosen the threads, then drain in a colander and run cold water over them. If using dry noodles, follow the instructions on the packet. Bring 8 cups of water to the boil. Add the wontans and a few drops of sesame oil, and simmer till the skins are soft. Drain and keep warm. Cut the duck into bitesize pieces. Mix the soya sauce, sherry, salt and pepper and set aside.

Heat the oil in a wok and stir-fry the lettuce leaves and spring onion. Add the soya sauce mixture and cook for 1 minute. Thicken with the cornflour paste and add the noodles, tossing gently. To serve, spread the noodles on a dish and place the cold duck pieces and drained wontans decoratively on top. Garnish with coriander leaves and chilli flowers.

## Hawker Style Noodles
*Dark Fried Hokkien Mee*

Serves 4–6

14 oz (400 g) thick egg noodles
1 tablespoon thick soya sauce
1 tablespoon light soya sauce
¼ teaspoon sugar

½ teaspoon salt
2 tablespoons vegetable oil
2 tablespoons sesame oil
2 cloves garlic, crushed
2 small onions, finely sliced
2 oz (50 g) pork, sliced (use Char Siew if you have some made up – see
   page 142)
2 oz (50 g) pork liver, sliced
3 oz (75 g) prawns, shelled and deveined
2 oz (50 g) squid, cleaned and sliced
2 oz (50 g) cockles
3 oz (75 g) spinach *or* Chinese green cabbage, shredded
2 fresh red chillies, seeded and sliced finely

Soak the noodles in boiling salted water until soft, then drain in a
colander and rinse under cold water. Fresh noodles, which are
obtainable in Chinese supermarkets, are ready for the frying stage.

Mix together the soya sauces, sugar and salt and set aside. Heat
both the oils in a wok and fry garlic and onions for 1 minute. Add the
pork, liver, prawns, squid and cockles and stir-fry for 1–2 minutes.
Add the spinach, chillies and soya mixture and fry for 3–4 minutes.
Add the noodles and continue to fry, stirring constantly but gently,
for about 5–7 minutes. If the noodles require more salt, add soya
sauce. The noodles should be dry and very dark in colour. Serve hot.

## Vegetarian Noodles                            *Serves 4–6*

I dedicate this recipe to my dear friend Roz, who adores my cooking,
had faith in me, and with her experience as a writer was able to give
me a lot of guidance.

14 oz (400 g) rice vermicelli
2 tablespoons sesame oil
6 cloves garlic, finely crushed
3 tablespoons black fermented soya beans, coarsely pounded
4 fresh red chillies, seeded and finely sliced
10 oz (300 g) beansprouts, tailed and washed
4 stalks each spring onion and Chinese celery, cut in 1-inch (2·5-cm)
   lengths (if Chinese celery is not available, use fresh chives)
a few coriander leaves, chopped

Soak the vermicelli in fairly hot water with salt and a few drops of oil till soft, then drain. Heat the oil in a wok until nearly smoking and quickly stir-fry the garlic, soya beans and chillies. Rinse the noodles under cold water, add to the pan, and stir-fry gently until the noodles are covered with the garlic mixture. Add the beansprouts, spring onion and Chinese celery, and stir-fry for a further 2–3 minutes. Serve hot, garnished with coriander leaves.

## Fried Broad Rice Noodles with Prawns   Serves 4–6
### Fried Kuih Teow with Prawns

1 lb (450 g) fresh Kuih Teow (flat broad rice noodles)
8 oz (225 g) large raw prawns, shelled and deveined
3 tablespoons vegetable oil
4 oz (100 g) mustard green, cut in 2-inch (5-cm) lengths
1 medium onion, sliced
3 stalks spring onion, cut in 1-inch (2·5-cm) lengths
1 teaspoon salt
1 tablespoon light soya sauce
½ teaspoon sugar
4 tablespoons chicken stock or water
1 fresh red chilli, seeded and finely sliced, for garnish

*Marinade*
½ teaspoon salt
½ teaspoon sugar
1 teaspoon sesame oil
1 teaspoon light soya sauce
dash of pepper

Soak the noodles in hot water with salt and a few drops of sesame oil. (If using dry noodles, follow the instructions on the packet.) Mix together the marinade ingredients, rub well over the prawns and leave to stand for 15 minutes. Heat 1 tablespoon of oil in a wok and stir-fry the mustard green for 1–2 minutes. Add 4 tablespoons of water and fry till the mustard green is tender. Remove from the pan with the juices and keep warm. Add 2 tablespoons of oil to the wok and fry the onion slices until lightly brown. Add the prawns and stir-fry until they are cooked and have turned pink. Add the spring onions and stir-fry for a further minute. Add the salt, soya sauce, sugar and chicken stock and bring to the boil. Add the noodles and stir-fry gently to prevent the noodles from breaking. Serve hot, with the mustard green arranged around the noodles and garnished with chilli slices.

## Fried Noodles with Seafood, Hunanese Style
*Serves 4–6*

1 lb (450 g) fresh egg noodles (if using dry noodles follow instructions on packet)
1 tablespoon light soya sauce
1 dessertspoon sesame oil
5 tablespoons oil
1 thumbsize piece fresh ginger, finely shredded
3 cloves garlic, finely chopped
8 oz (225 g) shelled prawns
12 fried squid balls, halved (available in Chinese supermarkets)
1 fish cake, cut in julienne strips (see pages 117–18)
3 oz (75 g) mustard green *or* Cos lettuce, blanched for 1 minute
2 tablespoons light soya sauce
½ teaspoon sugar
salt and pepper to taste
1 cup water
2 tablespoons cornflour
2 spring onions, chopped
1 fresh red chilli, finely sliced

If using fresh noodles, soak them in hot water to soften then drain in a colander and rinse under cold water. Mix together the tablespoon of soya sauce and the sesame oil, add to the noodles and toss well. In a wok heat 2 tablespoons of oil and add the noodles. Fry till the underneath is browned, then turn and brown the other side. Remove to a serving dish. In the same wok heat 3 tablespoons of oil and fry the ginger and garlic until fragrant. Add the seafood and greens and stir-fry for 2 minutes. Mix together the soya sauce, sugar, salt, pepper, water and cornflour, add to the pan, and bring to the boil. Pour over the noodles and serve hot, garnished with the chopped spring onion and finely sliced chilli.

# Cantonese Yong Chow
# Fried Rice

*Serves 4–6*

There are perhaps a dozen or more variations of fried rice in the Chinese cuisine, although I think the Cantonese variation is most popular. I recommend that the rice is cooked a day ahead, completely cooled and grains loosened.

12 oz (350 g) shelled prawns
3 tablespoons sesame oil
4 Chinese sausages, cut diagonally into thin slices
4 Chinese dried mushrooms, soaked until soft and caps finely chopped
2 oz (50 g) green peas
4 cups cooked rice
3 teaspoons light soya sauce
2 eggs, lightly beaten
3 spring onions, finely chopped

*Marinade*
1 teaspoon light soya sauce
salt and pepper
½ teaspoon sugar
1 teaspoon cornflour

Mix together the marinade ingredients, add the prawns, and leave for 10 minutes. Heat 1 tablespoon of sesame oil in a wok, and stir-fry the prawns for 1 minute. Add the Chinese sausage, mushrooms and peas, and fry for a further 2 minutes. Add the rice and mix well. Pour the soya sauce over the rice and fry, stirring constantly, till the rice is even in colour. Push the rice to the sides, making a well. Add the remaining sesame oil and pour in the beaten eggs. Fold in the rice and stir quickly till the egg has set. Garnish with the spring onions and serve hot.

## Wind Dried Duck and Rice, Cantonese Style

*Serves 4–6*

6 tablespoons sesame oil
1 thumbsize piece fresh ginger, finely sliced
2 cloves garlic, finely crushed
11 oz (300 g) dried duck, cut in small pieces (available in Chinese supermarkets)
4 light Chinese sausages, sliced diagonally
4 cups rice, washed and drained
1 fish stock cube
salt and pepper to taste
6 cups water (use same cup as for measuring rice)
1 onion, sliced, deep-fried and drained

Heat the oil in a large heavy pan and fry the ginger and garlic for 1 minute. Add the duck pieces and Chinese sausage and fry for 5 minutes. Reduce the heat. Add the rice, crushed stock cube, salt and pepper and stir well. Add the water, increase the heat and bring to the boil, then reduce the heat to the lowest, cover the pan and allow the rice to cook. This will take 20–30 minutes. Serve hot, garnished with the fried onion.

## Plain Rice with Roast Pork

*Serves 4–6*

### Char Siew Fan

On page 142 I have given the recipe for Char Siew, and you will see in this section how handy it is to have some in your freezer.

4 cups rice, washed and drained
6 cups water (use same cup as for measuring rice)
1 teaspoon salt
1 tablespoon margarine
2 tablespoons light soya sauce
2 tablespoons sesame oil
1 teaspoon honey
1 teaspoon sugar
salt and pepper

1 lb (450 g) roast pork, thinly sliced (see page 142)
½ cucumber, sliced diagonally

Put the rice, water, salt and margarine in a large pan and bring to the boil, then reduce the heat, cover the pan and allow the rice to cook until it is fluffy and all the water has evaporated. Turn off the heat and leave covered for 5 minutes. Mix together the soya sauce, sesame oil, honey, sugar, salt and pepper and stir-fry the pork slices until thoroughly coated with sauce. To serve, give each person a portion of rice and some slices of pork and cucumber. Pour some sauce over the rice and serve hot with a chilli sauce. Instead of rice you can serve boiled noodles tossed in the soya juice and garnished with roast pork slices, blanched beansprouts and mustard green or Cos lettuce.

## Rice with Mixed Meats and Mustard Green
*Serves 4–6*
### Choy Sum Fan

6 tablespoons vegetable oil
1 inch (2·5 cm) fresh ginger, finely shredded
4 cloves garlic, finely crushed
2 pig's kidneys, cored and sliced
2 oz (50 g) pig's liver, thinly sliced
12 oz (350 g) roast pork, sliced (see page 142)
4 oz (100 g) large prawns, shelled and deveined
1 lb (450 g) mustard green, cut in 1-inch (2·5-cm) lengths
4 tablespoons light soya sauce
6 tablespoons oyster sauce
salt and pepper to taste
2 tablespoons dry sherry
2 tablespoons sesame oil
2 teaspoons cornflour
4 tablespoons water
freshly cooked rice for 6 persons (3 cups rice to 4½ cups water)

Heat the oil in a wok and stir-fry the ginger and garlic until fragrant. Add the kidney and liver and fry for 2–3 minutes. Mix together all the remaining ingredients except the rice, add to the pan, and continue to fry on a moderate heat, taking care not to overcook the greens. Place a helping of rice on each plate and top with the meat and vegetable mixture. Serve hot with a light soup.

## Vegetarian Fried Rice, Cantonese Style

*Serves 4–6*

3 tablespoons vegetable oil
3 cloves garlic, finely crushed
4 Chinese dried mushrooms, soaked until soft and caps diced
8 oz (225 g) frozen stir-fry vegetables
3 eggs, lightly beaten
½ teaspoon five-spice powder
salt and pepper to taste
6 cups cooked rice, cooled and grains loosened
1 tablespoon light soya sauce
3 tablespoons sesame oil
4 stalks spring onion, finely chopped
1 fresh red chilli, seeded and finely sliced

Heat the vegetable oil in a wok and fry the garlic, mushrooms and mixed vegetables for 2–3 minutes. Add the eggs and fry till nearly set, stirring to break the egg into tiny pieces. Add the five-spice powder, salt and pepper and stir well. Add the rice and toss to mix the vegetables and eggs evenly. Sprinkle on the soya sauce, stirring constantly, and add the sesame oil slowly along the sides of the wok to prevent the rice sticking. Fry till the rice is an even colour. Serve hot, garnished with chopped spring onion and chilli slices.

## Steamed Savoury Rice
### Loh Mai Kai

*Serves 4–6 (8 as a starter)*

This is usually eaten as a snack, and if you prepare a double quantity you can freeze it for up to 3 months. To use frozen portions, thaw at room temperature and steam for 30 minutes.

8 pieces of foil, 12 inches (30 cm) square *or* 8 dried lotus leaves, softened in
  water overnight
sesame oil
1 teaspoon salt
1 teaspoon thick soya sauce
1 teaspoon light soya sauce
dash of pepper
½ teaspoon monosodium glutamate *or* 1 teaspoon sugar
4 tablespoons oil
6 oz (175 g) cooked chicken meat, cubed
6 oz (175 g) roast pork, cubed (see page 142)
6 oz (175 g) Szechuan duck (see page 132)
6 Chinese mushrooms, soaked until soft and caps quartered
1 Chinese sausage, sliced diagonally
1 oz (25 g) dried prawns, soaked until soft
9 oz (250 g) glutinous *or* long-grain rice, washed, steamed till cooked, and
  grains loosened

Prepare the foil pieces or lotus leaves by brushing with sesame oil on
one side. Mix together the salt, soya sauces, pepper and monosodium glutamate. Heat the oil in a wok over a medium heat, and
add the soya mixture. Add all the remaining ingredients except the
rice, and stir-fry for 2–3 minutes. Add the rice and stir-fry till it is
evenly coloured. Divide into eight portions and wrap in foil pieces or
lotus leaves. Steam the packets for 30 minutes over a high heat, and
serve hot with chilli sauce and mustard.

## Prawn Cakes, Peking Style                    Serves 4–6

I first tried this in a restaurant but have found it to be a favourite at
parties, either as an *hors d'oeuvre* or as a cocktail snack.

8 pieces medium sliced white bread
12 oz (350 g) shelled prawns
2 oz (50 g) pork fat
1 egg white
½ teaspoon salt
1 tablespoon cornflour
½ teaspoon dry sherry

1 oz (25 g) sesame seeds
oil for deep-frying

Remove the crusts from the bread and cut each slice into quarters. Mince together the prawns and the pork fat finely.

Mix together the egg white, salt, cornflour and sherry, add the minced prawns and mix well. Spread the mixture on to the bread squares. Sprinkle each square with sesame seeds, and pat gently to make them stick. Heat the oil in a wok and deep-fry the bread squares paste side down for 1 minute, then turn them and deep-fry for 1 minute on the other side. Drain on kitchen paper and serve hot.

# Condiments

## Chilli Sauce 1

6 cloves garlic, crushed
6 fresh red chillies, finely crushed
1 large tomato, skinned and mashed
1 large onion, finely sliced, deep-fried until crisp, and crushed
1 teaspoon cornflour
juice of 1 lemon
salt to taste
1 teaspoon sugar
6 tablespoons vegetable oil

Combine all the ingredients and bring to the boil. Cool and serve as an accompaniment with any savoury dish. You can prepare it in larger quantities, as it will store in the refrigerator for up to 4 weeks.

## Chilli Sauce 2

6 cloves garlic
1 thumbsize piece ginger
6 fresh red chillies
salt to taste
2 teaspoons sugar
¼ teaspoon turmeric
½ cup oil
½ cup vinegar

Grind together the garlic, ginger, chillies, salt, sugar and turmeric in a blender. Heat the oil and fry the ground ingredients for 2–3 minutes. Add the vinegar and bring to the boil. Cool thoroughly and store in airtight jars in a cool place. This sauce will store indefinitely.

## Chilli Sauce 3

10 tablespoons oil
2 oz (50 g) dried prawns, coarsely pounded
10 large dried chillies, seeded and crushed
pinch of salt

Heat the oil and fry the prawns and chillies until fragrant. Add the salt and leave to cool. Will store indefinitely in airtight jars.

## Chilli Sauce 4

10 tablespoons oil
10 fresh red chillies, seeded and finely ground
4 fl oz (110 ml) vinegar
4 oz (100 g) sugar
pinch of salt

Heat the oil and fry the chillies for 1–2 minutes. Add the vinegar, sugar and salt and boil till the sugar has dissolved. Cool and store in airtight jars. Will keep indefinitely. For a sweeter taste increase the amount of sugar.

# Sweets and Drinks

## Buboh Cha Cha
*Serves 4*

Handed down for many generations, this refreshing drink has retained a wistful nostalgia.

8 oz (225 g) yam
8 oz (225 g) sweet potato
4 tablespoons pearl sago
a 1-oz packet gelatine
1 pint (600 ml) hot water
sugar to taste
green and red food colouring
1 pint (600 ml) thick coconut milk
6 tablespoons sugar
finely crushed ice

Cook the yam and sweet potato separately in boiling water till soft, then cut into small pieces. Boil the sago until soft, then drain. Dissolve the gelatine in the hot water and sweeten to taste. Divide the dissolved gelatine between two dishes and colour one with green food colouring and the other with red. Cool and leave to set in the refrigerator. When set, cut in strips or triangular pieces.

In a pan bring coconut milk and sugar to the boil. Remove from the heat and cool, then chill in the refrigerator. To serve, divide the yam, sweet potato, sago and set jellies among 4–6 sweet bowls and pour on the coconut milk. Top each bowl with finely crushed ice just before serving.

## Almond Jelly with Lychees and Watermelon Balls
*Serves 4–6*

¾ cup loosely packed agar-agar (seaweed jelly) strands, soaked overnight
    in 4 cups warm water
6–8 tablespoons sugar
½ cup evaporated milk
¼ cup water

a few drops green food colouring
½ teaspoon almond essence
½ watermelon
1 tin chilled lychees, drained (reserve the syrup)

Bring the soaked agar-agar to the boil on a medium heat and simmer till all the strands have dissolved. Add the sugar, evaporated milk and water and bring back to the boil. Remove from the heat and add the green food colouring and the almond essence. Wet a large mould or 4–6 individual moulds and sieve the agar-agar mixture into them, not filling them to the brim. Cool and place in the refrigerator to set.

Scoop out the watermelon in balls and chill in the refrigerator together with the tin of lychees.

To serve, unmould the jelly into a large dish or individual dishes and decorate with the drained lychees and the watermelon balls. Pour some lychee syrup over each mould.

Almond jelly packets are now readily available from Chinese grocers. If you have difficulty in obtaining agar-agar, use a 1-oz packet of ordinary gelatine and follow the instructions on the packet. The food colouring used can be of your own choice.

## Pancakes Filled with Coconut                 Makes 8–10
## Kuih Da-Da

This is a popular *Nonya* (Straits Chinese) dish and makes a delicious variation for Pancake Day.

4 oz (100 g) plain flour
pinch of salt
2 eggs
½ pint (300 ml) coconut milk
a few drops green or blue food colouring
margarine

*Coconut Filling*
1 freshly grated coconut *or* 8 oz (225 g) desiccated coconut
8 tablespoons dark brown sugar
2 tablespoons white sugar
4 tablespoons water

Sift the flour with the salt, place in a large bowl, and make a well in the centre. Add the eggs and whisk with an electric whisk until the mixture is completely blended. Slowly add the coconut milk, continuing to whisk until the batter is smooth. Add a few drops of food colouring.

In a pan mix all the filling ingredients, and gently heat till all the sugar has dissolved. Keep warm. Heat a little margarine in a wok, pour in a ladle of pancake mixture and swivel the wok to make a thin pancake. When the edges begin to curl remove to a large plate, cooked side down. Put some coconut filling along the edge nearest to you and tuck in the left and right edges to make a rectangle. Roll up the pancake and serve hot. Repeat this procedure until all the batter and filling are used.

## Refreshing Mango Ice                    Serves 4–6

14 oz (400 g) tinned mango pulp
a few slices tinned mango, coarsely chopped
3 teaspoons honey
1 bottle lemonade *or* ice cream soda, chilled
caster sugar
4–6 maraschino cherries

Mix the mango pulp, mango pieces and honey. Divide among 4–6 sundae glasses. Freeze till firm. To serve, remove from the freezer and dip the rim of each glass in caster sugar. Top with lemonade or soda and decorate with maraschino cherries.

## Chinese Doughnuts                    Makes 8–10
### Kuih Keria

2 large sweet potatoes, peeled, boiled and mashed
6 fl oz (175 ml) thick coconut milk
pinch of salt
3 tablespoons rice flour
oil for deep-frying
4 oz (100 g) sugar
4 tablespoons water
icing sugar

Mix the mashed potato with the coconut milk, salt and flour until it forms a smooth dough. Divide the dough and shape into balls, the size of a golf ball. Slightly flatten each ball and cut a hole in the centre. Heat the oil in a deep pan and fry the doughnuts until golden brown. Drain and keep aside.

In another large pan heat the sugar and water and cook till the sugar begins to crystallize. Add the doughnuts and coat well with the syrup, then remove them from the pan and sprinkle with a little icing sugar. Cool and serve.


## Cantonese Creamed Peanuts

*Serves 4–6 (more if using as a dip)*

12 oz (350 g) shelled raw peanuts
4 oz (100 g) rice flour
2 pints (1·2 litres) water
5 oz (150 g) demerara sugar

Roast the peanuts in a dry pan till brown and allow to cool. Rub the peanuts to remove the skin, then grind them very finely. In a heavy pan mix the peanut powder and rice flour, add the water, and bring to the boil on a low heat, stirring continuously. Add the sugar and keep on a gentle boil till the sugar dissolves and the mixture has a creamy texture. If it is too thick add a little hot water, and add more sugar if you prefer a sweeter taste. Serve hot.

This can also be served cold as a dip with biscuit sticks.

## Chinese Tea

There are three main types of tea. The first is black or fermented, and is called 'red tea' by the Chinese. The second is green or unfermented tea, and the third is oolong or semi-fermented tea. All three come from the same tea bushes but are treated differently after picking. Nowadays these three varieties are further blended with herbs, flowers and fruits. My favourite blends are chrysanthemum and jasmine. The Chinese never add milk or sugar, and tea is drunk throughout the day, even sometimes as a toast. To make proper Chinese tea you must abide by two rules. Use an earthenware teapot and water that has been boiled just once. Ensure that the tea is stored in an airtight jar and away from any strong aromas from other items in your larder.

1 teaspoon Chinese tea of your choice
6 cups freshly boiled water

Infuse together in a teapot for 2–3 minutes and sip while still hot.

In Malaysia, teas of all sorts are available in cartons and they are drunk cold. Even the basic Chinese tea is iced to help you cool off.

I heard some time ago that one of the reasons why the majority of the Chinese are so slim is their large consumption of hot tea. They say that it helps split the fat contents in your body. My Chinese sister-in-law, who drinks Chinese tea by the gallon, definitely proves this point.

# Steamboat
# (Chinese Fondue)

No Malaysian cookery book can be considered complete without the inclusion of a 'steamboat', so allow me to introduce you to it. I have given this a separate section, as it is a mixture of all kinds of ingredients.

The traditional steamboat, also known as 'Mongolian hot pot', is a round metal chafing dish with a chimney in the centre surrounded by a deep bowl. This rests on a grid which is open on one side, and charcoal is placed in the grid to keep the stock in the bowl on a constant boil. The chimney releases excess steam and prevents the stock from boiling over. Steamboats are obtainable from Chinese shops, and nowadays electric and gas varieties are also available. You can also use a rice cooker (as I do) or a fondue set. If you have none of these, use a deep pan over an electric hot plate, although you may have to return it to the cooker to boost the temperature of the stock occasionally.

In Malaysia most restaurants serve steamboat dinners, but here they are available at only a few. They are enjoyed by every nationality in Malaysia, but each has its own variations – for example, the Malays will omit pork and the Hindus beef.

When I have a large number of guests I find a steamboat party ideal. It is great fun both for my guests and myself, as the only work is in the preparation – the guests do their own cooking. The steamboat can consist of just meat and vegetables, or seafood and vegetables, or can be a combination of everything.

As making the stock is the only cooking you have to do, you can give a lot of time to preparing the raw ingredients. Cut them finely to speed the cooking time, and arrange them attractively, considering colour schemes, so that when your guests arrive the display will boost their appetites, even though at this stage the food is still raw.

Provide each guest with a rice-bowl, a small plate, a sauce dish, a pair of chopsticks and a net spoon. Chinese utensils are now widely sold and they are not too expensive, so it will be worth your while investing in them. Of course, they can also be used when serving ordinary Chinese meals. For the guests who will not be able to manage chopsticks, provide skewers and cutlery. Traditionally, each guest is also provided with one raw egg beaten in a small bowl – the cooked ingredients, while hot, should be dipped in the beaten egg before being eaten. However, this is not a hard and fast rule so the choice is yours.

The steamboat, whichever version you are using, should be placed in the centre of the table, with all the dishes of prepared raw ingredients and sauces arranged round it. Provide a variety of sauces – soya sauce, wine vinegar, chilli sauces of various flavours and strengths, and mustard.

Before you invite your guests to the table, ensure that the stock is boiling. Each guest chooses his or her own ingredients, using chopsticks or skewers, and cooks them in the stock for 2–3 minutes or according to taste. Some will prefer the food rare, some medium and some well done. Advise your guests to use the net spoons for ingredients like quail's eggs, fish balls, etc., which are difficult to hold with chopsticks.

Do not rush a steamboat menu, and do not feel embarrassed if you have to ask your guests to pause for a while to enable you to re-heat the stock. This is all part of the enjoyment and it will also give your guests time to breathe and perhaps exchange a few gossips.

By the time all the raw ingredients have been cooked the stock will be very rich in flavour. The meal can be ended by drinking the stock as soup, perhaps with some cooked noodles or rice mixed in. When my family gets together for a steamboat we end with a competition. Using a lettuce or cabbage leaf floating on the hot stock, each member tries to poach a raw egg on it. The challenge is to see who can retrieve a fully poached egg.

When the guests cannot eat any more and if there are any stock and raw ingredients remaining, tidy the table leaving fresh rice-bowls, chopsticks, etc., and you will invariably find that they can have a little more after resting a while. The table will be messy but the messier the table the more successful your steamboat has been.

There is no necessity to serve drinks with a steamboat as you are consuming enough liquid, but the traditional drinks which you can serve are warm rice wine or authentic Chinese tea.

My suggested ingredients will serve up to 10 persons, but you can adjust the quantities and ingredients as you wish.

## Raw ingredients

4 chicken breasts, skinned, boned and thinly sliced (save skin and bones
    for the stock)
12 oz (350 g) tender beef, thinly sliced
12 oz (350 g) lean pork, thinly sliced
2 pig's livers, thinly sliced
12 oz (350 g) large raw prawns, shelled and deveined and left whole (save
    heads and shells for the stock)
12 oz (350 g) firm white fish, skinned, boned and cubed
12 oz (350 g) squid, cleaned and thinly sliced
2 fishcakes, cut into thin slices
20 fish balls, left whole
14 oz (400 g) tinned abalone, drained and thinly sliced
20 pieces fried beancurd, cut in half diagonally
12 oz (350 g) Chinese cabbage, cut into 2-inch (5-cm) lengths
12 oz (350 g) beansprouts, tailed, washed and thoroughly drained
20 boiled and shelled quail's eggs, left whole
10 raw eggs, placed in a basket (optional)

Prepare all the ingredients and arrange decoratively on plates and in dishes. Place on the table, leaving a space in the centre for the steamboat, and scatter small bowls of sauces here and there. Cover the dishes of raw ingredients with a damp cloth to prevent them from drying out.

## Stock ingredients

6 fl oz (175 ml) sesame oil
chicken bones and skin
prawn shells and heads
2 cloves garlic, crushed
2 inches (5 cm) fresh ginger, crushed
2 stalks celery, chopped
5 stalks spring onions, chopped
1 teaspoon monosodium glutamate
20 cups water
salt and pepper to taste

Heat 2 tablespoons of sesame oil in a large pan, and when nearly smoking fry the chicken bones and skin, the prawn shells and heads, the garlic and the ginger for 2–3 minutes. Add the celery, spring onions and monosodium glutamate and fry for another 1–2 minutes. Pour in the water, salt and pepper to taste, and bring to the boil. Simmer for 1–1½ hours. Strain the stock into the steamboat and bring to the boil on the table just before your guests are ready. Add the remaining sesame oil to the stock before your guests start cooking the raw ingredients.

# 4.
## Indian Cuisine

*Introduction*   It is difficult to generalize about the eating habits of Indians in Malaysia – there are Hindus, Christians, Muslims, Sikhs, Bengalis and even Ceylonese, and each community follows its own customs and traditions. One thing the entire Indian community has in common is the use of spices, and curries are the most important part of the cuisine. The majority of Indians in Malaysia are from South India, and are therefore Hindus, and it is their cuisine that I shall concentrate on.

In India itself there are several Hindu festivals, but the Indians in Malaysia celebrate mainly three of them. In January Thaipusam and Ponggal are celebrated. Thaipusam is connected with the fulfilment of vows. Severe penance is performed, and this includes tolerance of bodily pain and fasting for anything from a week to three months. This may seem cruel to the western world but it is founded in ancient history. When all the penances have been performed the vows are considered fulfilled. During this period Hindu households will cook only vegetarian food, even for those not partaking in any penance.

The second festival, Ponggal, is the harvest festival. It is celebrated for three days, the first day being the most important. On this day meals are cooked from the newly harvested rice and the new vegetables, which are now ready to eat. On the second day the festival is concentrated on cattle. This is their day, and their owner gives them special food, bathes them, and decorates them with saffron and vermilion masks and paints their horns with bright colours. On the third day, young unmarried girls will pray that they be found good husbands and as a token will wear new clothes and cook their own meals.

Finally, and the one celebrated with the greatest pomp, comes Deepavali or festival of lights, which usually falls during the month of October. Food preparations for this feast begin nearly two weeks in advance, to cater for all the nationalities who will visit their Hindu friends and partake in the celebrations. Both vegetarian and non-vegetarian meals are prepared, and the more prosperous families will feed the more needy ones in order to receive their God's blessings. Trays of sweetmeats are sent to friends and relatives, who in turn will refill the trays with their own sweetmeats before returning them. Little oil lamps flicker around the Hindu homes, turning areas where Hindu communities are concentrated into fairylands. Decorative patterns made from coloured rice flour are drawn on the entrance of the house to welcome Lord Krishna, who saved the Hindus from a tyrannical king centuries ago, and Lakshmi, the goddess symbolizing prosperity. The general Hindu greeting is *'Namaste'*, given with the palms joined together.

Although traditions are fading, the orthodox Hindu housewife still rises with the sun to prepare a substantial breakfast for her family. This usually consists of Dosai with chutney and a lentil curry, Apam, another variety of rice flour pancake, chappatis or puris with a vegetarian curry. The family always begin their breakfast by having coffee, which is taken strong with milk and sugar.

Breakfast is barely over when the housewife has to start preparations for lunch. This usually consists of one or two vegetable curries, a lentil curry, rice, pickles and *tayir* (yogurt). If some members of the family are not strict vegetarians they will eat their favourite non-vegetarian dishes outside the home. What is prepared for lunch is usually served again for dinner, with perhaps another fresh vegetable dish. Water is the main drink during meals.

For tea there will be curry puffs, pakoras, pisang goreng or just cakes and biscuits.

Meals are generally eaten from a *thali*, a large steel or brass plate, and the curries and condiments are served to individuals in tiny bowls on the *thali*, with space left for rice. For festive occasions banana leaves are used as plates. The banana plant is very versatile – it bears fruits, is fodder for the cattle, and the leaves are used to decorate the *mandap* or wedding altar. Besides all that, it saves the housewife a great deal of washing up. Indians generally eat with the fingers of their right hand only. This does not mean that crockery and cutlery are not favoured, however – the younger generation tend to prefer them.

Although several of the recipes in this section are South Indian, I have included some which are traditional to the other Indian communities in Malaysia. *'Santosh Sapad'* (Tamil)/*'Priti bhojan'* (Hindi) – Happy dining.

# Soups and Snacks

## Lentil Soup

*Serves 4–6*

6 oz (175 g) masoor dhal (red lentils)
4 tablespoons dessicated coconut
2 fresh green chillies, seeded and finely chopped
4 cloves garlic, crushed
salt to taste
1 small onion, finely chopped
handful fresh coriander leaves, finely chopped
lemon juice (optional)

*Ingredients to be ground together*
3 peppercorns
1½ teaspoons poppy seeds
½ teaspoon cumin seeds
4 almonds

Boil the masoor dhal with 1 pint (600 ml) of water until soft. Mash the dhal with a wooden spoon. Add all the other ingredients except the onions and some of the chopped coriander leaves. Bring back to the boil and simmer for 5 minutes. Serve hot, garnished with chopped onions and the remaining coriander leaves. Add a few drops of lemon juice if you wish.

## Meat or Vegetable Curry Puffs

*Makes 20–24*

A delicious tea-time snack.

*For filling*
Use the recipe for Minced Meat on page 212
or for Potato Fry on page 241.

*For pastry*
2 cups wholemeal flour
½ teaspoon salt

4 dessertspoons margarine
iced water

Sieve the flour into a large bowl with the salt. Add the margarine and mix until crumbly. Adding a little water at a time, mix to form a dough. Knead well. Form into balls the size of small walnuts, and roll out into thin pancakes about 4 inches (10 cm) in diameter. Fill each pancake with about 1 tablespoon of minced meat or vegetable filling. Fold over and wet the edges to seal, and pinch the edge with your finger tips or the tip of a fork. Heat some oil in a wok or chip fryer and fry four or five puffs at a time until both sides are evenly brown. Drain on kitchen paper and serve hot, with tomato ketchup mixed with a little chilli sauce.

## Rice and Lentil Pancakes    Makes 10–12
### Dosai

This is a very popular South Indian dish and is served for breakfast or as a snack. It is eaten on its own with a lentil curry and chutney, or filled with a dry potato curry. I also enjoy it on its own with sugar. The batter is now readily available from Indian grocers and sometimes even large supermarkets.

4 oz (100 g) long-grain rice, soaked in water overnight
1 oz (25 g) urad dhal (black gram), soaked in water overnight
ghee

Drain the rice and dhal and grind each separately to a fine paste in an electric blender. Mix together and leave in a warm place for 6–8 hours, then add enough water to make a creamy batter. Heat a flat griddle and brush with ghee. Pour a ladle of batter on the hot griddle and spread it out thinly with the back of the ladle. Cover with a lid and cook till the first side is golden brown, then turn and cook the other side, spooning a little more ghee on the griddle. Serve hot, folded in half, with lentil curry (see page 240) and chutney (see page 250) or potato fry (see page 241).

# Rice Dumplings
## Idlis

Makes 12–15

Another popular South Indian breakfast or snack dish. In the east special steamer trays are obtainable, but I find that egg poachers do the job perfectly. This batter is also now readily available from Indian grocers.

4 oz (100 g) long grained rice, soaked in water overnight
2 oz (50 g) urad dhal (black gram), soaked in water overnight
¼ teaspoon salt
ghee to grease egg poachers

Drain the rice and dhal and grind each separately to a fine paste in an electric blender. Mix together, add the salt, and leave in a warm place for 6–8 hours. If the mixture is too thick, add a little water to make it the consistency of double cream. Grease the egg poacher depressions with ghee and pour in the rice batter. Cover the pan and steam for 10–15 minutes. Serve hot with Sambhar (see page 240) and chutney (see page 250). For Masala Idlis, add finely chopped green chillies, coriander leaves and 1 or 2 chopped curry leaves to the mixture.

# Savoury Semolina
## Upma

Serves 4–6

Serve this hot, as a snack with coffee. The South Indians either sprinkle it with some caster sugar or eat it with a hot mango pickle.

3 tablespoons vegetable oil
1 oz (25 g) ghee *or* unsalted butter
1 teaspoon mustard seeds
1½ teaspoons urad dhal (black gram)
2 oz (50 g) cashew nuts
2 onions, finely chopped
2 tablespoons chopped coriander leaves (reserve 1 teaspoon for garnish)
2 green chillies, seeded and finely chopped
3–4 curry leaves, finely chopped

½ pint (300 ml) water
juice of 2 lemons
salt to taste
8 oz (225 g) semolina, dry roasted in a hot oven until brown

Heat the oil and butter in a heavy pan and fry the mustard seeds until they begin to pop. Put in the dhal and cashew nuts and fry for 1 minute. Add the onions, coriander leaves, chillies and curry leaves and fry until the onions are soft. Add the water, lemon juice and salt and bring to the boil. Simmer for 5 minutes. Gradually sprinkle in the semolina and cook for 5 minutes, stirring constantly, then cover the pan and cook gently till the mixture is dry and leaves the sides of the pan. Serve hot, garnished with the reserved coriander leaves.

## Savoury Vegetable Fritters
### Pakoras

*Serves 4–6*

Delicious as a tea-time snack or for a drinks party. Serve hot with mint chutney or tomato ketchup.

oil for deep-frying
1 large potato, parboiled and cut in thin round slices
1 aubergine, cut in thin round slices (soak in water till ready to use)
1 large onion, sliced in thick rings
a few fresh spinach *or* cabbage leaves, cut in 2-inch (5-cm) pieces
6 large green chillies, seeded and left whole

*Ingredients for batter*
8 oz (225 g) gram flour
½ teaspoon chilli powder
½ teaspoon turmeric powder
1 teaspoon coriander powder
½ teaspoon baking powder
salt to taste

Sift the batter ingredients together in a large bowl. Add enough water to make a thick smooth batter, and adjust the seasoning. Heat the oil in a wok. Dip the vegetables individually in batter and deep-fry until golden brown and crisp. Drain on kitchen paper, and serve hot.

## Savoury Potato Cakes
### Alu Petis

*Makes 8*

A delicious starter – or perhaps an eastern version of shepherd's pie. A favourite Muslim Indian dish.

2 lb (900 g) potatoes, peeled, boiled and mashed
1 teaspoon fresh coriander leaves, finely chopped
salt to taste
2 tablespoons oil
1 large onion, finely chopped
1 clove garlic, minced
1 thumbsize piece fresh ginger, minced
1 teaspoon coriander powder
½ teaspoon cumin powder
½ teaspoon garam masala
½ teaspoon turmeric powder
1 green chilli, finely chopped
1 teaspoon chopped mint
8 oz (225 g) lean minced beef
1 tomato, chopped
breadcrumbs for coating
1 egg, beaten
oil
lemon wedges for garnish

Mix together the mashed potato, coriander leaves and salt and set aside. Heat 2 tablespoons of oil and fry the onion, garlic and ginger until the onion is soft. Mix the coriander, cumin, garam masala, turmeric, chilli and mint to a paste with a little water, add to the pan, and fry until the oil rises. Add the minced beef and fry well until the meat is evenly brown. Add the tomato and some salt and simmer till the meat is cooked and dry.

Divide the mashed potato into 8 portions and make into balls. Flatten one ball on the palm of your hand and place a helping of mince in the centre. Gather the sides together and enclose the meat completely with potato. Flatten it a little. Coat with breadcrumbs, then dip in beaten egg and give a second coat of breadcrumbs. Shallow fry in hot oil till both sides are golden brown and crisp. Serve hot with lemon wedges.

# Poultry and Egg Dishes

## Chicken Curry with Potatoes                    Serves 4–6

2 tablespoons oil
a 3 lb (1·3 kg) chicken, skinned and cut into small pieces
a few curry leaves
salt to taste
2 inches (5 cm) lemon rind
1½ pints (900 ml) thick coconut milk
2 small onions, thinly sliced, deep-fried and drained
4 potatoes, peeled and each cut into 8 pieces
juice of 1 lemon

*Ingredients to be ground together*
3 red chillies, seeded
2 cloves garlic
1 thumbsize piece fresh ginger
¼ teaspoon ground cinnamon
½ teaspoon turmeric powder
1 teaspoon cumin powder
2 teaspoons coriander powder

Heat the oil and fry the ground ingredients until fragrant. Add the chicken, curry leaves, salt, lemon rind and half the coconut milk and bring to the boil. Lower the heat and add the remaining coconut milk, fried onions and potatoes. Simmer till the chicken and potatoes are cooked. Check the seasoning and discard the lemon rind. Add the lemon juice and serve hot with boiled rice, nan or warm freshly baked white bread.

## Ceylon Chicken Curry                    Serves 4–6

I have several very dear Ceylonese friends in Malaysia and have had great feasts in their homes. The main distinction between Indian curry and Ceylon curry is that when dry roasting whole spices for the latter they should be a few shades darker but not burnt.

2 teaspoons turmeric powder
2 teaspoons vinegar
2 teaspoons salt
a 3 lb (1·3 kg) chicken, jointed
4 tablespoons vegetable oil
2 large onions, finely sliced
4 cloves garlic, finely minced
2 inches (5 cm) fresh ginger, finely minced
6 fl oz (175 ml) thin coconut milk
6 fl oz (175 ml) thick coconut milk

*Ingredients to be ground together*
10 dried chillies (seeded for milder flavour)
2 tablespoons coriander seeds
1 tablespoon cumin seeds
1 teaspoon fennel seeds
1 teaspoon fenugreek seeds
a few curry leaves

Mix together the turmeric, vinegar and salt and marinade the chicken pieces for 1 hour.

Heat the oil and fry the onions till fairly dark brown. Add the garlic, ginger and chicken and stir well. Cover the pan and simmer for 10 minutes. Add the thin coconut milk and the ground spices and bring to the boil, then add the thick coconut milk and simmer till the chicken is tender and the gravy has a thick consistency. Check for salt, and serve hot with boiled rice.


## Chicken Kebabs                                    Serves 4–6
### Koli Kebabs

4 breasts of chicken, skinned and cut into bitesize pieces
4 crisp lettuce leaves, shredded
1 carrot, grated

*Marinade*
4 oz (110 ml) double cream
5 oz (150 ml) natural yogurt
2 inches (5 cm) fresh ginger, minced
4 cloves garlic, minced

1½ teaspoons five-spice powder
salt and pepper to taste
a few strands saffron soaked in 1 teaspoon warm milk*

Mix together the marinade ingredients, add the chicken, and leave to stand for 4 hours. Deep-fry the chicken pieces or grill them until tender. The remaining marinade can be heated in a shallow pan until thick and poured over the chicken pieces before serving. Serve the chicken on a bed of shredded lettuce and grated carrot, and pour over the marinade.

* Do not substitute saffron strands with saffron powder, as in this dish it is the flavour that is required, not the colour.

## Chicken in a Delicate Gravy
### Koli Sodhi

*Serves 4–6*

This dish originated as a coconut soup, but housewives began adding meat while retaining the spices. If you want to try it as a soup, omit the chicken.

a 3 lb (1·3 g) chicken, skinned and jointed
5 tablespoons oil
a few coriander leaves, finely chopped

*Ingredients for boiling*
½ teaspoon fenugreek
1 inch (2·5 cm) fresh ginger, crushed finely
3 cloves garlic, crushed finely
2 fresh green chillies, seeded and slit
2 dried red chillies, seeded and slit
1 large onion, thickly sliced
a few curry leaves
1 teaspoon turmeric powder
1 teaspoon coriander powder
7 oz (200 g) coconut cream, dissolved in 1 pint (600 ml) boiling water

*Ingredients for frying*
2 teaspoons mustard seeds
1 teaspoon fennel seeds

a few curry leaves
3 dried chillies

Put the chicken and all the boiling ingredients in a large pan. Bring to the boil, then reduce the heat and cook till the chicken is tender. Stir constantly to prevent the coconut curdling. Heat the oil in a frying pan and add all the frying ingredients. When the mustard seeds start to splutter, pour the contents of the frying pan over the chicken and cover for 2–3 minutes. Serve hot, garnished with chopped coriander leaves.


## Chicken Curry with Sour Milk

*Serves 4–6*

This dish is of Ceylonese origin.

¾ teaspoon turmeric powder
1 teaspoon coriander powder
1 teaspoon cumin powder
½ teaspoon ground black pepper
3 fl oz (85 ml) evaporated milk
4 fl oz (110 ml) water
2 teaspoons lemon juice
2 tablespoons vegetable oil
6 chicken drumsticks
6 chicken thighs
1 large onion, finely chopped
2 inches (5 cm) fresh ginger, finely minced
4 cloves garlic, finely minced
salt to taste
a few coriander leaves, finely chopped
2 green chillies, seeded and finely sliced

Mix the turmeric, coriander, cumin and pepper to a smooth paste with a little water. Mix together the milk, water and lemon juice. Heat the oil in a large heavy pan and fry the chicken pieces till evenly brown. Remove from the pan and keep warm. In the same oil fry the onion to a golden brown, then add the minced ginger and garlic and fry for a further 1–2 minutes. Add the paste of spices and when the oil rises add the chicken, the salt and the sour milk mixture. Simmer gently till the chicken is cooked. Garnish with the coriander leaves and chilli slices, and serve with rice or bread, with a vegetable curry or a salad as an accompaniment.

## Captain's Chicken
### Koli Kapitan

*Serves 4–6*

4 tablespoons ghee *or* unsalted butter
2 onions, finely sliced
1 inch (2·5 cm) fresh ginger, finely minced
2 cloves garlic, finely minced
3 green chillies, seeded and finely chopped
a 3 lb (1·3 kg) chicken, cut into small pieces
1 teaspoon turmeric powder
salt to taste
½ pint (300 ml) thick coconut milk
2 tablespoons almond flakes for garnish

Heat the ghee in a pan and fry the onions until soft. Add the ginger, garlic and green chillies and fry till fragrant. Add the chicken and fry till all the pieces are evenly browned. Add the turmeric, salt and coconut milk and bring to the boil, then reduce the heat and simmer till the chicken is tender and the gravy thick. Garnish with the almond flakes and serve hot.

## Chicken Masala
### Koli Masala

*Serves 4–6*

a 3 lb (1·3 kg) chicken, skinned and cut into pieces
salt and pepper to taste
oil for frying
3 onions, finely sliced
2 tablespoons vinegar *or* juice of 1 lemon
a few coriander leaves for garnish

*Ingredients to be ground together*
2 cloves garlic
1 thumbsize piece fresh ginger

2 tablespoons coriander powder
1 teaspoon cumin powder
1 teaspoon five-spice powder
1 teaspoon chilli powder or to taste
pinch of salt

Season the chicken with salt and pepper and fry till evenly brown. Drain and keep warm. Pour off the excess oil, leaving about 2 tablespoons in the pan, and fry the onions till soft. Add the ground ingredients and fry till the oil rises. Return the chicken to the pan and coat well. Add the vinegar, cover the pan, and simmer till the chicken is done. Garnish with coriander leaves and serve hot with boiled rice.


## Spiced Chicken with Yogurt
### Koli Khorma

*Serves 4–6*

½ pint (300 ml) natural yogurt
1 teaspoon turmeric
4 tablespoons vegetable oil
6 cloves
2 cardamoms
2 inches (5 cm) cinnamon quill
1 bay leaf
8 peppercorns
2 large onions, finely sliced
1 inch (2·5 cm) fresh ginger, finely minced
2 cloves garlic, finely minced
2 dry red chillies
a 3 lb (1·3 kg) chicken, skinned and jointed
1 lb (450 g) tinned chopped tomatoes
salt to taste

Beat the yogurt with the turmeric and set aside. Heat the oil in a large heavy pan and fry the cloves, cardamoms, cinnamon, bay leaf and peppercorns until fragrant. Add the onions and fry till golden brown. Add the ginger, garlic and red chillies and fry for 1–2 minutes. Add the chicken and fry till all the pieces are evenly brown. Reduce the heat and slowly add the yogurt mixture, stirring well. Add the tomatoes and salt to taste. Cover the pan and simmer the chicken till tender, then simmer uncovered for a further 10 minutes to thicken the gravy. Garnish as desired and serve hot with rice or nan bread.

Remember to warn the diners about the whole spices, for although edible, these have a strong taste.

## Chicken and Potato Stew    *Serves 4–6*
### Koli Urulaikizhangu

2 oz (50 g) ghee *or* unsalted butter
2 onions, finely sliced
a 3 lb (1·3 kg) chicken, skinned and jointed
1 pint (600 ml) hot water
salt to taste
4 medium potatoes, peeled and each cut into 6
lemon slices for garnish

*Ingredients to be ground together*
1 inch (2·5 cm) fresh ginger
2 cloves garlic
1 teaspoon five-spice powder
½ teaspoon chilli powder
1 fresh red chilli, seeded
a few fresh coriander leaves

Heat the ghee in a large pan and fry the onions until soft. Add the ground ingredients and fry till the ghee separates. Add the chicken pieces and stir well to coat the chicken with the spices. Add the hot water and salt and bring to the boil, then reduce the heat and add the potatoes. Cover and simmer till the chicken and potatoes are cooked. Garnish with lemon slices, and serve hot with boiled rice or white bread. Squeeze the lemon juice over before eating if you wish.

# Duck in a Spicy and Sour Gravy
## Vatthu Vindaloo

*Serves 4–6*

a 4 lb (2·2 kg) duckling, skinned and cut into small pieces
4 tablespoons oil
2 teaspoons sugar
lemon wedges for garnish

*Marinade*
8 dried red chillies, soaked and seeded
6 cloves garlic
1 thumbsize piece fresh ginger
½ cup vinegar
1 teaspoon turmeric powder
1 teaspoon coriander powder
2 teaspoons cumin powder
salt and pepper to taste

Grind all the marinade ingredients together, add to the duck pieces, and leave overnight. Heat the oil in a large pan and fry the duck pieces with their marinade until evenly browned. Reduce the heat, add a little hot water, cover the pan, and simmer till the duck is tender. Stir occasionally, and add a little more hot water if necessary during the cooking to prevent the duck burning. When the duck is tender add the sugar and mix well. Garnish with lemon wedges and serve hot with plain boiled rice.

# Duck Baked in a Casserole
## Vatthu Bake

*Serves 4–6*

A capon or a large roasting chicken can be used instead of duck.

a 4 lb (2·2 kg) duckling, skinned and cut into serving pieces
2 oz (50 g) ghee *or* unsalted butter
2 onions, finely sliced
2 cloves garlic, finely sliced
2 bay leaves

*Marinade*
½ teaspoon turmeric powder
1 teaspoon finely crushed ginger
1 teaspoon five-spice powder
½ teaspoon chilli powder
¼ teaspoon ground mace
salt to taste

Mix the marinade ingredients to a paste with a little water, add the duck pieces, and leave for 2 hours. Heat the ghee in a wok and fry duck pieces with their marinade till evenly brown. Transfer all the contents of the pan to a casserole dish. Top with onion and garlic slices, and tuck bay leaves in between the pieces of duck. Cover the casserole with a sheet of foil and a lid, and cook for 1–1½ hours in a pre-heated oven, 350°F/180°C. Serve hot with rice. (If you are using chicken the cooking time will be 50–60 minutes.)

## Pheasant Pickle

This recipe can be used for any game bird, or even for rabbit.

1 hung and dressed pheasant, jointed
3 tablespoons salt
3 cups cooking oil
juice of 3 lemons
8 medium onions, finely sliced
2 oz (50 g) garlic, finely minced
2 oz (50 g) chilli powder
½ pint (300 ml) vinegar
4 oz (100 g) ginger, finely shredded
2 oz (50 g) garam masala
4 oz (100 g) sugar

Place the pheasant and the salt in a large pan and cover with cold water. Bring to the boil, then simmer until no water is left. In a wok or large pan heat the oil and lemon juice. When it begins to smoke add the onions and garlic, and fry till golden. Add the chilli powder and the pieces of pheasant and fry for 2–3 minutes. Pour in the vinegar and bring to the boil once, then remove from the heat and fold in the ginger, garam masala and sugar. Allow to cool completely, and store in jars. It will keep in the refrigerator for a long time, and can be served as an accompaniment to any non-vegetarian meal. Serve cold or warmed. If the latter, warm only the portion required.


## Egg Curry                                                   *Serves 4–6*
### Muttai Kari

Serve with plain rice or nan bread, or as an accompaniment to Chicken Biryani, page 243.

1 tablespoon ground almonds
1 teaspoon chilli powder
1 teaspoon turmeric powder
1 tablespoon coriander powder
1 teaspoon cumin powder
4 tablespoons oil
1 large onion, finely sliced
2 cloves garlic, finely minced
14 oz (400 g) crushed tinned tomatoes
2 oz (50 g) creamed coconut dissolved in ½ pint (300 ml) hot water
a few curry leaves *or* 1 bay leaf
salt to taste
1 teaspoon gram flour *or* wholemeal flour
8 hard-boiled eggs, shelled and cut into half lengthwise
chopped coriander leaves for garnish

Mix the almonds, chilli, turmeric, coriander and cumin to a paste with a little water. Heat the oil and fry the onion until brown, then add the garlic and fry for 1 minute. Add the curry paste mixture and fry well. Add the tomatoes, coconut and curry leaves and bring to the boil, then add the salt and gram flour, lower the heat, and simmer for 20 minutes. If the gravy is too thick add a little hot water. Add the halved eggs and simmer for 5 more minutes. Garnish with coriander leaves and serve hot.

## Savoury Scrambled Eggs
### Muttai Bharth

Serves 4–6

This makes a delicious cocktail snack if served in vol-au-vents or on little cheese biscuits. The Indian Muslims prefer it with hot chappatis for breakfast, but it tastes just as delicious on freshly made toast. To make it a complete meal, serve on potato waffles.

2 tablespoons ghee or unsalted butter
1 onion, finely chopped
1 green chilli, finely chopped
a few fresh coriander leaves, finely chopped
1 firm tomato, finely chopped
¼ teaspoon turmeric powder
salt and pepper to taste
6 eggs, beaten

Melt the ghee on a medium heat and fry the onions, chilli, coriander leaves and tomato until the onions are soft. Add the turmeric, salt and pepper and mix well. Pour in the beaten eggs and continue to cook slowly, sitrring all the time to break up any lumps. Add more salt and pepper if necessary.

# Meat and Offal Dishes

## Dry Meat Curry
### Mutton Paretal

*Serves 6–8*

Everyone who visits my mother-in-law in Kelang gets to taste this delicious curry, especially on Christmas Day, when 20 kg of mutton are cooked. This is only one of 8 dishes prepared to feed nearly 300 people. Christmas Day in Kelang is something one does not forget in a hurry.

3 teaspoons chilli powder
4 tablespoons curry powder
1 teaspoon turmeric powder
salt to taste
pinch of monosodium glutamate
4 tablespoons oil
1 large onion *or* 8 Bombay onions, finely sliced
2 inches (5 cm) fresh ginger, finely minced
4 cloves garlic, finely minced
a few curry leaves
2 lb (900 g) mutton *or* lean lamb
6 fl oz (175 ml) thick coconut milk
2 large potatoes, peeled and cut into fairly large pieces
2 large tomatoes, finely chopped

Mix the chilli, curry powder, turmeric, salt and monosodium glutamate to a paste with a little water. Heat the oil in a wok and fry the onion until lightly browned. Add the ginger and garlic and fry for a further 1–2 minutes. Add the curry paste mixture and the curry leaves, and when the oil rises above the spices add the meat and fry well until evenly browned. Cover the pan and allow the meat to simmer in its own juices for about 10 minutes, then add the coconut milk and stir well. Add the potatoes and tomatoes, and simmer uncovered until the meat and potatoes are cooked. The gravy should be very thick. Serve hot with boiled rice or Appam (see page 248). Alternatively, serve cold with French bread and a green salad as a picnic dish.

## Tender Mutton with Onions
### Mutton Do Piyaza

*Serves 4–6*

One of the traditional recipes still used by the Indian Muslims in Malaysia.

1½ teaspoons honey
1 teaspoon vinegar
pinch of salt
1 lb (450 g) mutton *or* lean lamb, cut into large pieces
4 tablespoons ghee *or* unsalted butter
1 large onion, thickly sliced
1 inch (2·5 cm) fresh ginger, finely minced
6 cloves garlic, finely minced
2 teaspoons chilli powder
½ teaspoon turmeric powder
1 teaspoon cumin powder
½ teaspoon five-spice powder
4 fl oz (110 ml) natural yogurt, beaten until smooth
1 teaspoon salt
a few coriander leaves for garnish

Mix together the honey, vinegar and salt and rub well into the meat. Leave to marinade for about 4 hours. Heat the ghee on a medium flame and fry the onion until lightly browned. Add the ginger and garlic and fry till fragrant. Mix the chilli, turmeric, cumin and five-spice to a paste with 2 tablespoons of water and add to the pan. Fry till the ghee separates, then add the meat and fry till all the pieces are evenly coated. Stir in a little hot water and simmer, covered, till the meat is nearly tender. Reduce the heat and very slowly blend in the yogurt, stirring constantly. Add the salt. Simmer for a further 5–10 minutes. Garnish with coriander leaves and serve hot with plain boiled rice or pilau rice.

## Mutton Fry

*Serves 4–6*

This is a hot dish, and perhaps you should not try it until your palate has acquired a taste for chillies. It would not be the same if the quantity of chillies were reduced.

20–30 large dried red chillies
1 tablespoon five-spice powder
½ teaspoon turmeric powder
1 tablespoon salt
2 inches (5 cm) fresh ginger
2 lb (900 g) mutton *or* lean lamb, cut into bitesize pieces
2 ripe tomatoes, finely chopped
3–4 curry leaves
2 large onions, finely sliced, deep-fried until brown, and drained
juice of 1 lemon
a few cashew nuts, fried until golden and drained

Grind the chillies, five-spice, turmeric, salt and ginger with a little oil, and put in a saucepan with the meat, tomatoes and curry leaves. Add enough water to cover the meat. Bring to the boil, then simmer gently till the meat is nearly cooked and the water has almost evaporated. Add the fried onions and stir well. Just before serving, add the lemon juice. Garnish with the fried cashew nuts and serve hot with rice.

## Mutton Curry, Madras Style     Serves 4–6

1 lb (450 g) mutton *or* lean lamb, cut into bitesize pieces
2 inches (5 cm) cinnamon quill
1 teaspoon turmeric powder
salt to taste
6 fl oz (175 ml) thin coconut milk
6 fl oz (175 ml) thick coconut milk
juice of 1 lemon

*Ingredients to be ground together*
2 small onions
5 cloves garlic
2 inches (5 cm) fresh ginger
8 large dried chillies, seeded
2 teaspoons coriander powder
1 teaspoon cumin powder
1 teaspoon aniseed

Put the mutton, cinnamon, turmeric, salt and thin coconut milk in a large heavy pan and bring to the boil. Lower the heat and simmer for

10 minutes, then add the ground ingredients and the thick coconut milk and stir well. Simmer uncovered till the meat is tender and the gravy thick. Add the lemon juice, and serve hot with boiled rice or chappatis.

## Spicy Mutton in Rich Yogurt Gravy    Serves 4–6
## Mutton Khorma

As this dish requires a great deal of preparation, it is a good idea to make extra portions of the ground ingredients and freeze them in small cartons for future use.

4 tablespoons ghee
1 tablespoon oil
2 lb (900 g) mutton or lean lamb, cut into large pieces
½ pint (300 ml) natural yogurt, beaten well
a few coriander leaves

*Ingredients to be ground (see recipe)*
2 large dried red chillies
2 teaspoons coriander seeds
1 teaspoon cumin seeds
1 teaspoon desiccated coconut
6–8 almonds
2 teaspoons poppy seeds
1 teaspoon sesame seeds
2 cloves garlic
1 inch (2·5 cm) fresh ginger
1 large onion, sliced

First prepare the ground ingredients. Dry roast all the ingredients individually in a frying pan without oil until brown and aromatic. Allow to cool, then place in an electric blender and grind to a smooth paste, adding a few drops of oil to keep the mixture pliable.

Heat the ghee and oil gently in a heavy pan and fry the ground ingredients, stirring continuously to prevent them sticking, until the oil separates. Add 2 tablespoons of water and stir well. Continue to fry until the water evaporates. Add the meat pieces and stir well to coat each piece with the spices, then reduce the heat and slowly blend in the yogurt. Stir well, cover the pan, and cook till the meat is tender, stirring occasionally. A few minutes before removing from the heat, add the coriander leaves. The liquid should have been reduced to a thick gravy coating the meat. Serve hot with boiled rice or nan bread.

## Lamb in Green Herbs                     *Serves 4–6*
### Attu Erachi in Green Masala

3 lb (1·3 kg) breast of lamb
4 oz (100 g) fresh coriander leaves
4 green chillies, seeded
6 cloves garlic
4 tablespoons oil
2 onions, finely sliced
1 teaspoon turmeric powder
salt to taste

Ask the butcher to remove the skin and excess fat from the lamb and cut it into small pieces including the bone. Pound together the coriander leaves, chillies and garlic.

Heat the oil in a heavy pan and fry the onions till soft. Add the turmeric, salt and coriander mixture and fry for 1–2 minutes. Add the lamb pieces and fry till evenly coated. Add enough hot water to cover the meat and bring to the boil, then reduce the heat and simmer till the meat is tender and comes off the bone easily. Serve as a main dish with plain boiled rice, or as a soup with bread.

## Spiced Roast Leg of Lamb                *Serves 4–6*
### Raan Masala

This recipe is for a whole leg of lamb, but the meat can also be boned and cut in cubes before being marinaded, then threaded on skewers and grilled until done. Baste occasionally while grilling.

4 lb (1·8 kg) leg of mutton *or* lamb, skin and excess fat removed
8 cloves
salt to taste
almond flakes for garnish

*Marinade*
2 onions
4 cloves garlic
2 inches (5 cm) fresh ginger
1 tablespoon ground almonds
2 teaspoons ground coriander
1 teaspoon turmeric powder
2 teaspoons garam masala
1 teaspoon ground cumin
2 teaspoons chilli powder
juice of 1 lemon
4 oz (100 g) plain yogurt
2 tablespoons tomato purée

To make the marinade, mince together the onions, garlic and ginger. Mix together the rest of the marinade ingredients and add to the minced onion mixture. Make gashes all over the meat and push in the cloves. Spread the marinade mixture evenly over the meat, pushing it into the gashes. Cover, and leave for 4 hours.

Preheat the oven to 375°F/190°C. Place the meat on a roasting tray and sprinkle it with salt. Cover with foil and roast on the centre shelf of the oven for 2 hours or until the meat is tender, basting occasionally. Remove the foil for the last 10 minutes of the cooking time. Serve hot, garnished with almond flakes. Serve with nan bread (see page 247) or pilau rice (see page 243).

## Curried Minced Meat
### Kheema

Kheema is used regularly by Indian Muslims. You can use this basic recipe in several ways:

(1) Serve hot with fried eggs and freshly made toast. To make it look special, separate each egg and whisk the white till stiff. Heat 1 teaspoon of butter and pour in the egg white. When nearly set, pour

the yolk into the centre. Spoon hot butter over the white to cook. (*Serves 6–8*)

(2) Beat 2 eggs with 2 tablespoons of minced meat and fry like an omelette.

(3) Use as a sandwich spread.

(4) Add peas and diced potatoes while cooking, and serve with boiled rice or puris and natural yogurt. (*Serves 4–6*)

(5) Use as a curry puff filling (see page 191).

2 tablespoons oil
1 large onion, finely chopped
2 cloves garlic, finely minced
2 green chillies, finely chopped
1½ teaspoons curry powder
a few fresh coriander leaves, finely chopped
1 tomato, finely chopped, *or* 1 teaspoon tomato purée
1 teaspoon salt
1 lb (450 g) lean minced mutton *or* beef, washed in a sieve and drained

Heat the oil and fry the onion, garlic and chillies till the onion is soft. Add the curry powder, coriander leaves, tomato and salt and fry till the oil separates. Add the minced meat and stir well. Add a little water and simmer, covered, till the mince is cooked and dry. Serve according to one of the above suggestions.


## Indian Meat Loaf                              Serves 4–6
### Lagan ki Seekh

1 lb (450 g) lean minced lamb *or* mutton
1 large potato, peeled and grated
1 teaspoon cumin powder
1 tablespoon coriander powder
½ teaspoon chilli powder
½ teaspoon curry powder
a few coriander leaves, chopped
2 cloves garlic, finely minced
1 inch (2·5 cm) fresh ginger, finely minced
juice of 1 lemon
1 teaspoon salt
2 eggs

Well grease an 8-inch (20-cm) baking dish, using ghee if available. Mix all the ingredients except the eggs, and knead the mixture until well blended. Whisk one egg until fluffy and pour into the greased baking dish. Add the minced meat mixture and smooth it out evenly. Cook for 30 minutes in a pre-heated oven, 350°F/180°C. Beat the second egg, pour over the meat, and bake till the egg has set and the meat is cooked. Cut into 6 or 8 slices and serve hot with a green salad and lemon wedges.

## Meatball Curry                                  *Serves 4–6*
### Kofta Kari

For vegetable koftas, see page 232. Meat or vegetable koftas can be served on their own, without a curry sauce, as a snack or with cocktails.

*Meatballs*
1 lb (450 g) lean minced mutton *or* lamb
2 cloves garlic, finely minced
1 inch (2·5 cm) fresh ginger, finely minced
2 green chillies, seeded and finely chopped
handful of coriander leaves, finely chopped
1 small onion, finely chopped
1 egg
½ teaspoon turmeric powder
1 teaspoon garam masala
1 large potato, peeled and grated
1 teaspoon salt
oil for deep-frying

*Curry (same recipe applies to Vegetable Kofta on page 232)*
2 tablespoons vegetable oil
1 onion, finely chopped
2 cloves garlic, finely minced
1 inch (2·5 cm) fresh ginger, finely minced
½ teaspoon turmeric powder
½ teaspoon chilli powder
½ teaspoon five-spice powder
salt to taste

2 tablespoons tomato purée mixed with ½ pint (300 ml) hot water
¼ pint (150 ml) natural yogurt, beaten until smooth
chopped fresh coriander leaves and lemon wedges for garnish

First make the meatballs. Mix all the ingredients together with your hands and shape into small balls. Deep-fry until brown, drain, and set aside.

For the curry, heat the oil and fry the onion, garlic and ginger till the onion is light brown. Mix the turmeric, chilli, five-spice and salt to a paste with a little water, add to the pan, and fry till the oil separates. Pour in the tomato stock and bring to the boil, then reduce the heat and simmer for 10–15 minutes.

Gently place the koftas in the curry and simmer for a further 5 minutes. Now add the yogurt very slowly, stirring constantly but making sure you do not break the koftas. When the gravy has reached a creamy consistency remove the pan from the heat. Serve hot with boiled rice, and garnish with coriander leaves and lemon wedges.


## Malacca Pork and Liver Curry             *Serves 4–6*

A Portuguese-influenced curry, favoured by the Indian Christians in Malaysia.

1 lb (450 g) pork with some fat but no skin
½ lb (225 g) pork liver, rinsed well and drained
4 tablespoons cooking oil
2 teaspoons chilli powder
1 teaspoon cumin powder
1 teaspoon freshly ground black pepper
½ teaspoon ground cloves
1 inch (2·5 cm) fresh ginger, finely minced
4 cloves garlic, finely minced
salt to taste
4 fl oz (110 ml) malt vinegar
2 tablespoons tomato purée
2 teaspoons sugar

Parboil the pork and liver in 2 pints (1·2 litres) of water. Drain and reserve the stock. When cool enough to handle, cut the meat into small cubes. In a heavy pan heat the oil gently and add the spices, ginger, garlic, salt and the vinegar mixed with the tomato purée. Fry till the oil separates, then add the pork and liver and stir-fry for 2–3 minutes. Add 6 fl oz (175 ml) of the reserved stock and cook until the meat is done and the gravy is thick. Add more stock if necessary. Finally add the sugar, adjust the salt, fry for 1 minute and remove from the heat.

Serve hot with boiled rice. Alternatively, it can be stored in an air-tight jar and used as an accompaniment, either cold or warm. If the latter, gently reheat only the required portions.

## Pork Vindaloo                                    *Serves 4–6*

Another hot dish for those who enjoy spicy fare. This has a Portuguese influence and is popular in Malacca state, where 3,000 Portuguese still reside.

2 lb (900 g) pork
6–8 dried red chillies
6 fl oz (175 ml) vinegar
2 inches (5 cm) fresh ginger
4 cloves garlic
2 teaspoons cumin powder
2 teaspoons five-spice powder
2 teaspoons salt
2 teaspoons brown sugar
4 tablespoons oil

Remove the skin and excess fat from the pork and cut into bitesize pieces. Soak the chillies in the vinegar for 10–15 minutes, then blend to a smooth paste with the ginger, garlic, cumin and five-spice powder. Mix all the ingredients except the oil and allow the pork to marinade for 4 hours.

Heat the oil in a heavy pan and fry the pork pieces without their marinade, stirring well. When the pork is evenly brown, add the marinade and simmer till the meat is tender. Serve hot with boiled rice, or cold as a pickle with other mild curries.

## Brain Curry
Serves 4–6
### Moolai Kari

This curry is delicious served hot with Khichdi (see page 246).

4 calves' brains
½ teaspoon turmeric powder
4 tablespoons oil
2 tomatoes, finely chopped
salt to taste
a few coriander leaves for garnish

*Ingredients to be ground together*
4 cloves garlic
3 green chillies, seeded
4 oz (100 g) fresh coriander leaves
2 teaspoons cumin powder

Soak the brains in cold water for 24 hours, changing the water two or three times. Place them in a large pan with the turmeric and ½ teaspoon of salt and add enough water to cover. Bring to the boil, then reduce the heat and simmer for 10 minutes. Drain, and when cool enough to handle cut the brains into 4 pieces each.

Heat the oil in another pan and fry the ground ingredients until fragrant. Add the tomatoes and salt to taste and fry well. Return the brains to the pan, stir well, and simmer for 5 minutes. Serve hot, garnished with fresh coriander leaves.


## Kidneys with Spinach
Serves 4–6
### Pukkam with Pasala Keerai

8 lamb's kidneys
4 tablespoons oil
1 medium onion, finely chopped
1 inch (2·5 cm) fresh ginger, finely crushed
2 cloves garlic, finely crushed
½–1 teaspoon chilli powder
¼ teaspoon turmeric powder

1 teaspoon garam masala
1 tablespoon tomato purée
4 tablespoons plain yogurt, beaten well
1 lb (450 g) frozen spinach leaves, thawed, excess water squeezed out
salt to taste
tomato and lemon wedges for garnish

Cut the kidneys into small pieces, removing the core, and soak them in cold water for 1 hour. Place the kidneys and the water in a pan, add a pinch of turmeric, and bring to the boil once. Drain and set aside.

Heat the oil in a large pan and fry the onion, ginger and garlic until brown. Mix the chilli, turmeric and garam masala to a paste with 2 teaspoons of water, add to the pan, and fry till the water has evaporated. Mix the tomato purée with 4 tablespoons of water and add to the pan with the kidneys. Simmer till kidneys are nearly tender, then stir the yogurt in gently and mix well. Add the spinach and some salt and cook till the spinach has absorbed the gravy.

Garnish with tomato and lemon wedges, and serve with boiled rice, lentil curry (see page 240) and a pickle of your choice. I like a mild-sweet lemon pickle (see page 250).

# Seafood Dishes

## Fish or Prawn Pickle

When any of us visit home, my mother-in-law spends the last two days preparing fish and prawn pickles for her son and two daughters in the UK. On one visit I watched her, and attempted the recipe with 95 per cent success. (Hope Mum will forgive me if I omitted something.) Use bream, bass, mackerel, mullet or large raw prawns.

1 lb (450 g) firm fish *or* prawns
salt to taste
oil for deep-frying
6–8 curry leaves
½ teaspoon turmeric powder
1 teaspoon monosodium glutamate
pinch of sugar
6 fl oz (175 ml) malt vinegar

*Ingredients to be ground together*
10 large dry red chillies, seeded, soaked and drained
8 cloves garlic
1 oz (25 g) fresh ginger

Clean the fish and cut into 1-inch (2·5-cm) pieces, or shell and devein the prawns, discarding the heads. Rub well with salt, then rinse and dry thoroughly.

Heat the oil and deep-fry the fish pieces or prawns until nearly crisp. Drain and set aside. Pour off the oil, leaving about 5 tablespoons in the pan, reheat, and fry the ground ingredients until fragrant. Add the remaining raw ingredients and fry for a further 2–3 minutes. Add the prawns or fish and stir-fry until all the pieces are evenly coated and the oil has separated from the spices. Cool and bottle.

## Spiced Pomfret
Serves 4–6
### Masala Bawal

You can use sole instead of pomfret. Pomfrets are available frozen from Chinese and Indian grocers, but are becoming so popular that I have even been able to ask my local fishmonger to get me some.

2 large pomfrets
a little ghee

*Marinade*
6 fl oz (175 ml) natural yogurt
2 tablespoons coriander powder
1 tablespoon cumin powder
2 tablespoons chilli powder
¼ teaspoon ground white pepper
4 cloves garlic, finely minced
2 inches (5 cm) fresh ginger, finely minced
dash of red colouring *or* a few drops of cochineal
1 teaspoon salt
½ teaspoon black cumin seeds (optional)

Scale and clean the fish, removing any fins but leaving the head. Make 4 gashes on each side. Mix together the marinade ingredients and rub well over the fish and into the gashes. Allow to stand for 4 hours.

Place the fish on a rack in a grill tray and cook under a moderate grill for 15 minutes on each side. Remove and cool a little. Preheat the grill to maximum, replace the fish, brushed with a little ghee, and grill till each side is cooked and crisp. Serve hot, with lemon wedges, raw onion rings and tomato slices.

## Fish Cutlets
Serves 4–6
### Meen Cutlets

I greatly enjoyed this dish when I visited my Pracina Aunty in Batang Berjuntai. She is very loving and always smiling.

1¼ lb (550 g) skinned haddock *or* coley fillets, parboiled and mashed
2 medium potatoes, peeled, boiled and mashed
1 onion, finely chopped
2 green chillies, seeded and finely chopped
1 inch (2·5 cm) fresh ginger, finely minced
salt to taste
¼ teaspoon freshly ground black pepper
a few coriander leaves, finely chopped
2 eggs
fine breadcrumbs
oil for shallow frying

Place the fish, potato, onion, chillies, ginger, salt, pepper and coriander in a large bowl. Add 1 egg and mix well. Form the mixture into balls the size of golf-balls and flatten them into cutlets ½ inch (1 cm) thick. Beat the remaining egg. Dip the cutlets in the beaten egg and then in breadcrumbs. Heat the oil in a frying pan and shallow-fry the cutlets until golden and crisp on both sides. Drain and serve hot with tomato ketchup or a sweet mango chutney.

## Hot South Indian Fish Curry
*Serves 6–8*
### Meen Kari

2 tablespoons oil
5–6 curry leaves
1 large onion, finely chopped
1 inch (2·5 cm) fresh ginger, finely minced
6 cloves garlic, finely minced
2 tablespoons Madras curry powder
1 teaspoon chilli powder
½ pint (300 ml) thick coconut milk
salt to taste
2 tablespoons desiccated coconut, dry-roasted until brown and ground
2 lb (900 g) firm white fish, cleaned and cut into pieces 1 inch (2·5 cm) thick
juice of 1 lemon

Heat the oil in a large pan and fry the curry leaves until golden. Add the onion, ginger and garlic and fry till the onion is brown. Mix the curry powder and chilli to a paste with a little water, reduce the heat, and add to the pan. Fry till the oil separates. Add the coconut milk, salt and ground coconut and bring to a simmer, stirring continuously. Add the fish pieces and stir well. Simmer uncovered till the fish is cooked, stirring occasionally but gently to prevent the fish breaking up. Remove to a serving dish and sprinkle with lemon juice. Serve hot with boiled rice.

## Fish in Fresh Green Herbs
### Meen in Green Masala

*Serves 4–6*

3 tablespoons vegetable oil
1 large onion, finely sliced
2 teaspoons lemon juice
4 tablespoons water
1½ tablespoons salt
1½ lb (675 g) firm white fish fillets
lemon wedges for garnish

*Ingredients to be ground together*
4 tablespoons desiccated coconut
10–12 cloves garlic
½ teaspoon fenugreek seeds
1 teaspoon cumin powder
1 cup tightly packed coriander leaves
4 green chillies, seeded for milder flavour

Heat the oil in a wok or large frying pan and fry the onion till pale yellow and soft. Add the ground ingredients, reduce the heat, and fry for 5 minutes. Pour in the lemon juice, water and salt, and simmer for 5–10 minutes. Place the fish fillets in the pan and coat both sides with sauce. Cover and simmer till the fish is cooked. Serve hot, garnished with lemon wedges.

## A Mild South Indian Fish Curry
Serves 4–6
### Meen Moolee

Prawns can be used instead of fish in this recipe. If you are using raw prawns, simmer them in the sauce for 10 minutes or until they turn pink. Cooked prawns need only 5 minutes.

1 lb (450 g) firm white fish steaks
1 teaspoon salt
2 tablespoons vegetable oil
1 medium onion, finely chopped
1 inch (2·5 cm) fresh ginger, finely minced
1 clove garlic, finely minced
4 curry leaves
½ teaspoon turmeric powder
10 fl oz (300 ml) thick coconut milk
juice of 1 lemon

Rub the fish with the salt. Heat the oil in a wok or large pan and fry the onion, ginger, garlic, curry leaves and turmeric till the onion is soft and the raw smell disappears. Reduce the heat and add the coconut milk, stirring continuously. Simmer uncovered for 5 minutes. Add the fish steaks and continue simmering, uncovered, till the fish is cooked. Before removing from the heat add the lemon juice and adjust the seasoning. Serve hot with boiled rice.

## Fried Fish
Serves 4–6
### Tali Meen

Use mackerel, halibut, pomfret or any firm fish.

2 lb (900 g) firm fish, cut into 1-inch (2·5-cm) thick steaks
salt
½ teaspoon turmeric powder
½ teaspoon chilli powder
1 clove garlic, finely minced
lemon juice
4 tablespoons cornflour
oil for shallow frying

Rub the fish with salt, rinse, and dry thoroughly. Mix the turmeric, chilli and garlic to a thick paste with some lemon juice, adding salt to taste, and rub this paste into both sides of the fish pieces. Leave covered for 15–20 minutes, then put the pieces of fish in a plastic bag with the cornflour and shake to coat the fish evenly.

Heat the oil in a wok or frying pan and fry the fish on both sides until deep brown and crisp. Do not overcrowd the pan or you will find it difficult to turn the fish pieces over. Serve hot. A delicious accompaniment with lentil curry, vegetable sodhi, pickles and rasam.

## Delicately Pickled Fish Steaks                    *Serves 4*

This dish is served cold and should be prepared the day before serving, so that the liquid will set like aspic. It makes a delicious starter.

4 tablespoons oil
3 small onions, finely chopped
1 inch (2·5 cm) fresh ginger, finely minced
2 cloves garlic, finely minced
2 red chillies, seeded, and finely chopped
3 green chillies, seeded, and finely chopped
½ teaspoon turmeric powder
1 tablespoon ground coriander
¼ pint (150 ml) vinegar
4 curry leaves
pinch of sugar
salt to taste
4 thick cod *or* halibut steaks
lemon wedges

Heat the oil and fry the onions till golden brown. Add the ginger, garlic, red and green chillies, turmeric and coriander and fry for 3 minutes. Add the vinegar, curry leaves, sugar and salt to taste and bring to the boil. Put the fish into the pan and coat both sides with the sauce. Cook till the fish is done. Place in individual bowls or on a large platter and pour the juices over the steaks. Allow to cool in the refrigerator for 24 hours, then serve cold with lemon wedges.

# Lentils with Salt Fish
## Karavadu Parappu

*Serves 4–6*

This dish came about when my husband suddenly got a brainwave. We tried it and loved it.

8 oz (225 g) dried salted fish
4 oz (100 g) masoor dhal (red lentils), washed and drained
½ teaspoon turmeric powder
2 green chillies
½ pint (300 ml) water
oil for deep-frying
1 oz (25 g) creamed coconut
½ lb (225 g) green cabbage leaves, coarsely chopped
1 teaspoon mustard seeds
2 dried red chillies
1 clove garlic, crushed
3 curry leaves
salt to taste

Soak the fish for 5 minutes in water and dry thoroughly. Cut into cubes, checking that there are no scales. Place the dhal, turmeric powder, green chillies and water in a large pan and bring to the boil, then reduce the heat and simmer till the lentils are soft. While the lentils are cooking, deep-fry the salt fish cubes until golden and crisp. Drain and set aside.

When the lentils are soft, mash them with a wooden spoon and add the creamed coconut and cabbage. Cook till the cabbage is tender, adding a little hot water if necessary. In a small frying pan heat 4 tablespoons of the oil in which you fried the salt fish, and fry the mustard seeds, dried chillies, garlic and curry leaves till the seeds begin to pop. Pour this mixture over the lentils, cover, and leave for 5 minutes. Add salt to taste and fold in the fish pieces. Serve hot with boiled rice.

## Prawn and Okra Curry                    Serves 4–6
### Eral and Vendaikai Kari

Okra makes a lovely combination with fish or meat. You can try the same recipe using lean lamb instead of prawns, and omitting the blacan. Add the lamb with the thin coconut milk.

1 large onion
1 piece blacan, stock cube size
2 tablespoons chilli powder
1 teaspoon turmeric
6 tablespoons oil
8 oz (225 g) small okras, washed, dried and left whole
2 cups thin coconut milk (see pages 24–5)
3–4 curry leaves
salt to taste
pinch of sugar
1 lb (450 g) large raw prawns, shelled and deveined
1 cup thick coconut milk (see pages 24–5)

Grind together the onion, blacan, chilli and turmeric. Heat the oil in a pan and stir-fry the okra for 3–4 minutes. Drain and set aside. Reheat the oil and fry the onion mixture until the raw smell disappears. Add the thin coconut milk, curry leaves, salt and sugar and bring to the boil. Simmer for 10 minutes, then add the prawns, okra and thick coconut milk and simmer till the prawns are cooked. Check the seasoning, and serve hot with rice.

## Sour Prawn Curry                    Serves 4–6
### Puli Eral

The prawns we can buy here are usually cooked. Raw prawns are available from Chinese supermarkets, but are expensive. If you are using cooked prawns, do not add them to the curry till the last 2–3 minutes or they will become tough and dry.

1 piece tamarind, golfball size
10 fl oz (300 ml) hot water
2 tablespoons sugar
¼ teaspoon salt
¼ teaspoon freshly ground black pepper
1 lb (450 g) raw prawns, shelled and deveined
5 tablespoons oil

*Ingredients to be ground together*
1 large onion, finely sliced
4 cloves garlic
8 candlenuts *or* 16 blanched almonds
1 teaspoon turmeric powder
1 teaspoon chilli powder
1 piece blacan, stock cube size

Soak the tamarind in the hot water till soft, then squeeze and strain the juice. Mix together the sugar, salt and pepper, add the prawns, and leave for 15 minutes.

Heat the oil in a pan and fry the ground ingredients on a medium heat until the raw smell of onion disappears. Add the tamarind juice and season to taste. Bring to the boil and simmer for 5 minutes, then add the prawns and simmer for a further 5 minutes or until the prawns curl and turn pink. (If using cooked prawns simmer for 2–3 minutes only.) Serve hot with boiled rice.

## Fried Prawns
### Tali Eral

*Serves 6–8*

An expensive dish, but worth trying at least once.

2 lb (900 g) large raw prawns
2 teaspoons chilli powder
½ teaspoon salt
1 tablespoon cornflour
oil for shallow frying

Shell the prawns, leaving the tail tips on, and carefully devein. Mix the chilli powder, salt and cornflour in a plastic bag, add the prawns, and shake to coat evenly. Heat the oil in a wok and fry the prawns in 2 or 3 batches until crisp and done. Drain well on kitchen paper. Serve with lemon pickle (see page 250) or tomato ketchup mixed with a hot chilli sauce.

# Vegetable and Lentil Dishes

## Ceylon Mixed Vegetables
*Serves 4–6*

oil for deep-frying potatoes
6 small potatoes, peeled and halved lengthwise
2 tablespoons ghee *or* unsalted butter
1 onion, finely chopped
1 teaspoon chilli powder
½ teaspoon turmeric powder
2 ripe tomatoes, finely chopped
salt to taste
4 leaves cabbage, coarsely sliced
20 whole beans, stringed and halved
1 large carrot, peeled and sliced
1 teaspoon cinnamon powder

Heat the oil in a deep pan and fry the potatoes till golden brown and cooked, turning them occasionally to brown them evenly. Drain and keep warm. Using another pan heat the ghee gently and fry the onion until soft. Mix the chilli and turmeric to a paste with a little water, add to the pan, and fry till the ghee separates. Add the tomatoes and salt and cook for 1–2 minutes, then add remaining vegetables except the potatoes and stir well. Add a few drops of water, cover the pan, and simmer till the vegetables are tender. Stir in the potatoes, and serve hot, sprinkled with the cinnamon.

## Golden Pumpkin Curry
*Serves 4–6*

1 lb (450 g) pumpkin, skinned and seeds removed
4 tablespoons ghee *or* vegetable oil
1 large onion, finely chopped
1 inch (2·5 cm) fresh ginger, finely minced
1 clove garlic, finely minced
½ teaspoon fennel seeds
3–4 curry leaves

2 fresh red chillies, seeded and coarsely chopped
½ teaspoon mustard seeds
1 teaspoon turmeric powder
4 fl oz (110 ml) thick coconut milk
salt to taste
a few fresh coriander leaves, chopped, for garnish

Cut the pumpkin into cubes and sprinkle with a little salt. Heat the ghee or oil in a pan and fry the onion, ginger, garlic, fennel seeds, curry leaves and chopped chillies until the onion is soft. Stir in the pumpkin, mustard seeds and turmeric. Fry for 1–2 minutes, then reduce the heat and pour in the coconut milk. Cook uncovered for 7–10 minutes, or until the pumpkin is tender and a little mushy. Add salt to taste. Serve hot, garnished with coriander leaves. This curry is delicious with hot chappatis or puris.

## Lentil Curry with Snake Gourd    *Serves 4–6*
### Parappu with Pudalankai

South Indians use snake gourd to make a variety of dishes. If you find it difficult to obtain, marrow or courgettes can be used instead.

4 oz (100 g) masoor dhal (red lentils)
1 medium snake gourd
3–4 curry leaves
1 fresh green chilli, left whole
2 cloves garlic, finely minced
1 teaspoon turmeric powder
1 large onion, finely sliced
½ pint (300 ml) thin coconut milk
2 ripe tomatoes, quartered
6 fl oz (175 ml) thick coconut milk
salt to taste
4 tablespoons ghee *or* vegetable oil
1 teaspoon mustard seeds
4 large dried chillies

Wash the lentils, soak them in water for 1–2 hours, and drain. Remove the pith from the snake gourd and cut the flesh into bitesize pieces. Place the lentils, curry leaves, green chilli, garlic, turmeric and half the onion in a heavy pan. Pour in the thin coconut milk and bring to the boil. Reduce the heat and simmer till the lentils are soft. (This can be done in a pressure cooker – it will take only 6–8 minutes.) Add the snake gourd and tomatoes and cook till the gourd is tender. Stir in the thick coconut milk and salt to taste.

In a pan heat the ghee or oil and fry the remaining onion till brown. Add the mustard seeds and dried chillies. When the mustard seeds begin to pop, pour the mixture over the lentils and stir well. Serve hot with rice and a dry meat or fish curry.

## Indian Vegetable and Fruit Salad           *Serves 4–6*
## Rojak

4 oz (100 g) beansprouts, tailed, washed and drained
½ cucumber, thinly sliced but not peeled
1 turnip, thinly sliced
4 Chinese cabbage leaves, shredded and blanched for 1 minute
6 pieces fried beancurd, cut in half diagonally
1 green mango *or* 1 green apple, thinly sliced
8 spinach fritters, cut in slices (see page 194)
2 red chillies, seeded and finely chopped
2 spring onions, finely chopped

*Sauce ingredients*
6 dried chillies, seeded
1 onion, finely chopped
3 tablespoons oil
½ teaspoon turmeric
juice of 1 lemon
2 oz (50 g) roasted peanuts, coarsely ground
1 teaspoon sugar
salt to taste

Arrange all the vegetables and fruits decoratively on a large platter and garnish with the chillies and spring onions. To make the sauce, grind together the chillies and onion and fry in the oil until fragrant. Add the turmeric, lemon juice, peanuts, sugar and salt, and stir well. If too thick, add a little water. Pour into a sauce bowl and serve with the vegetable platter. Alternatively you can toss everything together and serve in a large salad bowl.

## Spicy Okra
### Masala Vendakai

*Serves 4–6*

This is how okra is prepared in my in-laws' home, and you will notice how they have used dried prawns and blacan, which is never done in India. If you are a strict vegetarian, omit the prawns and blacan.

1 teaspoon tamarind
4 tablespoons boiling water
4 tablespoons vegetable oil
8 oz (225 g) okra, cut into slanted slices, deep-fried and drained
salt to taste

*Ingredients to be ground together*
1 oz (25 g) dried prawns, soaked for 5 minutes and drained
1 clove garlic
1 small onion
½ teaspoon chilli powder
½ teaspoon turmeric powder
1 piece blacan, garlic clove size
1 teaspoon sugar

Soak the tamarind in the boiling water till soft, then strain off the juice. Heat the oil in a wok and fry the ground ingredients until the raw smell disappears. Add the tamarind juice and simmer for 1–2 minutes. Add the fried okra slices and stir-fry for 3–4 minutes. Season, and serve hot.

## Vegetable Ball Curry
### Sabzi Kofta Curry

*Serves 4–6*

People are consciously using vegetables more and more in their daily meals, and Indian cuisine can provide a wide range of everyday vegetable recipes.

1 lb (450 g) packet frozen stewing vegetables
4 leaves cabbage, finely shredded
1 potato, peeled and grated

1 onion, finely chopped
1 tablespoon curry powder
4 cloves garlic, finely crushed
2 tablespoons cornflour
a few coriander leaves, finely chopped
1 green chilli, seeded and finely chopped
½ teaspoon five-spice powder
salt and pepper to taste
oil for deep-frying

1 curry recipe (page 214)

In a large pan of salted water, boil the stewing vegetables and cabbage until they are soft and can be crushed with a fork. Drain and cool, then place in a large mixing bowl together with all the other ingredients except the oil and curry. Mix to a dough-like texture, and shape into balls the size of golfballs. Heat the oil in a wok and fry the vegetable balls until golden. Drain, carefully add to the curry, and simmer for 5 minutes. Serve hot with rice or puris.

The vegetable koftas can be served on their own, for a coffee party or as a cocktail snack.


## Cauliflower Curry

Serves 4–6

4 tablespoons oil
1 cauliflower, broken into florets
6 fl oz (175 ml) thick coconut milk

*Ingredients to be mixed to a paste*
1 teaspoon chilli powder
1 tablespoon coriander powder
1 teaspoon cumin powder
1 teaspoon mustard powder
1 teaspoon turmeric powder
juice of 1 lemon
salt and pepper to taste
1 tablespoon gram *or* wheat flour
4 tablespoons water

Heat the oil and fry the spice paste until the oil separates. Add the cauliflower and stir well. Reduce the heat, cover the pan, and simmer until the cauliflower is half cooked. Add the coconut milk and stir well. Adjust the seasoning. Simmer until the cauliflower is cooked, stirring regularly. Serve hot with boiled rice.


## Indian Style Mixed Vegetable Curry

*Serves 4–6*

4 tablespoons vegetable oil
½ teaspoon mustard seeds
2 dried red chillies, seeded and coarsely broken
1 onion, finely chopped
2 cloves garlic, finely minced
8 kalonji (onion) seeds
½ teaspoon cumin seeds
1 teaspoon coriander powder
½ teaspoon turmeric powder
pinch of asafoetida (optional)
8 small whole okra
20 whole beans, stringed and cut into 2-inch (5-cm) lengths
1 carrot, peeled and cut into 2-inch (5-cm) lengths
2 oz (50 g) peas
4 white cabbage leaves, finely sliced
2 tablespoons tomato purée
6 tablespoons water
1 teaspoon sugar
salt to taste

Heat the oil and fry the mustard seeds and chillies till the seeds begin to pop. Add the onion, garlic, kalonji, cumin, coriander, turmeric and asafoetida, and fry till the onion is soft. Add all the vegetables and stir till well blended with the spices. Mix the tomato purée with the water and add to the pan with the sugar and salt. Simmer till vegetables are done, adding a little hot water if necessary. Check the seasoning and serve hot.

# Tomato Broth
## Tomato Rasam

*Serves 4–6*

Rasam is a thin, highly spiced broth which is exclusively a South Indian preparation. It is served as a final course, as it is said to aid digestion, and I find it also helps a lot when one is feeling low with a cold or flu. This is one of many different versions.

2 tablespoons oil
10 fl oz (300 ml) tomato juice
10 fl oz (300 ml) water
salt to taste
1 small onion, finely chopped
1 green chilli, seeded and finely chopped (optional)
fresh coriander leaves, chopped
juice of 2 lemons

*Ingredients to be mixed together*
2 cloves garlic, crushed but unpeeled
1 teaspoon freshly ground black pepper
6 peppercorns
4 dried chillies
6–8 curry leaves
pinch of asafoetida (optional)
½ teaspoon turmeric powder
½ teaspoon cumin powder

Heat the oil on a low heat and gently fry the spice mixture for 1–2 minutes. Pour in the tomato juice and water and bring to the boil. Add salt to taste, and more black pepper if necessary. Simmer for 20 minutes, then strain and bring back to the boil. Just before serving, add the chopped onion, chilli and fresh coriander and stir in the lemon juice. Serve piping hot in small bowls.

Alternatively, the onion, chilli and coriander leaves can be added while the broth is simmering. Strain, and serve hot in teacups, adding lemon juice to suit individual taste.

## Fried Aubergine
### Katrikai Tali

*Serves 4–6*

A delicious accompaniment to a vegetarian menu of lentil curry, rice, rasam and pickles – economical yet nutritionally complete.

2 medium aubergines
½ teaspoon chilli powder
1 teaspoon turmeric powder
salt to taste
oil for shallow frying

Wash the aubergines and cut them into ¼-inch (6 mm) thick rings. Soak them in water until needed, then drain them well and pat them dry with kitchen paper. Mix together the chilli, turmeric and salt and rub the aubergine slices on both sides with this mixture. Heat the oil in a frying pan until nearly smoking, and fry the slices of aubergine, a few at a time, until golden brown on each side. Drain well and serve hot.

## Mixed Vegetables in Coconut and Yogurt
### Aviyal

*Serves 4–6*

This is one of the most popular South Indian dishes, and is often prepared for mass feedings at celebrated Hindu temples. The vegetables traditionally used are gourds, raw banana, yam, aubergine, beans, raw mango, drumsticks, cucumber, potato, carrots, peas, and pumpkin. Use whatever is available, in proportions according to your choice.

½ pint (300 ml) water
1 lb (450 g) mixed vegetables, cut into bitesize pieces
½ green mango, sliced (optional)
5 fl oz (150 ml) natural yogurt, 2 or 3 days old
3–4 curry leaves

*Ingredients to be ground together*
4 tablespoons desiccated coconut
2 cloves garlic
3 fresh green chillies, seeded
1 teaspoon cumin seeds
1 teaspoon salt

Bring the water to the boil in a large pan and simmer the vegetables until half done. Reduce the heat and add the coconut mixture, mango, yogurt and curry leaves, and continue to simmer till the vegetables are fully cooked. Serve hot.

## Corn on the Cob Curry                    *Serves 4–6*
### Mokkacholum Kari

A particular favourite of my sons. Do not hesitate to use your fingers – after biting off the kernels suck the cob, which will have absorbed the delicious curry juices.

½ teaspoon turmeric
1 teaspoon five-spice powder
½ teaspoon chilli powder
½ teaspoon garam masala
1 teaspoon coriander powder
3 tablespoons ghee *or* oil
4 frozen corn cobs, thawed and each cut into 4 pieces
1 onion, finely chopped
1 inch (2·5 cm) fresh ginger, finely minced
2 cloves garlic, finely minced
½ pint (300 ml) yogurt, well beaten
½ teaspoon sugar
salt to taste
lemon wedges and chopped fresh coriander leaves for garnish

Mix the turmeric, five-spice, chilli, garam masala and coriander to a paste with 4 tablespoons of water. Heat the ghee or oil in a wok or large pan, and fry the corn till brown on all sides. Drain and set aside. In the same wok fry the onion, ginger and garlic, and when light brown add the spice paste. Cook for 2 minutes, then reduce the heat and gently pour in the yogurt, stirring continuously to prevent curdling. Add the sugar, and salt to taste. Return the corn to the wok, stir well, cover, and cook till the corn is tender. Serve hot, garnished with lemon wedges and chopped coriander. Have extra paper napkins handy.

## Curried Tomatoes                                    Serves 4–6
### Tamatar Kari

1½ lb (675 g) firm red tomatoes
½ teaspoon cumin powder
1 teaspoon coriander powder
½ teaspoon mustard seeds
½ teaspoon chilli powder
3 tablespoons vegetable oil
1 onion, finely chopped
3 cloves garlic, finely minced
2 green chillies, seeded and finely chopped
a few fresh coriander leaves, chopped
2–3 curry leaves
½ teaspoon sugar
4 fl oz (110 ml) thick coconut milk
salt to taste

Place the tomatoes under a hot grill until the skins burst, then peel and finely chop them. Mix the cumin, coriander, mustard seeds and chilli powder to a paste with a little water. Heat the oil in a wok and fry the onion, garlic, chillies, coriander leaves and curry leaves till the onion is soft. Reduce the heat, add the chilli mixture, and fry until the oil separates. Add the tomatoes and sugar and simmer for 5 minutes, then pour in the coconut milk and stir well. Add salt to taste. Cook uncovered for a further 10–15 minutes, and serve hot with boiled rice.

## Cucumber Cooked in Coconut Milk   *Serves 4–6*
## Cucumber Sodhi

In the West, we use cucumber mainly in salads and as a garnish, but the vegetarian Indians have found a way of making it into a curry. This is a mild dish which makes a good accompaniment to hot and spicy curries.

4 oz (100 g) creamed coconut
4 fl oz (110 ml) hot water
½ teaspoon turmeric
1 teaspoon salt
1 teaspoon sugar
1 large cucumber, cut into small pieces without peeling

*Ingredients for 'tarka' (final fry) (see page 30)*
4 tablespoons oil
2 dried red chillies
1 teaspoon mustard seeds
1 teaspoon cumin seeds
2–3 curry leaves
4 cloves garlic, finely crushed

Dissolve the coconut in the hot water and bring to the boil with the turmeric, salt and sugar. Reduce the heat and add the cucumber. Cook for 10 minutes, then remove from the heat and set aside. In a frying pan heat the oil and fry the dried chillies, cumin and mustard seeds till the mustard seeds start to pop. Reduce the heat, add the curry leaves and garlic, and fry till the garlic is golden brown. Pour this mixture over the cucumber and stir well. Serve hot.

## Plain Cooked Dhal (Lentils)   *Serves 4–6*
## Parappu

Dhal is whole gram, split and husked. Many varieties are available, and it is essential in a vegetarian diet because it is high in protein. The South Indians serve dhal daily, even at weddings and other auspicious feasts, and if asked why they reply, 'Can there be a marriage without dhal?'

4 oz (100 g) tur dhal (greased variety) *or* red lentils
½ pint (300 ml) water
½ teaspoon turmeric powder
1 green chilli, left whole
salt to taste
4 tablespoons vegetable oil
½ onion, finely sliced
2–3 curry leaves
a few coriander leaves, chopped

Pick over and wash the dhal, and put it in a large pan with the water, turmeric and chilli. Bring to the boil, then reduce the heat and simmer till the dhal is very soft. This will take 35–45 minutes, but if you have a pressure cooker it can be done in 10–12 minutes. When the dhal is soft, mash it to the consistency of thick pea soup. Add salt to taste. Heat the oil in a frying pan and fry the onion and curry leaves until the onion is golden brown. Pour over the dhal and stir well. Reheat before serving, and garnish with chopped coriander leaves.


## Lentil Curry with Vegetables                    *Serves 4–6*
## Sambhar

This is usually served with Idlis (see page 193) and Dosai (see page 192). The mixed vegetables can be chosen from the following: aubergines, peppers, okra, carrot, marrow, beans and potatoes.

2 oz (50 g) desiccated coconut
2 green chillies, seeded
2 cloves garlic
a few fresh coriander leaves
4 oz (100 g) masoor dhal (red lentils)
1 oz (25 g) channa dhal (yellow split beans)
1 pint (600 ml) water
½ teaspoon turmeric powder
1 tablespoon coriander powder
1 teaspoon cumin powder
2 tablespoons vegetable oil
pinch of asafoetida (optional)
1 lb (450 g) mixed vegetables, cut into bitesize pieces

4 tablespoons tamarind juice (see page 44) *or* juice of 1 lemon
salt to taste

*Ingredients for 'tarka' (final fry) (see page 30)*
2 tablespoons oil
½ teaspoon mustard seeds
¼ teaspoon fenugreek seeds
2 dried red chillies
2–3 curry leaves

Dry roast the coconut, chillies, garlic and coriander leaves in a frying pan, then cool and grind to a paste. Set aside. Mix the dhals with the water, turmeric, coriander, cumin, oil and asafoetida and cook till the dhals are soft. Mash with a fork or wooden spoon, adding some water if too thick. Add the vegetables, tamarind juice, ground coconut paste and salt to taste. Mix well and simmer till the vegetables are cooked.

In a frying pan heat 2 tablespoons of oil and fry the 'tarka' spices until the mustard seeds begin to pop. Pour over the dhal, cover the pan, and leave for 5 minutes. Reheat before serving and stir well. Serve hot with Idli and Dosai.

All lentil curries tend to thicken if cooked in advance. Add a little water to adjust the consistency before reheating.


# Potato Fry                                    Serves 4–6
## Urulaikizhangu Bharth

This recipe can also be used to fill curry puffs (see page 191), but in that case cut the potatoes into small dice.

3 tablespoons vegetable oil
2 onions, finely chopped
2 cloves garlic, finely minced
1 green chilli, seeded and finely sliced
½ teaspoon cumin seeds
½ teaspoon turmeric powder
1 tablespoon sesame seeds, dry roasted, cooled and ground
1 teaspoon poppy seeds, dry roasted, cooled and ground
1 lb (450 g) potatoes, boiled, peeled and cubed

salt to taste
juice of 1 lemon
a few fresh coriander leaves, chopped

Heat the oil and brown the onions. Add the garlic and green chilli
and fry till aromatic. Reduce the heat, add the cumin, turmeric,
ground sesame and ground poppy and fry well. Add the potatoes
and gently stir to coat evenly with the spices. Season with salt.
Sprinkle with lemon juice and coriander leaves and serve hot. Serve
with Dosai (see page 192), as a snack or as a main vegetarian dish.

# Rice and Bread Dishes

## Fragrant Rice
### Plain Pilau

*Serves 4–6*

4 cups Basmati *or* long-grain rice
pinch of saffron
4 tablespoons milk
4 tablespoons ghee
4 cloves
2 inches (5 cm) cinnamon quill
6 cups water (use same cup as for measuring rice)
salt to taste
fried almond flakes and cashew nuts for garnish
2 hard-boiled eggs, quartered

Wash the rice in 3–4 changes of water and drain well. Mix the saffron and milk and set aside. Heat the ghee in a large heavy saucepan and fry the cloves and cinnamon until aromatic. Reduce the heat and gently stir-fry the drained rice. Add the water and salt and bring to the boil, then reduce the heat to the minimum, cover the pan, and simmer till the rice is half done. Remove the lid, quickly pour the saffron mixture at random over the rice, cover again, and cook till the rice is ready. It takes about 20–25 minutes after coming to the boil. Turn off the heat and leave the pan to stand without removing the cover for 5 minutes. Serve hot, garnished with almond flakes, cashew nuts and egg quarters.

## Rice Layered with Meat or Chicken
### Mutton or Murgh Biryani

*Serves 4–6*

4 large onions, finely sliced, deep-fried until crisp and brown, and drained
3 lb (1·3 kg) mutton, cut into large pieces, *or* meaty chicken pieces, skinned
4 cups Basmati rice, picked and washed

8 cups water (use same cup as for measuring rice)
1 teaspoon black cumin seeds
2 inches (5 cm) cinnamon quill
1 teaspoon salt
a few strands of saffron
4 tablespoons warm milk
4 fl oz (110 ml) milk
6 tablespoons ghee

*Marinade*
5 oz (150 ml) natural yogurt
2 tablespoons tomato purée
1 tablespoon salt
2 tablespoons garam masala
2 inches (5 cm) fresh ginger, finely minced
6 cloves garlic, finely minced
2 tablespoons lemon juice

Crush the deep-fried onions, leaving aside a small quantity for the garnish. Mix the crushed onions with all the marinade ingredients and rub well into the mutton or chicken. Leave aside for 8–10 hours, or preferably overnight. Put the rice, water, cumin seeds, cinnamon and salt in a large pan and bring to the boil. Reduce the heat and simmer until the rice is half-cooked. Drain well. Soak the saffron in the warm milk.

In a large pan with a tight-fitting lid place the mutton or chicken with the marinade. Cover with the half-cooked rice and evenly pour the 4 fl oz (110 ml) milk over the rice. Heat the ghee and pour along the sides of the pan. Make deep holes with a skewer and into each hole pour a little of the saffron and milk mixture. Cover the pan, first with a sheet of foil and then with a lid. Put on a medium heat and let it cook till you hear the ghee sizzling inside. Reduce the heat and cook until the rice is fluffy. Do not uncover the pan to check, but sprinkle a little cold water on the outside of the pan and if it sizzles away very fast your biryani is done. Serve hot, with egg curry and yogurt salad.

# Sweet Saffron Rice
## Kesarbath

*Serves 4–6*

This dish is usually prepared for feast days and auspicious events like weddings. It is also served to temple priests as a token by those who visit the temple to make special vows. It is sometimes eaten with a little paruppu (plain lentil curry), but this is an acquired taste of the South Indians.

10 cashew-nuts
2 oz (50 g) sultanas
a few strands of saffron
2 tablespoons ghee
2 inches (5 cm) cinnamon quill
2 cloves
2 cups long-grain rice, washed, rinsed 3 times and drained
3 cups water (use same cup as for measuring rice)
1 teaspoon lemon juice
6 tablespoons sugar

Fry the nuts and sultanas until the sultanas puff up, and drain. Soak the saffron in 2 teaspoons of warm water. Heat the ghee in a heavy saucepan with a tight-fitting lid, and fry the cinnamon and cloves until fragrant. Add the rice and gently fry for 4–5 minutes. Add the water, lemon juice and sugar and bring to the boil, then reduce the heat, cover the pan and simmer for 10 minutes. Add the saffron mixture, cashew-nuts and sultanas, and gently stir with a fork. Replace the lid and simmer for a further 10 minutes, then remove from the heat and leave covered for 5 minutes. Fluff the rice gently with a fork and serve hot.

If possible, remove the whole spices before serving or warn diners – there is no harm in eating them but the taste is very strong. This rice is delicious when served hot with whipped cream.

## Lemon Rice
### Elumichampazham Sadam

*Serves 4*

A fascinating title, but just a basic method adopted by South Indians to use up left-over rice. (*Elumichampazham* = lemon juice; *Sadam* = cooked rice.) I enjoy it so much that I often prepare extra rice in order to have some left over. Serve with any curry of your choice.

3 tablespoons ghee *or* unsalted butter
1 teaspoon mustard seeds
2–3 curry leaves, coarsely broken
1 teaspoon urad dhal (black gram) (optional)
4 cups cooled cooked rice, grains loosened
2 green chillies, seeded and finely chopped
juice of 2 lemons
salt to taste

Heat the ghee and fry mustard seeds, curry leaves and dhal until the dhal turns golden brown and the mustard seeds begin to pop. Reduce the heat, add the rice and chillies, and fry gently until the rice is coated with ghee and has a shine. Remove from the heat. Sprinkle the lemon juice all over the rice and mix well. Check seasoning, and serve hot.

## Rice Cooked with Lentils
### Khichdi

*Serves 4*

2 cups long-grain rice
½ cup masoor dhal (red lentils)
2 tablespoons ghee *or* unsalted butter
1 small onion, thinly sliced
1 inch (2·5 cm) fresh ginger, finely crushed
1 clove garlic, finely crushed
2 green chillies, left whole
4 cups water
½ teaspoon salt

Wash the rice and masoor dhal three or four times and drain. Heat the ghee in a deep pan and fry the onion, ginger, garlic and green chillies until the onion is light brown. Add the rice and dhal and stir-fry for a few minutes. Pour in the water and add the salt. Bring to a quick boil, then reduce the heat, cover the pan tightly, and allow to simmer till the rice and dhal are fluffy and tender. This will take about 20 minutes. Remove from the heat and allow to stand for 5 minutes without removing the lid. Serve hot with a curry and a yogurt salad. Indian Muslims favour this with Brain Curry (see page 217).

## Leavened Bread
*Makes 8*
### Nan

2 lb (900 g) plain flour
2 teaspoons salt
1 egg
1 teaspoon unsalted butter
1 teaspoon sugar
5 fl oz (150 ml) milk
2½ level teaspoons baking powder
1 egg yolk, beaten
1 teaspoon white poppy seeds
1 teaspoon sesame seeds
oil for deep-frying

Sift the flour with the salt. In a large bowl mix together the egg, butter and sugar till creamy, then add the milk and baking powder. Mix well until smooth. Gradually add the flour and mix to form a spongy dough. Cover the bowl with a damp cloth and leave to rise in a warm place for about 2 hours.

Divide the dough into 8 portions and gently roll each out to the size of a tea plate, sprinkling with dry flour if necessary. Brush each nan with beaten egg yolk and sprinkle with poppy and sesame seeds. When all the portions have been rolled out, heat the oil in a large pan and fry one nan at a time over a moderate heat. Do not turn the nan, but ladle oil from the sides until it puffs up. Drain well and serve hot with any meat, vegetable or lentil curry. To keep the nans warm, wrap in a clean kitchen towel until required.

## Unleavened Deep-fried Bread                    *Serves 4–6*
### Puris

1 lb (450 g) wholemeal flour
1 teaspoon salt
1 tablespoon ghee
lukewarm water
oil for deep-frying

Sieve the flour and salt into a large bowl and rub in the ghee. Make a well, pour in about 1 cup of lukewarm water, and gradually mix to a firm dough, adding more water if necessary. Knead the dough for at least 10 minutes, then cover and leave to rest for 1 hour.

Divide the dough into balls the size of a golfball and roll out into thin pancakes, sprinkling on dry flour to prevent them sticking to the board. When all have been rolled out, heat the oil in a wok and when nearly smoking fry one puri at a time over a medium to high heat. When one side is brown, turn and fry the other side, gently patting the puri and pouring on hot oil to encourage it to puff up. When golden brown on both sides, drain on absorbent paper and serve hot.

To make chappatis follow the same procedure, but when the chappatis are rolled out, roast them individually on a hot griddle until both sides are evenly brown, pressing the sides to encourage them to puff. Serve hot, brushing with ghee on the side that was roasted first. To keep them warm, stack the chappatis and wrap them in a thick kitchen towel. If you are worried about cholesterol, serve the chappatis without brushing them with ghee.

## Rice Flour Pancakes                            *Makes 8–10*
### Appam

These are simpler to make than ordinary pancakes. They are delicious with vegetable or lentil curries, or – my favourite – hot with sugar.

5 fl oz (150 ml) natural yogurt, 2 or 3 days old
10 fl oz (300 ml) water

½ teaspoon baking powder
½ teaspoon salt
1 cup rice flour
ghee for frying

Mix together the yogurt, water, baking powder and salt. (You can use 15 fl oz (450 ml) of thick coconut milk instead of the yogurt and water.) Add the rice flour and beat till smooth, then cover and leave overnight to rise.

Whisk the batter to trap air and make it light. Heat a wok or *kuali** and add ghee to grease the base. When hot, pour in 2–3 tablespoons of batter. Swivel the wok or *kuali* to allow some of the batter to settle on the sides in a thin film, leaving the centre a little thick. Cover and allow the pancake to cook for 2–3 minutes. When it is crisp on the sides and fully set in the centre, remove from the pan and serve hot. To keep pancakes warm, wrap them in greased foil and keep in a warm place.

* A *kuali* is like a wok but smaller and heavier. If you do not have either, use a small non-stick frying pan on which a lid will fit.

# Condiments and Accompaniments

## Chutney

This is served with Dosai (see page 192) and Idlis (see page 193).

4 fl oz (110 ml) natural yogurt
2 tablespoons desiccated coconut
1 green chilli, seeded and finely chopped
½ teaspoon salt
2 tablespoons vegetable oil
¼ teaspoon urad dhal (black gram)
1 dried red chilli, left whole
a few curry leaves
¼ teaspoon mustard seeds

Mix together the yogurt, coconut, chilli and salt in a heatproof bowl. Heat the oil in a small frying pan over a medium heat and fry the urad dhal, red chilli, curry leaves and mustard seeds. When the mustard seeds start to pop, pour the mixture over the yogurt and fold in.

## Sweet Lime Pickle

Some years ago I went on a frantic diet. I was drinking the juice of two lemons each day, but it broke my heart to waste the peels because I knew back home they would be used for pickling. I tried this recipe, and although I don't need to diet any more I have a regular supply of pickle for my family and friends.

6 yellow limes (or lemons with thin peels)
4 tablespoons salt
8 tablespoons demerara sugar
2 tablespoons chilli powder

Cut each lime into four pieces and try to remove as many pips as you can. From each piece squeeze out some of the juice into a jar. Put all the lime pieces into the jar and cover with the salt. Cover the jar and shake well. Place the jar in a warm but bright place till the peels become soft and turn a light brown colour. This can take any length of time, depending on the warmth the jar gets, but please don't try to speed the process by putting it in the oven. Keep shaking the jar occasionally.

When the limes are soft add the sugar and chilli powder and return the jar to the warm place. When the sugar has dissolved, the pickle is ready. I keep preparing this in rotation so that I never run out of it.

## Yogurt Salad
### Pachadis

Serves 4–6

In Southern India, yogurt spiced with various vegetables and fruit is called *pachadi* – a cousin to the North Indian *raitha*. It should be fairly thick, as South Indians generally eat off banana leaves. The recipe gives the basic ingredients, but before the final fry you can blend any one of these into the yogurt: chopped coriander leaves, thinly sliced cucumber, boiled and cubed potato or sweet potato, green peppers, tomatoes, bananas, deep-fried and drained aubergine or onions.

5 oz (150 g) set natural yogurt
1 green chilli, finely sliced
½ teaspoon salt
2 tablespoons desiccated coconut, soaked in 1 tablespoon hot water and cooled
1 tablespoon oil
½ teaspoon mustard seeds
½ teaspoon cumin seeds
pinch of paprika

Mix together the yogurt, chilli, salt and coconut. Add any vegetables or fruit you wish (see above). Heat the oil in a small frying pan and fry the mustard and cumin seeds until the mustard seeds pop. Pour this mixture over the yogurt and fold in. Sprinkle a pinch of paprika on top to make it colourful.

## Cucumber and Peanut Salad                    *Serves 4–6*

My husband used to enjoy this in his bachelor days, when he dined at some of his Hindu friends' homes.

1 cucumber, peeled and sliced in julienne strips
2 oz (50 g) roasted peanuts, coarsely ground
2 green chillies, seeded and finely sliced
a few coriander leaves, finely chopped
juice of 1 lemon
pinch of sugar
salt to taste

*Ingredients for 'tarka' (final fry) (see page 30)*
1 tablespoon oil
½ teaspoon mustard seeds
½ teaspoon cumin seeds
2 dried red chillies, seeded and broken into small pieces

In a large heatproof bowl toss the cucumber, peanuts, green chillies, coriander leaves, lemon juice, sugar and salt. In a small frying pan fry the 'tarka' ingredients until the mustard seeds begin to pop. Pour over the cucumber and fold in. Chill, and serve as an accompaniment to either a non-vegetarian or a vegetarian menu.

## Mango Pickle
### Mangai Pickle

3 lb (1·3 kg) firm green mangoes
8 oz (225 g) salt
2 oz (50 g) fenugreek seeds
2 oz (50 g) coriander seeds
4 oz (100 g) cumin seeds
2 oz (50 g) garlic
6 fl oz (175 ml) vinegar
2 pints (1·2 litres) mustard *or* vegetable oil
2 oz (50 g) mustard seeds
5 oz (150 g) chilli powder

12 whole red chillies
6 tablespoons sugar

Cut the mangoes into small pieces without peeling them. Cut through the seed, but discard it if it is too hard. Put the mangoes in a large glass bowl and sprinkle with the salt. Cover the bowl with a muslin cloth and leave it in a warm, bright place for 6 days. If the sun is hot, 3 days on a window-sill will do.

Soak the fenugreek, coriander, cumin and garlic in 2 fl oz (55 ml) of vinegar, then purée in an electric blender. Heat the oil till it smokes and add the mustard seeds, chilli powder and whole red chillies. When the mustard seeds begin to pop, reduce the heat, add the puréed mixture, and fry till the mixture separates from the oil. Add the mangoes and mix well. Allow to cool, then add the remaining vinegar and the sugar.

Bottle in sterilized jars and store in a warm place for 1 month before using. This pickle will store and mature for years.


# Tomato Pickle
## Thakkalipazham Pickle

This should be prepared a week before serving. It will keep in the refrigerator or cool larder for a considerable time.

10 fl oz (300 ml) mustard *or* vegetable oil
15 cloves garlic, finely crushed
8 oz (225 g) sugar
2 tablespoons salt
10 fl oz (300 ml) vinegar
4 lb (2·2 kg) firm salad tomatoes, quartered

*Ingredients to be ground in an electric blender*
20 large red chillies, seeded, soaked and patted dry
2 oz (50 g) fresh ginger
2 teaspoons turmeric powder
6 teaspoons cumin seeds
a little oil

Heat the mustard or vegetable oil until smoking, add the ground ingredients, and fry well till the oil separates. Reduce the heat and add the garlic, sugar, salt and vinegar. Stir continuously. When the sugar has dissolved, add the tomatoes and cook till they are pulpy and the oil separates. Check the salt, leave to cool, and store in airtight jars.

A word of advice if you are using mustard oil: while it is heating it gives out a pungent smoke which irritates the eyes, so keep a window open and stand well back.

# Sweets and Drinks

## Indian Ice Cream
## Kulfi

Serves 4–6

A firm favourite. The Indians in Malaysia have altered the authentic recipe slightly – this method is easier, though the taste is the same. Evaporated milk is very widely used in Malaysia.

1 pint (600 ml) milk
a 14·5 fl oz (410 ml) tin evaporated milk
7 oz (200 g) demerara sugar
pinch of cardamom powder *or* nutmeg
a few drops of rose water

Put the milk and evaporated milk in a pan and boil till thick. Add the sugar and cardamom and mix well. Add the rose water. Leave to cool, then pour into individual moulds or ice cube trays and freeze. Remove from the freezer 1 hour before serving.

This is the basic recipe, but you can add chopped pistachio or almonds, or chopped pieces of fresh or tinned mango. Serve like ordinary ice cream, but in smaller quantities as it is richer and creamier.

## Mango Sorbet

Serves 4–6

a 15 oz (425 g) tin mango pulp
a few drops of lemon juice
a little grated lemon *or* orange rind
4 egg whites (size 3)
2 oz (50 g) caster sugar

Mix the mango pulp, lemon juice and lemon rind. Beat the egg whites with the sugar until peaks form. Fold in the mango pulp, mixing gently with a wooden spoon. Put in a shallow box and freeze. When half frozen, remove from the freezer, whisk the sorbet in a blender or mixer, and freeze again.

Remove from the freezer 30–45 minutes prior to serving. Scoop out either into individual serving bowls or on to a bed of chilled fresh or tinned mango slices.

## Buttermilk Drink　　　　　　　　　*Serves 4*
### Mor

1 large carton plain yogurt
1 pint cold water
salt and pepper to taste
pinch of sugar
pinch of cumin powder
1 small onion, finely chopped
1 green chilli, very finely chopped

In a blender whisk the yogurt and water until smooth. Add the salt, pepper, sugar and cumin powder and whisk for 1 minute more. Chill well in the refrigerator. Serve in individual glasses, garnished with onion and chilli to suit individual taste.

For a sweet version, whisk the yogurt and water with 6 teaspoons of sugar, ½ teaspoon of cumin powder, a pinch of salt and a dash of pepper.

## Green Gram Pudding　　　　　　　*Serves 4–6*
### Moong-Dhal Payasam

My Clara Aunty in Kuala Selangor is the master of this dish. When we visit her there is usually about a gallon of this delicious pudding simmering away for us to help ourselves as and when we please.

4 oz (100 gm) moong dhal (split green gram), washed and drained
¾ pint (450 ml) water
6 fl oz (175 ml) thick coconut milk
10 teaspoons brown sugar, or to taste
6 fl oz (175 ml) creamy milk
1 oz (25 g) sultanas

1 oz (25 g) almond flakes
¼ teaspoon cardamom powder *or* grated nutmeg

Roast the dhal in a dry pan for a few minutes. Put in a large pan with the water and bring to the boil, then reduce the heat and simmer till the dhal is very soft. Add the coconut milk and sugar, and continue to simmer till the sugar dissolves. Add the milk, sultanas and almonds and bring to the boil, then continue boiling for 10 minutes, stirring continuously. Remove from the heat and fold in the cardamom or nutmeg. Serve hot in a teacup and provide a spoon.


## Vermicelli Pudding

### Semia Payasam

*Serves 4–6*

Hindus serve this at weddings and big social events, and Muslims serve it after the thirty days of fasting of Ramadan are over.

4 oz (100 g) fine vermicelli
a few saffron strands
3 teaspoons warm milk
2 tablespoons ghee *or* unsalted butter
1 oz (25 g) sultanas
2 tablespoons almond flakes
¾ pint (450 ml) milk, Jersey if possible
4–6 tablespoons sugar
3 dates, seeded and shredded
½ teaspoon cardamom *or* nutmeg powder

Roast the vermicelli in a dry frying pan till golden brown. Dissolve the saffron in the warm milk. Heat the ghee in a heavy pan and fry the sultanas and half the almonds until the sultanas become puffy. Add the roasted vermicelli and the ¾ pint (450 ml) of milk and bring to the boil. Reduce the heat, add the sugar, dates, saffron and cardamom or nutmeg, and simmer till thick and creamy. Serve hot or cold, decorated with the remaining almond flakes.

In the East, pink rose petals are also used as an edible decoration. Add more sugar if you have a sweet tooth.

## Rice Pudding
### Pal Payasam

*Serves 4–6*

This pudding is regularly prepared by the South Indians as an offering to Lord Krishna. Only cows' milk is used, as Lord Krishna was famous for stealing the cream from *gopis* (village girls) who were churning the cows' milk to make butter.

a few saffron strands
3 teaspoons warm milk
¼ cup pudding rice, washed and soaked overnight
1 cup water
1 pint (600 ml) creamy milk
8 tablespoons sugar, or to taste
½ teaspoon cardamom powder *or* grated nutmeg

Dissolve the saffron in the warm milk. Place the rice and water in a large pan and bring to the boil, then reduce the heat, cover the pan, and simmer till the rice is soft. Add the 1 pint (600 ml) of milk and sugar and continue to simmer till thick and creamy in consistency. Add more sugar if necessary. Remove from the heat and fold in the cardamom powder and saffron. Serve hot or cold. Puris (see page 248) are also served with this pudding, but this is an acquired taste.

## Steamed Coconut Cake
### Puttu

*Serves 4–6*

My mother-in-law makes a special effort to prepare this when my husband goes home. Puttu is available from stalls and hawkers, but none of them taste like Mum's. It is traditionally steamed in a broad bamboo stick, but I use a jelly mould.

8 oz (225 g) rice flour
1 teaspoon salt
1½ cups freshly grated coconut
2 oz (50 g) soft brown sugar
2 ripe bananas, thinly sliced and sprinkled with lemon juice

Sift the rice flour with the salt and place in a large bowl. Sprinkle on a little water at a time and mix till crumbly. Fold in 1 cup of the grated coconut. Line a jelly mould with the remaining coconut. Put in the flour mixture and flatten it out evenly. Place the mould in a hot steamer and steam for 15–20 minutes. Serve hot with the brown sugar and banana slices.

## *Coconut Fudge*                                        *Serves 8–10*
### *Thengai Khadi*

If you have used freshly grated coconut to prepare coconut milk, do not throw away the gratings – you can make this delicious fudge. Children love it, and it is ideal for birthday parties. If you are using coconut already used for coconut milk, soak the gratings in 1 cup of fresh milk, but this is not necessary if you are using coconut freshly grated for this recipe.

sugar, equal to 1½ times weight of grated coconut
4 fl oz (110 ml) water
1 freshly grated coconut
1 teaspoon ghee
½ teaspoon rose *or* vanilla essence
a few drops of red food colouring

Bring the sugar and water to the boil in a large pan, and cook till it has a syrupy consistency. Add the remaining ingredients and cook till the mixture is thick and leaves the sides of the pan. Pour into a greased tray and flatten evenly. While still warm, cut into pieces in the tray, but leave to cool completely before removing them.

You can use different food colourings to make a colourful display.

## Coconut Custard
Serves 4–6
### Vattalappam

A Ceylonese favourite, although of Malay origin.

3 fl oz (85 ml) water
4 oz (100 g) palm sugar *or* dark brown sugar
12 fl oz (350 ml) thick coconut milk
4 eggs, lightly beaten
5 fl oz (150 ml) evaporated milk
1 tablespoon rose water
pinch of clove powder
½ teaspoon cardamom powder
¼ teaspoon ground mace

Bring the water to the boil in a pan and dissolve the sugar. Leave to cool, then stir in the coconut milk, beaten eggs and sugar syrup. Strain the mixture and add the remaining ingredients. Pour into individual heatproof bowls or terrines, and put these in a baking dish with water reaching half-way up the sides. Bake in a preheated oven, 300°F/150°C, till the custard sets. This will take about 1–1¼ hours. Remove from the oven and chill the custards well before serving.

## Semolina Cake
Serves 4–6
### Halwa

Ideal as a tea-time snack or for coffee parties.

6 oz (175 g) ghee *or* unsalted butter
4 oz (100 g) sugar
1 oz (25 g) sultanas
1 oz (25 g) almond flakes (reserve a few for decoration)
½ pint (300 ml) milk
¼ pint (150 ml) water
½ teaspoon cardamom powder *or* grated nutmeg
a few drops of yellow food colouring (optional)
6 oz (175 g) semolina, dry-roasted till light brown

Heat the ghee or butter in a heavy pan and fry the sugar, sultanas and almonds until the sugar has melted. Stir in the milk, water, cardamom and food colouring and leave on a low heat. Add the roasted semolina and fold in with a wooden spoon. Cook until the mixture is thick and leaves the sides of the pan, then spread in a shallow greased dish and flatten evenly. Sprinkle with the remaining almond flakes. When cool, cut into diamond or square shaped pieces.

## Indian Bread Pudding
### Double ka Mitha

*Serves 4–6*

a few strands of saffron
4 tablespoons warm milk
8 slices white bread, crusts removed
6 fl oz (175 ml) melted ghee *or* unsalted butter
4 oz (100 g) marzipan, softened
6 oz (175 g) sugar
6 fl oz (175 ml) water
2 pints (1·2 litres) milk
1 teaspoon rose water
almond flakes for decoration

Dissolve the saffron in the warm milk. Cut each slice of bread into 2 pieces, and fry them in the ghee on a low heat till they are a golden colour on both sides. Drain well. While hot, spread each piece with a little marzipan. Make a syrup with the sugar and water and keep it on the heat. Add the pieces of bread and cook till all the liquid has evaporated. Add the 2 pints (1·2 litres) of milk, a cup at a time, and simmer gently. When all the milk has been used the pudding should be soft and moist. Remove from the fire and add the saffron and rose water. Heat any left-over ghee and pour over the pudding. Serve warm, decorated with almond flakes.

# 5.
# Menu Suggestions

# Malay menus

1. *Informal dinner*

| | |
|---|---|
| Otak-Otak | 75 |
| Kambing Rebusan | 66 |
| Kacang Buncis Goreng | 87 |
| Sambal Nanas | 90 |
| Nasi (plain boiled rice) | 27 |

2. *Formal dinner*

| | |
|---|---|
| Sop Kambing | 55 |
| Ayam Makanan Panggang | 61 |
| Rendang Telur | 65 |
| Lontong | 83 |
| Nasi Minyak | 95 |
| Salad in Santan | 91 |
| Acar | 89 |
| Agar-Agar Drink | 109 |

3. *Seafood menu*

| | |
|---|---|
| Tom Yam Kung | 56 |
| Udang and Ikan Bilis Sambal | 77 |
| Ikan Bawal Rebusan | 74 |
| Gadoh-Gadoh | 82 |
| Nasi Goreng | 92 |
| Hot Ikan Sambal | 74 |
| Lychee Pudding | 107 |

## 4. *Festive menu*

| | |
|---|---|
| Daging Lembu Rendang | 69 |
| Opor Ayam | 63 |
| Bergedel | 72 |
| Sayur Lodeh | 86 |
| Rojak | 81 |
| Nasi Beriyani | 92 |
| Sambal Buah Tomat | 105 |
| Acar Timun | 90 |
| Roti Kirai | 103 |
| Nanas Sirap | 106 |
| Roti Pudding | 111 |

# Chinese menus

1. *Fun menu*      Steamboat      182

2. *Informal Chinese
dinner*
     Chicken Rice      129
     Choy Sum with Oyster
       Mushrooms      155
     Mixed Vegetable Soup      120
     Almond Jelly with Lychees
       and Watermelon      177

3. *Formal dinner*
     Braised Duck      132
     Crispy Fried Chicken      125
     Roast Pork in White Wine      137
     Fish with Chinese Broccoli      151
     Vegetarian Noodles      166
     Yong Chow Fried Rice      169
     Beancurd and Fish Ball Soup      117
     Refreshing Mango Ice      179

## 4. Festive Dinner

| | |
|---|---:|
| Fried Sharks' Fins | 153 |
| Prawns in Honey | 144 |
| Braised Chicken with Black Fungus | 127 |
| Pork Cooked Twice | 134 |
| Cabbage Hearts with Larp Cheong | 161 |
| Stuffed Peppers and Chinese Mushrooms | 157 |
| Duck and Wontan Lomein | 165 |
| Vegetarian Fried Rice | 172 |
| Duck Soup with Salted Vegetables | 117 |
| Authentic Chinese Tea | 181 |
| Warm Rice Wine | |

# Indian menus

**1. Vegetarian menu**

| | |
|---|---|
| Mor | 256 |
| Vegetable Kofta Curry | 232 |
| Fried Aubergines | 236 |
| Aviyal | 236 |
| Parappu | 239 |
| Pachadis | 251 |
| Pickle (Mango or Lime) | 250, 252 |
| Arasi (plain boiled rice) | 27 |

**2. Informal dinner**

| | |
|---|---|
| Mutton Curry, Madras Style | 209 |
| Fried Fish | 223 |
| Cucumber Curry | 239 |
| Pilau Rice | 243 |
| Tomato Pickle | 253 |
| Mango Sorbet | 255 |

**3. Tea party**

| | |
|---|---|
| Curry Puffs | 191 |
| Upma | 193 |
| Pakoras | 194 |
| Kheema Sandwiches | 212 |
| Spiced Scrambled Eggs on Toast | 206 |
| Puttu | 258 |

## 4. *Festive dinner*

Savoury Potato Cakes                195
Biryani (Mutton or
    Chicken)                         243
Raan Masala                          211
Egg Curry                            205
Fried Prawns                         227
Mixed Vegetable Curry                234
Pachadis                             251
Pickle (Mango or Lime)      250, 252
Halwa                                260

# Multi-racial menus

I often serve a mixture of all the three Malaysian cuisines. Here are a few suggested menus.

1. **Multi-racial buffet**

| | |
|---|---|
| Prawn Balls | 145 |
| Rojak Malay Style | 81 |
| Satay with Accompaniments | 81 |
| Mutton Fry | 208 |
| Appam | 248 |
| Nonya Chinese Cabbage with Dried Red Chillies | 155 |
| Tropical Fruit Salad (fresh or tinned) | 38 |
| Chinese Tea and/or Nanas Sirap | 106, 181 |

2. **Multi-racial dinner**

| | |
|---|---|
| Cold Aspic Prawns | 145 |
| Fried Sesame Chicken | 124 |
| Mee Siam | 98 |
| Lagan ki Seekh | 213 |
| Parappu with Snake Gourd | 230 |
| Pilau Rice | 243 |
| Soto Ayam | 55 |
| Pisang Besriam | 107 |

## 3. *Multi-racial tea party*

| | |
|---|---:|
| Tiga Lapis Sandwich | 101 |
| Curry Puffs | 191 |
| Pakoras | 194 |
| Fried Wontans with Chilli Sauce | 119 |
| Goreng Pisang | 109 |
| Kuih Da-Da | 178 |

# Index

Abalone
    in steamboat, 184
    with oyster mushrooms,
        Cantonese style, 152
*Acar*, 89
*Acar Timun*, 90
*Agar-agar*, 32
    in almond jelly with lychees and
        watermelon balls, 177
*Agar-agar Minuman*, 109
*Aji-no-moto* (monosodium
        glutamate), 40
Almond, 33
    jelly with lychees and
        watermelon balls, 177
*Alu Petis*, 195
Anchovies
    dried, 32
        deep-fried, 88
        seasoned with pineapple, 90
        with fresh prawns in a rich
            chilli sauce, 77
        paste, 33
Aniseed, 32
*Appam*, 248
Asafoetida, 32
*Assam Ikan Bulu Meehoon*, 99
*Attu Erachi in Green Masala*,
        211
Aubergine, fried, 236
*Aviyal*, 236
*Ayam curry*, 60
*Ayam Makanan Panggang*, 61
*Ayam sambal*, 64

*Baghar*, 30
*Bah Kuk Tea*, 32, 121
Bamboo shoots, 32
    with salted beancurd, 156

Banana
    fritters, 109
    steamed with coconut sauce, 107
Bass
    in fish pickle, 219
    steamed, 150
Batter
    for banana or sweet potato
        fritters, 109
    for savoury vegetable fritters,
        194
Bay leaves, 40
Beancurd
    and fish ball soup, 117
    cakes, fried, with beansprouts,
        157
    salted, with bamboo shoots, 156
    with chicken livers and snow
        peas, 130
    with straw mushrooms, 85
Bean paste, 33
    hot, with fried pomfret,
        Szechuan style, 147
Beans
    black, fermented
        with squid, 151
        with steamed pork ribs,
            Cantonese style, 135
    French or runner
        in fried long beans, 87
    long, fried, 87
Beansprouts, 33
    salad, 160
    with fried beancurd cakes, 157
    with salted fish, 83
Beef
    CHINESE DISHES
    hot and spicy, Straits Chinese
        style, 140

Beef (cont'd)
  in steamboat, 184
  steaks, ginger, 139
  tender fried, Szechuan style, 139
  INDIAN DISHES
  in curried minced meat, 212
  in savoury potato cakes, 195
  MALAY DISHES
  braised in soya sauce, 70
  in *Satay*, 58
  in tender meat with vegetables,
    68
  tender, in aromatic gravy, 69
  with sweet dessicated coconut,
    71
*Bergedel*, 72
*Blacan*, 33
Bombay duck, 37
  in beansprouts with salted fish,
    83
Brain curry, 217
Brazil nuts, 33
Bread
  Chinese dishes, 173
  Indian dishes, 247–8
  Malay dishes, 100–102
Bread pudding
  Indian, 261
  with coconut milk, 111
Bream
  fried, with hot bean paste,
    Szechuan style, 147
  in fish pickle, 219
  steamed, 150
Broccoli, Chinese
  with braised quails, Hunanese
    style, 131
  with simmered fish, 151
Broth, tomato, 235
*Buah Kelapa Bengka*, 111
*Buboh Cha Cha*, 177
Buttermilk drink, 256

*Cabai Merah Ayam*, 62
Cabbage, Chinese, 35

and pork balls casserole, 136
crisp, with a sweetsour flavour,
    Szechuan style, 158
in oyster mushroom sauce, 155
Straits Chinese style, 155
with Chinese sausage, Cantonese
    style, 161
with fish cake, 149
Cake
  semolina, 260
  steamed coconut, 258
Candlenuts, 33
*Cantonese Bee Hoon with Mixed
    Meat*, 164
Cardamom, 33
Carp, steamed, 150
Cauliflower curry, 233
Celery, 33
*Cendol*, 112
*Char Siew*, 142
  in hawker style noodles, 166
*Char Siew Fan*, 170
Chicken
  CHINESE DISHES
  and pineapple salad, 123
  crispy five-spice, Cantonese
    style, 125
  fried sesame, Szechuan style,
    124
  in black soya sauce, 124
  in hot and sour soup, 118
  in rice noodles with mixed meat,
    164
  in steamboat, 184
  in steamed savoury rice, 173
  in stir-fried mixed meat,
    Cantonese style, 141
  livers, with beancurd and snow
    peas, 130
  Nonya, with dried red chillies,
    128
  porridge, 121
  rice, 129
  satin, Cantonese style, 127
  spicy lemon, 127

wings, sweet and sour, 126
INDIAN DISHES
and potato stew, 202
baked in a casserole, 203
captain's, 200
curry, Ceylon, 196
curry with potatoes, 196
curry with sour milk, 199
in a delicate gravy, 198
kebabs, 197
layered in rice, 243
Masala, 200
spice, with yogurt, 201
MALAY DISHES
cooked with red chillies, 62
crispy, of Pinang, 60
curry, mild, 63
grilled, spicy, 61
in egg noodles in sweet potato
    gravy, 97
in Malay fried rice, 92
in *Satay*, 58
in spiced yellow rice, 92
livers, in beancurd with straw
    mushrooms, 86
shredded, spicy, 64
soup, spicy, 55
with condensed tomato soup, 60
Chillies
dried
    sauces, 34, 175–6
    with Nonya chicken, 128
fresh, 34
    flowers, 34
    sauces, 34, 104–5, 175–6
    with chicken, 62
*Chilli sambal*, 104
Chinese taste powder, 35
Choy Sum (flower spinach) in
    oyster mushroom sauce,
    155
*Choy Sum Fan*, 171
Chutney, *see also* Pickles, 250
Cinnamon, 35
Cloves, 36

Cockles, in hawker style noodles,
    165
Coconut
and chilli sauce, 104
and yogurt with mixed
    vegetables, 236
cake, steamed, 258
custard, 260
    baked, 111
filled pancakes, 178
fudge, 259
sauce with steamed banana, 107
sweet dessicated, with beef, 71
with stewed fish, 74
Coconut milk
how to make, 24–5
salad in, 91
with bread pudding, 111
with cucumber, 239
Cocktail snacks
CHINESE DISHES
abalone with oyster mushrooms,
    Cantonese style, 152
fried beancurd cakes with
    beansprouts, 157
prawn balls, 145
prawn cakes, Peking style, 173
INDIAN DISHES
meatballs, 214
savoury scrambled eggs, 206
savoury vegetable fritters, 194
MALAY DISHES
beef patties, 72
crispy chicken of Pinang, 60
spicy shredded chicken, 64
whitebait fritters, 79
Cod
in sweet and sour fish, 148
steaks, delicately pickled, 224
Coley
cutlets, 220
in beancurd and fish ball soup,
    117
Condiments and accompaniments,
    *see* Pickles, Sauces

Coriander, 36
Corn on the cob curry, 237
Courgettes with lentil curry, 230
Crab
  claws, chilli, 146
  curry, 78
Cucumber
  and peanut salad, 252
  cooked in coconut milk, 239
  pickle, 90
*Cucumber Sodhi*, 238
Cumin, 36
Curried tomatoes, 238
Curry, 30–31
  INDIAN DISHES
  brain, 217
  cauliflower, 233
  chicken, Ceylon, 196
  chicken, with potatoes, 196
  chicken, with sour milk, 199
  corn on the cob, 237
  cucumber cooked in coconut
    milk, 239
  curried minced meat, 212
  dry meat, 207
  egg, 205
  fish, hot South Indian, 221
  fish, mild South Indian, 223
  golden pumpkin, 229
  lentil, with snake gourd, 230
  lentil, with vegetables, 240
  Malacca pork and liver, 215
  meatball, 214
  mixed vegetable, 234
  mutton, Madras style, 209
  pork vindaloo, 216
  potato, as filling for pancakes,
    193
  prawn and okra, 226
  puffs, meat or vegetable, 191
  sour prawn, 226
  vegetable ball, 232
  MALAY DISHES
  chicken, mild, 63
  crab, 78

  dry liver, 72
  egg, 65
  fish head, 76
  lamb, 69
  rich potato, 88
  spicy squid and prawn, served
    with rice, 93
  vegetable, 83
Curry leaves, 36
Curry powder, 37
Custard, coconut, 260
  baked, 111


*Daging Lembu Rendang*, 69
*Daging Masak Sayur*, 66
*Dark Fried Hokkien Mee*, 165
*Dosai*, 192
*Double ka Mitha*, 261
Doughnuts, Chinese, 179
Drinks
  CHINESE
  *Buboh Cha Cha*, 177
  Chinese tea, 181
  INDIAN
  buttermilk drink, 256
  MALAY
  *Cendol*, 112
  ice and nut drink, 106
  jelly drink, 109
  pineapple syrup, 106
Dry-roasting method for spices, 29
Duck
  CHINESE DISHES
  braised spiced, Straits Chinese
    style, 132
  Cantonese style roast, with
    wontan and noodles, 165
  crispy Szechuan, 132
  in steamed savoury rice, 173
  porridge, 121
  soup, with salted vegetables, 117
  sweet, Straits Chinese style, 133
  wind dried, and rice, Cantonese
    style, 170

INDIAN DISHES
  baked in a casserole, 203
  in a spicy and sour gravy, 203
  MALAY DISHES
  spicy, 65
*Duck and Won Tan Lomein*, 165
Dumplings
  rice, 193
  soup, 119

*Easy Laksa*, 97
Eggs
  CHINESE DISHES
  in steamboat, 184
  quail's, in steamboat, 184
  INDIAN DISHES
  curry, 205
  savoury scrambled, 206
  MALAY DISHES
  curry, 65
  spicy, 66
*Elumichampazham Sadam*, 246
*Eral and Vendaikai Kari*, 226

Fennel, 37
Fenugreek, 37
Festivals
  Chinese, 115
  Hindu, 189
  Muslim, 53
Fillings
  coconut, for pancakes, 178
  curried minced meat, for
    sandwiches or puffs, 212
  for curry puffs, 191
  for wontan skins in dumpling
    soup, 119
  potato, for curry puffs, 241
Final fry (of spices), 30
  for cucumber and peanut salad,
    252
  for cucumber cooked in coconut
    milk, 239
  for lentil curry with vegetables,
    241

Fish (*see also* cod, coley, halibut,
    mackerel, etc.)
  CHINESE DISHES
  fried pomfret with hot bean
    paste, Szechuan style, 147
  fried shark's fin, 153
  porridge, 121
  simmered, with Chinese
    broccoli, 151
  squid curls, 151
  squid with fermented black
    beans, 151
  steamed, 150
  sweet and sour, 148
  white, in steamboat, 184
  dried, 37
  INDIAN DISHES
  curry, hot South Indian, 221
  curry, mild South Indian, 223
  cutlets, 220
  fried, 223
  in fresh green herbs, 222
  pickle, 219
  spiced pomfret, 220
  steaks, delicately pickled, 224
  MALAY DISHES
  filling, savoury, for fried
    sandwiches, 100
  head curry, 76
  hot spicy, 74
  stewed in coconut, 74
  wrapped in foil, 75
  salted
    with beansprouts, 83
    with lentils, 225
  sauce, 37
    for spaghetti, 97
Fish balls
  and beancurd soup, 117
  in spicy noodles with seafood,
    163
  in steamboat, 184
  to make, 118
  with rice vermicelli in a sour
    gravy, 99

Fish cakes
  in fried noodles with seafood,
      Hunanese style, 168
  in spicy noodles with seafood,
      163
  in steamboat, 184
  with Chinese cabbage, 149
Five-spice powder, 38
Fondue
  Chinese (steamboat), 182–5
    stuffed vegetable, 159
*Fresh Ikan Bilis Goreng*, 79
*Fried Coconut Sambal*, 104
*Fried Kuih Teow with Prawns*, 167
Fritters
  banana, 109
  savoury vegetable, 194
  sweet potato, 110
  whitebait, 79
Fruit (*see also* banana, melon,
      pineapple, etc.)
  Chinese dishes, 159
  Indian dishes, 231
  Malay dishes, 81, 106–9
  varieties, 38
Fudge, coconut, 259

*Gadoh-Gadoh*, 82
Game pickle, 204
*Garam Masala*, 38
Garlic, 39
Ginger, 39
*Goreng Pisang*, 109
Gourd, snake, with lentil curry,
    230
Green gram pudding, 256
*Gula Melaka*, 110

Haddock cutlets, 220
Halibut
  fried, 223
  in sweet and sour fish, 148
  steaks, delicately pickled, 224
  stewed in coconut, 74
*Halwa*, 260

*Hei-ko*, 33, 39
Herbs, 32–45
  fresh green, with fish, 222
  green, with lamb, 211
  grinding of, 24
*Hot Ikan Sambal*, 74
*Hum Choy*, 42

Ice and nut drink, 106
*Ice Kacang*, 106
Ice cream
  Indian, 255
  refreshing mango ice, 179
*Idlis*, 193
*Ikan Bawal Rebusan*, 74
*Ikan Kepala Kari*, 76
*Ikan Roti Goreng*, 100
*Ikan Telur Sambal*, 79
*Itik Rempah*, 65

Jackfruit
  custard, 108
  syrup, 108
*Jaggery*, 41
Jelly drink, 109

*Kacang Bhendi*, 85
*Kacang Buncis Goreng*, 87
*Kambing Rebusan*, 66
*Karavadu Parappu*, 225
*Kari Kambing*, 69
*Katrikai Tali*, 236
*Kesarbath*, 245
*Ketam Kari*, 78
*Kheema*, 212
Kidney
  pig's, in rice with mixed meats
      and mustard green, 171
  with spinach, 217
*Kofta Kari*, 214
*Koli Kapitan*, 200
*Koli Kebabs*, 197
*Koli Khorma*, 201
*Koli Masala*, 200
*Koli Sodhi*, 198

*Koli Urulaikizhangu*, 202
Kuali, to use, 249
*Kuih Da-Da*, 178
*Kuih Keria*, 179
*Kuih Teow*, 167
*Kulfi*, 255

*Lagan Ki Seekh*, 213
*Laksa*, 163
Lamb and mutton
  INDIAN DISHES
  curry, Madras style, 209
  dry meat curry, 207
  fry, 208
  in curried minced meat, 212
  in green herbs, 211
  in Indian meat loaf, 213
  in meat layered with rice, 243
  spiced roast leg of, 211
  spicy, in rich yogurt gravy, 210
  tender, with onions, 208
  MALAY DISHES
  curry, 69
  in *Satay*, 58–9
  in tender meat with vegetables,
    68
  soup, 55
  stewed, 66
Laurel leaves, 40
Lemon
  juice, 40
  rice, 246
Lemon grass, 40
Lentils
  and rice pancakes, 192
  plain cooked, 239
  red
    and salt fish, 225
    cooked with rice, 246
    curry with snake gourd, 230
    curry with vegetables, 240
    plain cooked, 239
    soup, 191
Lime, 40
  pickle, 250

Liver
  chicken, with beancurd and snow
    peas, 130
  curry, dry, 72
  pig's
    and pork curry, Malacca, 215
    in hawker style noodles, 165
    in rice noodles with mixed
      meat, 164
    in rice with mixed meats and
      mustard green, 171
    in steamboat, 184
    in stir-fried mixed meat,
      Cantonese style, 141
    with assorted vegetables, 143
*Loh Mai Kai*, 172
*Lontong*, 83
Lychee
  pudding, 107
  with almond jelly and
    watermelon balls, 177

Macadamia nuts, 33
Mackerel
  fried, 223
  fried, with hot bean paste,
    Szechuan style, 147
  in fish pickle, 219
  in fried sandwiches with a
    savoury fish filling, 100
  in spaghetti with a fish sauce, 97
*Mangai Pickle*, 252
Mango
  ice, refreshing, 179
  pickle, 252
  sorbet, 255
*Manjal*, 45
Maple syrup, 41
Marinade
  for Cantonese Yong Chow fried
    rice, 169
  for chicken kebabs, 197
  for crispy chicken of Pinang, 60
  for crispy Szechuan duck, 132
  for duck baked in a casserole, 204

Marinade (cont'd)
  for duck in a spicy and sour
      gravy, 203
  for fried broad rice noodles with
      prawns, 167
  for ginger beef steaks, 139
  for pork steaks, Cantonese style,
      135
  for prawns in honey, 144
  for rice layered with meat or
      chicken, 244
  for roast pork in white wine,
      Peking style, 137
  for Satay, 58
  for satin chicken, Cantonese
      style, 127
  for spiced pomfret, 220
  for spiced roast leg of lamb, 211
  Hunanese, for braised quails and
      Chinese broccoli, 131
Marrow, with lentil curry, 230
Masala Bawal, 220
Masala Vendaki, 232
Meat (see also beef, lamb and
      mutton, pork)
  CHINESE DISHES, 134–43
  mixed, with rice and mustard
      green, 171
  mixed, stir-fried, Cantonese
      style, 141
  mixed, with rice noodles, 164
  INDIAN DISHES, 207–18
  curried minced, 212
  curry, dry, 207
  curry puffs, 191
  layered with rice, 243
  loaf, 213
  meatball curry, 214
  MALAY DISHES, 67–72
  tender, with vegetables, 68
Meen Cutlets, 220
Meen in Green Masala, 222
Meen Kari, 221
Meen Moolee, 223
Mee Rebus, 97

Mee Siam, 98
Mee Sup Masakan, 57
Melon, in prawns in honey, 144
Memasak Daging Lembu, 70
Menus
  Chinese, 267–8
  Indian, 269–70
  Malay, 265–6
  multi-racial, 271–2
  planning, 31
Milk, sour, with chicken curry, 199
Mokkacholum Kari, 237
Monosodium glutamate, 40
Moolai Kari, 217
Moong-Dhal Payasam, 256
Mor, 256
Mullet, in fish pickle, 219
Mung (green) beansprouts, 33
Mushrooms
  Chinese dried, 35
  oyster, 40
    sauce, with Chinese cabbage,
        155
    with abalone, Cantonese style,
        152
  straw, 40
    with beancurd, 85
Mustard green, 41
  with hot sauce, 84
  with rice and mixed meats, 171
Mustard seeds, 40
Muttai Bharth, 206
Muttai Kari, 205
Mutton do Piyaza, 208
Mutton Khorma, 210
Mutton or Murgh Biryani, 243
Mutton Paretal, 207

Nan, 247
Nanas Sirap, 106
Nasi Beriyani, 92
Nasi Goreng, 92
Nasi Kunyit, 95
Nasi Lemak, 93
Nasi Minyak, 95

New Year, Chinese, 115
Noodles, 28–9
  CHINESE DISHES, 163–8
  fried, with prawns, 167
  fried, with seafood, Hunanese
    style, 168
  hawker style, 165
  in Cantonese style roast duck,
    with wontan, 165
  rice, with mixed meat, 164
  spicy, with seafood, 163
  vegetarian, 166
  MALAY DISHES, 96–100
  egg, in sweet potato gravy, 97
  savoury rice vermicelli, 98
  soupy, 57–8
  spaghetti with a fish sauce, 97
  vegetarian fried, 96

Offal, *see* kidneys, liver, etc.
Okra
  and prawn curry, 226
  savoury, 85
  spicy, 232
Onion, 41
  flakes, deep-fried, 41
  with tender mutton, 208
Onion seeds, 41
*Opor Ayam*, 63
*Otak Otak*, 75
Oyster sauce, 41

*Pachadis*, 251
*Pakoras*, 194
Palm sugar, 41
*Pal Payasam*, 258
Pancakes
  filled with coconut, 178
  for chicken with condensed
    tomato soup, 61
  lacy, 103
  rice and lentil, 192
  rice flour, 248
  thick, 102
*Parappu with Pudalankai*, 230

Pastry, for curry puffs, 191
Paté, roe, 79
Peanuts, 41
  and cucumber salad, 252
  Cantonese creamed, 180
  oil, 42
Peas, snow, with chicken livers and
    beancurd, 130
Pestle and mortar, to use, 24
Pheasant pickle, 204
Pickle
  chutney, 250
  cucumber, 90
  fish, 219
  Malacca pork and liver, 216
  Malay mixed vegetable, 89
  mango, 252
  pheasant or game, 204
  pork vindaloo, 216
  prawn, 219
  sweet lime, 250
  tomato, 253
*Pinang Ayam*, 60
Pineapple
  and chicken salad, 123
  in salad in coconut milk, 91
  syrup, 106
  with seasoned dried anchovies,
    90
*Pisang Besriam*, 107
*Pisang Rajah*, 109
*Plain Pilau*, 243
Plum sauce, 41, 42
Pomfret
  fried, 223
  fried, with hot bean paste,
    Szechuan style, 147
  in fish stewed in coconut, 74
  spiced, 220
Pork
  CHINESE DISHES
  balls, and Chinese cabbage
    casserole, 136
  cooked twice, 134
  crispy, Peking style, 137

Pork (cont'd)
 dumplings, 138
 in filling for wontan skins, for
  dumpling soup, 119
 in fried shark's fin, 153
 in hawker style noodles, 165
 in hot and sour soup, 118
 in rice noodles with mixed meat,
  164
 in rice with mixed meats and
  mustard green, 171
 in steamboat, 184
 in stir-fried mixed meat,
  Cantonese style, 141
 in stuffing for mixed vegetables,
  Cantonese style, 158
 liver, with assorted vegetables,
  143
 ribs, steamed, with fermented
  beans, Cantonese style, 135
 roast, 142
 roast, in steamed savoury rice,
  173
 roast, in white wine, Peking
  style, 137
 roast, with plain rice, 170
 soup with Chinese herbs, 121
 steaks, Cantonese style, 134
 INDIAN DISHES
 and liver curry, Malacca, 215
 vindaloo, 216
Potato
 and chicken stew, 202
 cakes, savoury, 195
 curry, as filling for pancakes, 192
 fry, 241
 rich curry, 88
 with chicken curry, 196
Potato, sweet, *see* Sweet potato
Poultry, *see* chicken, duck, etc.
Prawn
 CHINESE DISHES
 balls, 145
 cakes, Peking style, 173
 chilli, 146

cold aspic, 145
fried, with Chinese sausages, 144
in bamboo shoots with salted
 beancurd, 156
in Cantonese Yong Chow rice, 169
in fillings for wontans in
 dumpling soup, 119
in fried noodles with seafood,
 Hunanese style, 167
in hawker style noodles, 165
in honey, 144
in pork dumplings, 138
in rice noodles with mixed meat,
 164
in rice and mixed meats and
 mustard green, 171
in spicy noodles with seafood,
 163
in steamboat, 184
in steamed savoury rice, 173
in stir-fried mixed meat,
 Cantonese style, 141
in stuffing, for mixed vegetables,
 Cantonese style, 158
king, baked in salt, Cantonese
 style, 146
with fried broad rice noodles,
 167
dried, 42
INDIAN DISHES
and okra curry, 226
curry, mild South Indian, 223
curry, sour, 226
fried, 227
pickle, 219
MALAY DISHES
and spicy squid curry served
 with rice, 93
fresh, and dried anchovies in a
 rich chilli sauce, 77
in Malay fried rice, 93
in savoury rice vermicelli, 98
in three layered sandwich, 101
paste chilli sauce, 105
soup, acidy, 56

Pudding (*see also* Sweets)
  green gram, 256
  Indian bread, 261
  rice, 258
  vermicelli, 257
*Pudding Chempedak*, 108
*Pukkam with Pasala Keerai*, 217
*Puli Eral*, 226
Pumpkin curry, golden, 229
*Puris*, 248
*Puttu*, 258

Quail
  braised, with Chinese broccoli,
    Hunanese style, 131
  eggs, in steamboat, 184

*Raan Masala*, 211
Rabbit pickle, 204
*Rendang Limpa*, 72
*Rendang Telur*, 65
Rice, 26–8
  CHINESE DISHES
  and wind dried duck, Cantonese
    style, 170
  Cantonese Yong Chow fried, 169
  chicken, 129
  glutinous, in chicken porridge,
    122
  plain, with roast pork, 170
  steamed savoury, 172
  vegetarian fried, Cantonese
    style, 172
  with mixed meats and mustard
    green, 171
  INDIAN DISHES
  and lentil pancakes, 192
  cooked with lentils, 247
  dumplings, 193
  fragrant, 243
  layered with meat or chicken,
    243
  lemon, 246
  pudding, 258
  sweet saffron, 245

  MALAY DISHES
  fried, 92
  glutinous yellow, 95
  scented fried, 95
  served with a spicy squid and
    prawn curry, 93
  spiced yellow, 92
  squares, pressed, 59
Rice flour pancakes, 248
Rice sticks, *see* Vermicelli
Roe paté, 79
*Rojak*, 81, 159, 231
*Roti Canai*, 102
*Roti Kirai*, 103
*Roti pudding*, 111

*Sabzi Kofta Curry*, 232
Saffron, 42
  rice, sweet, 245
Sago
  in *Buboh Cha Cha*, 177
  pudding, 110
*Salad in Santal*, 91
Salads
  chicken and pineapple, 123
  Chinese vegetable and fruit, 159
  cucumber and peanut, 252
  in coconut milk, 91
  Indian vegetable and fruit, 231
  Malay vegetable, 82
  Malay vegetable and fruit, 81
  yogurt, 251
Salmon, in fish head curry, 76
Salt, to correct an excess of, 31
Salted vegetables, 42
*Sambal*, 42
*Sambal Blacan*, 105
*Sambal Buah Tomat*, 105
*Sambal Nanas*, 90
*Sambhar*, 240
Sandwiches
  fried, with a savoury fish filling,
    100
  three layered, 101
*Satay*, 58

*Satay sauce*, 58
Sauces
  black soya, with chicken, 124
  chilli, 175–6
  rich, with fresh prawns and dried
      anchovies, 77
  coconut, with steamed banana,
      107
  for vegetable and fruit salad,
      231
  oyster mushroom with Chinese
      cabbage, 155
  *Satay*, 58
Sausage, Chinese, 35
  in Cantonese Yong Chow fried
      rice, 169
  in steamed savoury rice, 173
  in wind dried duck and rice,
      Cantonese style, 170
  porridge, 121
  with fried prawns, 144
  with green cabbage, Cantonese
      style, 161
*Sayur Bunga with Sambal*, 84
*Sayur Lodeh*, 86
*Sayur Mee Goreng*, 96
Screwpine leaves, 43
Seafood, 29 (*see also* Fish, Prawns,
      etc.)
  Chinese dishes, 144–53, 163,
      168
  Indian dishes, 219–28
  Malay dishes, 74–80, 97–9,
      101
*Semia Payasam*, 257
Semolina
  cake, 260
  savoury, 193
*Sereh* powder, 40
*Serunding Daging Lembu*, 71
Sesame oil, 43
Sesame seeds, in fried sesame
      chicken, Szechuan style,
      124
*Shao Mai*, 138

Shark's fin, 43
  fried, 153
Shrimp paste, 39
Sole
  fried, with hot bean paste,
      Szechuan style, 147
  spiced, 220
  steamed, 150
*Sop Kambing*, 55
Sorbet, mango, 255
*Soto Ayam*, 55–6
*Sotong Masak Hitam*, 77
Soup
  CHINESE DISHES, 117–22
  chicken porridge, 121
  duck, with salted vegetables, 117
  dumpling, 119
  hot and sour, 118
  mixed vegetable, 120
  pork, with Chinese herbs, 121
  INDIAN DISHES
  coconut, 198
  lentil, 191
  tomato broth, 235
  MALAY DISHES, 55–8
  acidy prawn, 56
  mutton, 55
  soupy noodles, Malay style, 57
  spicy chicken, 55
Soya
  beancurd, 43
  beans, fermented, 43
  beansprouts, 33
  sauce, 43
    with chicken, 124
Spaghetti with a fish sauce, 97
Spices, 24, 29–30, 32–45
Spinach
  mustard green, 41
    with hot sauce, 84
  with kidneys, 217
Squid
  balls, in fried noodles with
  seafood, Hunanese style,
  168

curls, 151
fresh, in a dark sauce, 77
in hawker style noodles, 165
in steamboat, 184
in stir-fried mixed meat,
    Cantonese style, 141
spicy, and prawn curry, served
    with rice, 93
with fermented black beans, 151
Stains, curry, removal of, 31
Star anise, 43
Starters (*see also* Cocktail snacks)
    CHINESE DISHES
    abalone with oyster mushrooms,
        Cantonese style, 152
    fried beancurd cakes with
        beansprouts, 157
    prawn cakes, Peking style, 173
    steamed savoury rice, 172
    INDIAN DISHES
    delicately pickled fish steaks, 224
    savoury potato cakes, 195
    MALAY DISHES
    beef patties, 72
    pineapple with seasoned dried
        anchovies, 91
    *Satay*, 58
    vegetable and fruit salad, 81
    vegetable salad, 82
    whitebait fritters, 79
Steamboat, 182–5
Stuffing
    for Chinese vegetable fondue,
        160
    for mixed vegetables, Cantonese
        style, 158
Sugar, raw, 41
Sweet basil, 40
Sweet potato
    fritters, 110
    gravy with egg noodles, 97
    in *Buboh Cha Cha*, 177
    in Chinese doughnuts, 179
Sweets
    Chinese, 177–80

Indian, 255–61
Malay, 107–8, 109–11

*Tali Eral*, 227
*Tali Meen*, 223
Tamarind, 44
*Tamatar Kari*, 238
*Tarka* (final fry), 30
*Taucheo*, 43
*Taugeh*, 83
*Tauhu Goreng Lagi Cendawan
    Jerami*, 85
Tea, Chinese, 181
*Telur Masakan*, 66
*Terasi*, 33
*Thakkalipazham pickle*, 253
*Thengai Khadi*, 259
*Tiga Lapis Sandwich*, 101
*Tofu*, 43
Tomato
    broth 235
    pickle, 253
    sambal, 105
*Tomato Rasam*, 235
*Tom Yam Kung*, 56
Treacle, 41
Trout, steamed, 150
Turmeric, 45

*Ubi Kentang Kari*, 88
*Udang and Ikan Bilis Sambal*, 77
*Upma*, 193
*Urulaikizhangu Bharth*, 241

*Vattalappam*, 260
*Vatthu Bake*, 203
*Vatthu Vindaloo*, 203
Vegetables (*see* Cabbage,
        Mushrooms, etc.)
    salted, 42
        with duck soup, 117
    CHINESE DISHES
    and fruit salad, Chinese, 159
    braised monk's, 154
    fondue, Chinese stuffed, 159

Vegetables (cont'd)
  mixed stuffed, Cantonese style, 157
  soup, mixed, 120
  INDIAN DISHES
  and fruit salad, Indian, 231
  ball curry, 232
  Ceylon mixed, 229
  curry puffs, 191
  fritters, savoury, 194
  mixed curry, Indian style, 234
  mixed, with coconut and yogurt, 236
  with lentil curry, 240
  MALAY DISHES
  and fruit salad, Malay, 81
  curry, Malay style, 83
  mixed, Malay style, 86
  pickle, Malay mixed, 89
  salad, Malay, 82
Vermicelli, 29
  pudding, 257
  rice, in spicy noodles with seafood, 163
  rice, in vegetarian noodles, 166
  rice, savoury, 98
  rice, with fish balls in a sour gravy, 99

*Ve-tsin* (monosodium glutamate), 40

Watermelon balls with almond jelly and lychees, 177
*Wei Fen*, 35
Weights and measures, 23
Whitebait fritters, 79
Whiting, fried, with hot bean paste, Szechuan style, 147
Wok, choosing and using a, 20–21
Wontan skins, 45
  in Cantonese style roast duck with noodles, 165
  in fried wontan soup, 119
*Wu Hsiang Fen*, 38

Yam, in *Buboh Cha Cha*, 177
Yogurt
  and coconut with mixed vegetables, 236
  as accompaniment for curry, 30
  gravy, rich, with spicy mutton, 210
  salad, 251
  with spiced chicken, 201
*Yong Tau Foo*, 159

# FOR THE BEST IN PAPERBACKS, LOOK FOR THE

In every corner of the world, on every subject under the sun, Penguin represents quality and variety – the very best in publishing today.

For complete information about books available from Penguin – including Pelicans, Puffins, Peregrines and Penguin Classics – and how to order them, write to us at the appropriate address below. Please note that for copyright reasons the selection of books varies from country to country.

**In the United Kingdom:** Please write to *Dept E.P., Penguin Books Ltd, Harmondsworth, Middlesex, UB7 0DA*

If you have any difficulty in obtaining a title, please send your order with the correct money, plus ten per cent for postage and packaging, to *PO Box No 11, West Drayton, Middlesex*

**In the United States:** Please write to *Dept BA, Penguin, 299 Murray Hill Parkway, East Rutherford, New Jersey 07073*

**In Canada:** Please write to *Penguin Books Canada Ltd, 2801 John Street, Markham, Ontario L3R 1B4*

**In Australia:** Please write to the *Marketing Department, Penguin Books Australia Ltd, P.O. Box 257, Ringwood, Victoria 3134*

**In New Zealand:** Please write to the *Marketing Department, Penguin Books (NZ) Ltd, Private Bag, Takapuna, Auckland 9*

**In India:** Please write to *Penguin Overseas Ltd, 706 Eros Apartments, 56 Nehru Place, New Delhi, 110019*

**In Holland:** Please write to *Penguin Books Nederland B.V., Postbus 195, NL–1380AD Weesp, Netherlands*

**In Germany:** Please write to *Penguin Books Ltd, Friedrichstrasse 10–12, D–6000 Frankfurt Main 1, Federal Republic of Germany*

**In Spain:** Please write to *Longman Penguin España, Calle San Nicolas 15, E–28013 Madrid, Spain*

**In France:** Please write to *Penguin Books Ltd, 39 Rue de Montmorency, F-75003, Paris, France*

**In Japan:** Please write to *Longman Penguin Japan Co Ltd, Yamaguchi Building, 2–12–9 Kanda Jimbocho, Chiyoda-Ku, Tokyo 101, Japan*